JAPONISME AND THE BIRTH OF CINEMA

JAPONISME AND THE BIRTH OF CINEMA

DAISUKE MIYAO

Duke University Press   Durham and London   2020

© 2020 Duke University Press
The text of this book is licensed under a Creative Commons AttributionNonCommercial-NoDerivatives 4.0 International License: https://creativecommons.org/licenses/by-nc-nd/4.0/
Designed by Drew Sisk
Typeset inPortrait Text, ITC Caslon 224, and ITC Avant Garde by Westchester Publishing Services

Open access edition funded by the National Endowment for the Humanities.

Library of Congress Cataloging-in-Publication Data
Names: Miyao, Daisuke, author.
Title: Japonisme and the birth of cinema / Daisuke Miyao.
Description: Durham : Duke University Press, 2020. | Includes bibliographical references and index.
Identifiers: LCCN 2019050720 (print) | LCCN 2019050721 (ebook)
ISBN 9781478008538 (hardcover)
ISBN 9781478009429 (paperback)
ISBN 9781478008873 (ebook)
Subjects: LCSH: Lumière, Auguste, 1862–1954. | Lumière, Louis, 1864–1948. | Motion pictures, French—Japan—History. | Motion pictures—France—History—19th century. | Motion pictures—Japan—History—19th century. | Japonism—France. | Orientalism—France. | Art, Modern—Japanese influences. | Art and motion pictures—France. | Culture in motion pictures.
Classification: LCC PN1993.5.F8 M59 2020 (print) | LCC PN1993.5.F8 (ebook) | DDC 791.430944052—dc23
LC recordavailableathttps:/ /lccn.loc.gov/2019050720
LC ebookrec ordavailableathttps:/ /lccn.loc.gov/2019050721

ISBN 978-1-4780-9167-7 (other)

Cover art: Auguste and Louis Lumière (camera operator unknown), *Panorama pendant l'ascencion de la tour Eiffel* (1897 or 1898). © Institut Lumière.

For Yoko

CONTENTS

Acknowledgments ix
Introduction 1

1 The À Travers Cinema: Japonisme and the Lumière Brothers' Films 17

2 Japonisme and Nativized Orientalism: The Lumière Brothers' "Japanese Films" 59

3 Japonisme and Internalized Orientalism: Cinematographer Shibata Tsunekichi and the Birth of Cinema in Japan 99

Epilogue Japonisme and the Birth of a Female Star in Hollywood and in Japan 127

Notes 145
Bibliography 183
Index 197

ACKNOWLEDGMENTS

It all started in Lyon, the home of the Lumière brothers. I understand that it is impossible to pinpoint the origin of cinema. But I clearly know the origin of this book. It was in Lyon. It was in 2012. I was on sabbatical and had an incredible opportunity to spend a year at the Université Jean Moulin Lyon 3 as a visiting researcher. As a film historian, the first place I visited in Lyon was, of course, the famous factory where the Lumière brothers made their film on March 19, 1895. Then I started watching their 1,428 films at the Institut Lumière one by one. I was instantly hooked.

First, I'd love to thank Laurie Wilson, the resident director through IE3 Global at the Université Lumière Lyon 2. It was Laurie who made it all possible, helping me and my wife with our visa issues, finding an apartment for us near the Institut Lumière, welcoming us with a fabulous dinner (with, of course, plenty of wine and cheese), and so on and so forth. Thank you so very much, Laurie! I must also thank Laura Hampton, the Study Abroad Program Director for IE3 Global at the Oregon State University. It was Laura who strongly recommended me to go to Lyon. I am grateful for the generous invitation to the Université Jean Moulin Lyon 3 by Corrado Neri, Claire Dodane, and Sophie Veron.

Laurie connected us to a number of film people and food lovers in Lyon, and we became very good friends. Our life there and the resulting book owe to them tremendously: Martin Barnier, Vincent Renner, Philippe Chapuis and Dominique Perrin, Aurélie Sauvignet and Alessandro Martini, Mirella and René Rolland, Barbara Schaff (with Elspeth and Harry), Yvette Dumont, Maenosono Nozomu, Fukuda Momoko, Ann Shriver and Larry Lev.

Without the help and support from Armelle Bourdoulous and Jean-Marc Lamotte of the Institut Lumière, it would have been impossible to complete this book. They have given me exceptional access to valuable materials. And more importantly, they have been very patient with my incomprehensible French.

My project also involved extensive research in France, Japan, and the United States. I have been very fortunate to be assisted by many people at various institutions. I thank above all the late Charles Silver and Frances Hui at the Museum of Modern Art Film Study Center in New York, Irie Yoshiro,

Kamiya Makiko, and Okada Hidenori at the National Film Archive of Japan, Ueda Manabu of Kobe Gakuin University, Kasai Hisako at the Tsubouchi Memorial Theatre Museum of Waseda University, and Jin Moon at the Geisel Library of the University of California, San Diego.

Special thanks go to Ken Wissoker of Duke University Press. Ken has been enthusiastic about this project from the very beginning. I am truly honored to work with him again and am already looking forward to the next opportunity! I thank Josh Tranen and Susan Albury for patiently guiding me through the book's production.

Another special thanks go to Gabriel Weisberg, the founder of *Journal of Japonisme*, which published my article "Japonisme and the Birth of Cinema: A Transmedial and Transnational Analysis of the Lumière Brothers' Films" in its inaugural issue in February 2016. Gabe was the one who saw a book-length project in the article and convinced me to do so. I also thank Brill, particularly Inge Klompmakers, for their generosity.

I am deeply grateful to Charles Affron, Michael Allan, Paul Anderer, Dudley Andrew, Eric Cazdyn, Alain Cohen, Aaron Gerow, Carol Gluck, Elise Hansen, Jane M. Gaines, Derek Gottlieb, Tom Gunning, Charlie Keil, Rob King, Hiroshi Kitamura, Jin-kyung Lee, Laura Lee, Ping-hui Liao, Munakata Kenji, Kurt Newman, Markus Nornes, Stefan Tanaka, Takuya Tsunoda, Christena Turner, Janet Whitmore, Kiju Yoshida, and Mitsuhiro Yoshimoto, who kindly read sections of this book or discussed ideas with me at various stages and gave me valuable comments and encouragements. I also thank enthusiastic audiences of my talks at the College Art Association; the College of William and Mary; Columbia University; Florida State University; Nihon University; the University of British Columbia; the University of California, Berkeley; the University of California, Los Angeles; and Yale University.

Both the University of California, San Diego, and the University of Oregon provided me with generous research support. In particular, I would like to thank Marianne McDonald, Cristina Della Coletta, Stephanie Jed, and Yingjin Zhang at UCSD and Mike and Keri Aronson, Steven Brown, Steve Durrant, Maram Epstein, Hilary Fisher, Sangita Gopal, Alison Groppe, Kaori Idemaru, Kathleen Karlyn, Dong Hoon Kim, Sandra S. Mefoude Obiono, HyeRyoung Ok, Priscilla Peña Ovalle, and Akiko and Glynne Walley at UO for their support. My research assistants at UCSD did fantastic jobs. Thank you, Stephanie Gomez Menzies, G. Victor LeGrand, Norell Martinez, and Pai Wang.

NEH Summer Stipend provided me with precious time and funding at the early stage of this project. An earlier version of the epilogue of this book appeared in a different form in *The Oxford Handbook of Japanese Cinema* (2014).

The piece has been substantially revised to be consistent with the arguments of this book. I thank Oxford University Press for their generosity.

Ito Hiromi-san, thank you for making our move to San Diego poetic and fantastic. Denise McKenna, John McMurria, Marion Wilson, and Nitin Govil, you made our life in New York lovely and are making our life in San Diego joyful. Cheers! (I am holding a glass of IPA.)

I was not able to discuss this project with the late Robert Sklar, my advisor, but he inspires me forever.

Lastly but importantly, this book is written for the loves of my life: Yoko, Dica (who crossed the Rainbow Bridge), Dot, and Hoku. Thank you for traveling with me to Lyon and back. You are truly global citizens. Dot and Hoku even have EU passports now!

INTRODUCTION

It was in 1897. Or maybe that was in 1898. A cinematographer from the company of the Lumière brothers, Auguste (1862–1954) and Louis (1864–1948), placed a motion picture camera, the Cinématographe Lumière, in an elevator of the Eiffel Tower and photographed a view from there.[1] This film, known as *Panorama pendant l'ascencion de la tour Eiffel* (Panoramic View during Ascension of the Eiffel Tower), is a visual record of a modern technological experience: a view from an electrically operated fast machine that takes a rider to the top of a metal tower in two brief shots, one of approximately fifteen seconds and the other thirty seconds.

Apparently, this film is a typical example of *actualités*, or actuality films. Film historians tended to call Lumière cinema actualités because they captured moments of life around the turn of the twentieth century, using footage of such current events, places, and things as French ceremonies, military parades, a president's visit to various locations, and travelogue footage of foreign countries. Arthur Lenning claimed that they were "nothing more than motion picture snapshots" that were "the recording of unadjusted, unarranged, untampered reality."[2]

But as early as 1979, analyzing twenty-eight Lumière films that were available for viewing at the Museum of Modern Art, the film historian Marshall Deutelbaum claimed that "there is little reason to continue to regard them as naïve photographic renderings of natural events which happened to occur before the camera." Deutelbaum's main argument is limited to the narrative structure of Lumière films that, according to him, use "ancillary actions to signal the beginning and end of central action, and, thereby create a strong sense of closure."[3] *Panorama pendant l'ascencion de la tour Eiffel* appears to begin when the elevator has started to move and end when it is about to stop. In that sense, Deutelbaum argues, the film has a certain narrative structure.

If we look a little closer, in addition to the narrative structure we notice that *Panorama pendant l'ascencion de la tour Eiffel* creates an attraction of its own that goes beyond *actualité* because of its careful composition. The film is basically divided into two planes: in the first, we see numerous metal bars that form the tower moving across the frame from the top to the bottom; in the second, we see the Palais du Trocadéro, which would be demolished for the Exposition

Figure I.I. © Institut Lumière, *Panorama pendant l'ascencion de la tour Eiffel*, 1897 or 1898.

Internationale in 1937 and replaced by the Palais de Chaillot. As each of these metal bars, coming from different directions, passes by, especially in the second shot, in which the camera slightly tilts downward and changes its direction to the low angle, the Palais du Trocadéro gradually changes its position while Pont d'Iena comes in sight. Eventually, the Seine also becomes visible at the bottom of the frame.[4]

The film historian Komatsu Hiroshi claimed in 1991 that Lumière films "probably adopted the significance of directionality of lines in paintings to their photographs" because the dominant discourse of the time about ideal photography was "to reproduce paintings."[5] Lumière films, according to Komatsu, "brought such artistic inclination in photography" to their Cinématographe and "graphically enhanced the directionality of lines by the movements of objects as a mass."[6] Already in their 1894 essay on photography, the Lumière brothers opposed the prevailing view that photography could not be an art form because it represented nature as it is. They pointed to directionality of lines and shadows as the elements that would have artistic effects in photog-

Figure I.2. Henri Rivière, "Dans la Tour" ("In the Tower"), from *Les trente-six vues de la tour Eiffel* (Paris: Eugène Verneau, 1902). Color lithograph. Achenbach Foundation. 1983.1.2.25. Fine Arts Museum of San Francisco. © 2019 Artists Rights Society (ARS), New York/ADAGP, Paris.

raphy. As they argued, "Composition and chiaroscuro should be satisfactory in order for a tableau to formulate a good impression" and claimed that the first priority should be "composition" that would contain "unity and balance."[7]

When we juxtapose the film *Panorama pendant l'ascencion de la tour Eiffel* with the work of Henri Rivière (1864–1951), a printmaker and photographer, we realize that the Lumière brothers' films were not simply *actualité* but should be located in the contexts of pictorialist photography as well as within the trend of Japonisme in art.[8] *Japonisme* was the term coined by the French critic Philippe Burty in 1872 to describe the influence of Japanese art and culture on European fine art starting roughly in the 1860s.

When the Lumière brothers screened their first films in Paris in December 1895, Rivière was a stage director of a puppet shadow theater under the name "Ombres chinoises" at a famous cabaret, Le Chat Noir. From 1886 to 1897, the year that the café closed, he created forty-three shadow plays. One of his inspirations was Japanese art. As did a number of impressionist and postimpressionist painters, Rivière encountered Japanese art through *ukiyo-e* (pictures of the floating world) woodblock prints.[9] Heavily influenced by the woodblock prints of Katsushika Hokusai (1760–1849), Rivière recorded the building of the Eiffel Tower with a series of thirty-six sketches from 1888 throughout the 1890s. The work was loosely based on Hokusai's popular serial of ukiyo-e prints, *Fugaku sanjūrokkei* (*Thirty-Six Views of Mt. Fuji*, ca. 1830).[10] Rivière's work was then published as a collection of lithographs, *Les trente-six vues de la tour Eiffel* (Thirty-Six Views of the Eiffel Tower) in 1902, only four or five years after *Panorama pendant l'ascencion de la tour Eiffel* was filmed. Rivière was also a pictorialist photographer whose prints were often based on his own photographic works.

The close graphic and compositional affinity between *Panorama pendant l'ascencion de la tour Eiffel* and Rivière's work in the series of *Les trente-six vues de la tour Eiffel* informs us that the Lumière brothers used motion picture cameras to depict the world in the way that Japanese ukiyo-e did, by way of the impressionist and postimpressionist painters and printmakers, including Rivière. Their films were not simply "the recording of unadjusted, unarranged, untampered reality" but indicated strong graphic awareness and vigilant compositional artificiality.[11]

In fact, when the Lumière brothers produced and exhibited their first films in 1895, France was in the midst of the popularity of Japonisme on a massive scale. It is said that printmaker Félix Henri Bracquemond discovered Hokusai's woodcut sketchbook series *Manga* (published 1814–78), which was supposedly used as packing material in a box of porcelain imported from Japan, as early as 1856.[12] The great wave of Japanese art began with the 1867 Exposition Universelle in Paris. Painters began to find inspiration in Japanese woodblocks, challenging the illusionism of perspectival depth found in conventional composition since the Renaissance. The supply of Japanese woodcuts was reaching its peak in Paris by the mid-1880s.[13] Then, according to the art historian Klaus Berger, "The decisive turning-point in the history of Japonisme" was the exhibition *Maîtres de l'estampe japonaise* (Masters of Japanese Printmaking) organized by art dealer Samuel Bing, the founder of the 1888 periodical *Le Japon artistique* (*Artistic Japan*), at the Ecole des Beaux-Arts, Paris, from April 25 to May 22, 1890. The Japanese sources, including 763 woodcuts, which had previously been accessible only to avant-garde artists such as the impressionists and collectors, were exhibited in public. "In the decade that followed," writes Berger, "it became harder for an avant-garde artist to avoid the lure of Japanese art than to succumb to it."[14]

This book explores the connections between Japonisme and early cinema. Japonisme surely influenced European fine art, but it also had a significant impact on the emergence of cinema in Europe and Japan in the late nineteenth century to early twentieth century. This link has never been explored in depth. The focal point is the films of the Lumière brothers between 1895 and 1905. My arguments are based on my close viewings of 1,428 Lumière films at the Institut Lumière in Lyon, France.[15] When I watched those 1,428 films one by one, I was not simply enjoying revisiting the moments of life and sights of history between 1895 and 1905. Instead, to begin with, I was hooked by the unique stylistic elements, particularly the aesthetic compositions, that those films adopted. Without knowing Rivière's work, I intuitively thought about the style of impressionism and about the acknowledged influence that ukiyo-e by Hokusai and Utagawa Hiroshige (1797–1858), among others, had on those French artists.[16]

When I encountered a film such as *Panorama pendant l'ascencion de la tour Eiffel*, my eyes could not help constantly moving back and forth between a distant view of the Paris landscape and a mobile close view of the grid of the tower itself. Clearly, Lumière films, in which this sort of composition with objects looming into the foreground dominates, are at odds with the order recession of perspective-driven images. To be more exact, these films stimulate a more physiological and corporeal sense of vision.

It was the film historian André Gaudreault who suggested that it would be more productive to discuss Lumière films by comparing them "synchronically with other work from the cultural practice" from which they were derived because what the Lumière brothers did was "amalgamate themselves with these products."[17] While Gaudreault's main focus was the relationship between Lumière cinema and a theatrical tradition in France, the aesthetic composition of Lumière films required them to be "synchronically" located in a much broader field of communal sensibility among various media: namely, Japonisme.

I consider Japonisme as the "nodal point in a transmedial network" among painting, photography, theater, and newly emerging cinema, among others, in the late nineteenth to the early twentieth century.[18] This is certainly a revision of (as well as an extension to) the existing history on Lumière films and beyond, "with a wider scope of pertinent phenomena and more inclusive in its understanding of the visual and material culture" that is relevant to a historical analysis of those films, if I may use the words of the film historian Thomas Elsaesser.[19] This book corresponds to what Elsaesser proposes as "film history as media archeology." What Elsaesser means by this concept is the activity of recovering "diversity" and "multiplicity" of trajectories in cinema's past "firmly embedded in other media practices, other technologies, other social uses, and above all as having—throughout its history—interacted with, been dependent on, been complemented by, and found itself in competition with all manner of entertainment forms, scientific pursuits, practical applications, military uses."[20] I see Japonisme as a significant example of, at least, "other media practices, other technologies, other social uses" and of other "entertainment forms" and "scientific pursuits."

Furthermore, when I was watching Lumière cinema at the Institut Lumière, I was amazed at the fact that there was a more explicit encounter between the Lumière Company and Japan during the height of Japonisme. Among the 1,428 films, I found thirty-three films made in Japan. This number itself was impressive because no film was shot in any other part of Asia, except French Indochina.

I was also surprised at the diversity of topics that these films dealt with. As I discuss in chapter 3, it has been widely believed that the earliest surviving Japanese film was *Momijigari* (*Maple Viewing*, 1899), which documented a performance of two acclaimed Kabuki actors, Ichikawa Danjurō IX and Onoe Kikugorō V. Historians have agreed that during the first decade of the twentieth century, Japanese-made films basically reproduced the Kabuki stage. However, the thirty-three Lumière films, which were produced between 1897 and 1899, revealed that the first "Japanese films" were not made by the Japanese but by French cinematographers and that their contents were not just about traditional Japanese theatrical plays. It was still true that some Lumière films reproduced theatrical performances, but the main focus of these films appeared to be on the everyday life of ordinary Japanese people. There were films of street scenes. There were others that depicted the work of farmers and of geisha. There were even a couple of films that displayed the village of Ainu, the indigenous people in Hokkaido, a northern island of Japan.

Perhaps what intrigued me most during my extensive viewing of Lumière films was a much more complicated image of Orientalism observable in those films. In his seminal work *Orientalism*, Edward Said clarified how Europe described the Orient and authorized a certain view of it.[21] European people tended not to view non-Western cultures as they were but accepted them only after transforming them into acceptable forms. In other words, the Orient was imagined and presented as an ahistorical, timeless, and closed entity, while a temporality such as progress or development was an attribute of the West. There was a clear dichotomy between the progress of Europe and the retreat or difference of the other regions, between the subject that viewed and its object that was viewed.

Instead of Orientalism being something that the West did to the passive East, these films by the Lumière Company revealed moments when the Orientalist imagination was somewhat contested. First, those films indicated a multipronged adaptation by French cinematographers of artistic techniques that originated in Japan and were exported to France, whereupon they underwrote the sense of composition; second, those films captured a dialogic moment where French cinematographers and Japanese people communicated with each other.

Preceding Lumière cinema, the Japonisme of late nineteenth-century Europe, with its grounding in a specific compositional regime for visual culture, played a significant role in such a reconfiguration of Orientalism. The art historian Geneviève Lacambre claims that there were four distinct stages in the reception of Japanese art in France:

1. Introduction of Japanese motifs into a repertoire of eclecticism, an addition that did not replace any other specific decorative motif
2. Preferential imitation of these exotic or naturalistic motifs, with naturalistic motifs being assimilated particularly quickly
3. Imitation of refined techniques from Japan
4. Analysis of the principles and methods that one can discover from Japanese art and their application[22]

In Lacambre's view, Japonisme was not merely imitation but encompassed an analysis and application of principles and methods discovered in Japanese aesthetics and techniques. If we follow her argument, the first three stages of her diachronic categorization should not be regarded as Japonisme but as variations of Orientalism. Japonisme emerged only when French artists started incorporating the principles and methods learned from Japanese art or started trying to penetrate the minds of Japanese artists and to communicate with them. Orientalism was a one-directional gaze from the West toward the East, but Japonisme was a two-way conversation. As I demonstrate in this book, although Lumière cinema maintained the Orientalist fantasy, the Cinématographe Lumière also captured moments when the monologue of Orientalism turned into a dialogue by way of Japonisme.

To put it differently, the link between Lumière cinema and Japonisme engages me with two recent tendencies in the historical study of late nineteenth-century to early twentieth-century art: visual cultural studies and "new art history." Visual cultural studies explore the problematic relationships between visual culture and science technology inspired by the thoughts of the philosopher and historian Michel Foucault, as well as others. The aesthetic composition of some of the Lumière films, which presumably had a close connection to that of the ukiyo-e woodblock prints, can be discussed in relation to the scientific analysis of the human body and the physiology of the eye. This is a realm of visual cultural studies that examines how the sense of vision was incorporated into the modern scopic regime throughout the nineteenth century.

"New art history" examines art forms from sociopolitical perspectives based on empirical research on historical documents. It has revealed the historical contexts behind the themes of realist, impressionist, and postimpressionist painters, such as the emergence of the bourgeoisie, urbanization, industrialization, and the colonization of Africa and Asia, and clarified the relationship between art and society in the nineteenth century. Lumière films clearly participated in the French colonization of Africa and Asia. Two layers of colonialism are observable in Lumière cinema. The first was to record the process of colonization. Those films that captured the French president's visit to specific locations in Africa were typical examples of this type. The second was to authenticate the Orientalist imagination. Those films that were produced in Africa and Asia were the examples. Cinema was—and still is—the perfect medium for immediate archiving because of its nature of compiling static moments and its function of mechanical reproduction. It could instantly freeze time and leave non-Western objects timeless. The "Japanese films" by the Lumière Company were obviously an outcome of sociopolitical conditions of the time of French imperialism. But because of the function of mechanical reproduction, Lumière cinema ended up recording dialogic moments between French cinematographers and Japanese people.

In the following three chapters I tell three pieces of one story: Japonisme-generated conversations and negotiations in the transnational flow of cinema during the period of global imperialism. As I addressed in my previous book, *The Aesthetics of Shadow: Lighting and Japanese Cinema* (2013), when I use the term *negotiation*, I have in mind an influential essay by the cultural theorist Stuart Hall, "Encoding/Decoding."[23] Hall proposes three decoding strategies in the practice of reading and making sense of cultural texts.[24] Negotiated reading is more ambivalent than dominant reading, which would presume no active intervention at all on the part of the decoder, or oppositional reading, which would understand the preferred way of reading the text's code but reject it. Again, I do not consider the notion of negotiation to be a simple form of resistance. Although I am concerned about historically specific struggles and conflicts among groups of people, I do not want to presuppose a binary structure between domination and resistance. Some people could be in politically or economically dominant positions and others in receptive ones, but such relationships were by no means unchanging. For instance, as I have demonstrated in my book on Sessue Hayakawa, the Japanese star in Hollywood (2007), and in a chapter that discusses Hayashi Chōjirō, the most popular star among female spectators of the late 1920s and the 1930s, in *The Aesthetics of Shadow*, a popular star's audience could be extremely passive to the presumed ideal of capitalist ideology and tremendously active at the same time.[25] Such an audience could be cooperative in reinforcing the dominant ideology by not passively but consciously participating in the construction of the star's official image. Simultaneously, his or her perception—or the affect—of the onscreen image of the star was direct and physical and diminished the distance between the actor and himself or herself. The notion of negotiation grasps such simultaneity, coexistence, and dialogism without ignoring the power relations—global power relations—in the cultural sphere. Along this line of thought, I consider Japonisme to be a generator of negotiations.

In chapter 1, I argue that Lumière films need to be understood within their contemporary media ecology of photography, painting, and cinema, all under the sway of the compositional principles of Japonisme and the new idea of a kinetic and corporeally grounded realism that arose from it. A certain number of Lumière films did not simply represent the fantastic image of Japan as a part of the prevailing discourse of Orientalism but incorporated or even enhanced the techniques of Japanese art with its new photographic technology of duration. In other words, those films went beyond Orientalism as a result of transnational and transmedial dialogue and negotiation in the context of Japonisme.

The optical connection between Lumière films and impressionist paintings was pointed out by the filmmaker Jean-Luc Godard as early as 1967 and by the art historian Steven Z. Levine in 1978.[26] The museum at the Institut Lumière in Lyon also has an exhibit that compares some Lumière films with impressionist and postimpressionist paintings: Édouard Manet's *La musique aux Tuileries* (*Music in the Tuileries*, 1862) is coupled with the film *Champs-Elysées* (1896), Claude Monet's *La gare Saint-Lazare* (*The Saint-Lazare Train Station*, 1877) is paired with *L'Arrivée d'un train à La Ciotat* (*Arrival of a Train at La Ciotat*, 1897), and Paul Cézanne's *Les joueurs de cartes* (*The Card Players*, 1890–92) is placed next to *Partie d'écarté* (*Card Game*, 1896). The wall label reads as follows:

> Antoine [Lumiére (1840–1911), the father of the brothers and the painter/photographer/photochemical industrialist] was probably at the origin of the pictorial taste of his two sons. The "views" of Lumière belong to the revolution of the gaze made by Impressionism: figuration of the invisible (the light, the wind . . .), the inaccessible (the clouds, the high snow-covered peaks . . .), the intangible (the smoke, the vapors . . .). The photographic

fixation of each photogram that passes through the camera reconstructs the movement of beings and things, but also restores the vibration of the particles of light. The agitation of the atoms of the pellicular material forms a stellar surface on which the contours of bodies, objects and their shadows are outlined, echoing pointillist research. The framing of the Lumière "views" does not probably stem from a deliberate desire to make art. Nevertheless, the views meet the iconography of their time, and in particular that which is attached to the atmospheric representation of the city and natural spaces, the observation of the crafts of the end of the nineteenth century, and the visible effects of the industrial revolution. Many echoes of Manet, Monet, Millet, Cézanne, and photographers of pictorialism are observable in the Lumiere "views."[27]

Based on the discourse that connects Lumière films to impressionism and postimpressionism, the city of Lyon held an exhibition titled "Impressionnisme et naissance du cinématographe" (Impressionism and Birth of the Cinématographe) in 2005.

In this book, whose title is inspired by this exhibition, I go further than simply comparing impressionism and Lumière films. Not only suggesting the thematic and stylistic connection between Japonisme and Lumière films, I argue that the impact of Japonisme on impressionist and postimpressionist artists was even enhanced in Lumière cinema.

The prevailing discourse on the Lumière films has been that the technology of the motion picture camera is able to extract instants in continuous movements ("the recording of unadjusted, unarranged, untampered reality").[28] But to me, one of the major attractions of Lumière films is the coexistence of the instants captured by the mechanical eye of the camera and the attempt by the cinematographers to reproduce bodily actions. In other words, Lumière films are a representative of industrialization and mechanization, but at the same time they intended to maintain or to restore the physicality of artists. I argue that the Lumière brothers and their cinematographers shared the contemporaneous obsession among impressionist and postimpressionist painters and printmakers about how to instantly *and* physically capture the movements of living things in the world. What impressionist and postimpressionist painters valued most in ukiyo-e was the method of sketching and composition that not only captured moments and movements of the environment instantly but also physically mobilized the eyes of the spectator.

In *Suspensions of Perception: Attention, Spectacle, and Modern Culture* (1999), the art historian Jonathan Crary states, by quoting the French critic Roland

Barthes, "I am not interested in recovering a primary or 'authentic' meaning that is somehow immanent to these works [by Manet, Georges Seurat, and Cézanne]; rather . . . by examining them I hope to construct some of the field of their exterior, to multiply the links to this exterior, 'to remain attentive to the plural' of these paintings, where 'everything signifies ceaselessly and several times.'"[29] My aim in the first chapter is to construct a multiplicity of links between Lumière films to their exterior by way of Japonisme. While the "space-drained (but hardly flat) images" of the paintings of Manet, Seurat, and Cézanne "are inseparable from emerging machine forms of 'realism' and optical verisimilitude," as Crary claims, I argue that Lumière films tackle the problem of how to reinvent corporeal experiences and representational practices.[30]

Throughout chapter 1 I survey the Lumière corpus and examine films, including *Panorama pendant l'ascencion de la tour Eiffel*, in which the composition of coexisting the distant and the close dominates. I propose the term "the *à travers* cinema" to describe this type of Lumière cinema, referring to the concept of the à travers, which Monet and Cézanne adopted from ukiyo-e prints and used in their work to emphasize the contrast between the frontal layer and the back and to mobilize human eyes or emphasize the transient nature of eyes. With the camera's duration, the act of mobilization is strengthened in the à travers cinema.

In chapter 2, I examine the thirty-three Lumière films produced in Japan and identify how the Orientalist fantasy was contested when it encountered the reality of Japan. As I have suggested earlier, there were two layers in Lumière cinema in its attitude toward non-Western culture. The first layer surely resided in the one-directional Orientalist fantasy that prevailed in Europe in the nineteenth century. The Lumière Company sent out a number of cinematographers all over the world to develop a repertoire of films, including picturesque landscapes, such as the pyramids of Egypt, as well as exotic objects and people of the French colonies or Japan, that would cater to that fantasy. Newspapers of the period tended to cover the travels of the Lumière cinematographers as an imperial conquest and marveled at how "the entire world" might soon be "the conquest of the Cinématographe Lumière."[31] Then there was the second layer in the midst of Japonisme, in which the Lumière cinematographers dialogically incorporated the techniques of Japanese art into their work, as extensively discussed in chapter 1. These two layers also existed in the Lumière films made in Japan.

The apparent protagonists of chapter 2 are Constant Girel (1873–1952) and Gabriel Veyre (1871–1936), two cinematographers whom the Lumière Company sent to Japan. The official goal of Girel and Veyre appeared to be to capture the "everyday life" of Japanese people and "daily scenes" in Japan. Obviously, though, both of them had their own Orientalist fantasy and, consciously or not, wanted to materialize it in their photographic experiences in Japan. Doubtlessly in their work, Japanese people and landscapes were repeatedly placed in timeless spheres in the manner of Orientalism (the first layer).

At the same time, those two cinematographers were familiar with Japonisme and had already incorporated the concept of à travers in their films before they arrived in Japan. They made transmedial efforts to reproduce the style of impressionist paintings in animated form. Thus, in addition to reflecting their Orientalist imagination toward Japan in their films, they attempted to rearticulate, or authenticate, the ukiyo-e-style, high-contrast composition, and the concept of à travers in the original Japanese landscape with Japanese people (the second layer).

Furthermore, the third layer of an attitude toward non-Western culture came to exist in the "Japanese films" by Girel and Veyre. Actual Japanese people were not living in a timeless place. But because of cinema's innate status as a medium of duration, the Cinématographe Lumière ended up capturing the actuality of Japan. In these "Japanese films," Japanese people were no longer simply passive objects of the controlling Orientalist gaze but became somewhat empowered beings. Thus, Lumière cinema developed into a site of negotiation between the French cinematographers and the Japanese people in front of the camera. The dialogic moments between the photographer and the photographed were captured there. Here, accidentally or not, Orientalism and actualités clashed because of Japonisme. Because Japonisme was in vogue, the Lumière Company sent its cinematographers to Japan. As a result, the project of a monologic Orientalist fantasy turned into a fully dialogic work.

In this regard, two hidden protagonists of chapter 2 are a Japanese industrialist, Inabata Katsutarō (1862–1949), who was a classmate of the Lumière brothers at La Martinière Institute in Lyon, and an anonymous Japanese geisha. When they appeared in the Lumière Company's "Japanese films," the Cinématographe Lumière recorded moments of negotiation between those two Japanese people and the two French cinematographers. I argue that the notion of "nativized Orientalism," conscious acts of self-exoticization of the non-European people for the Orientalist gaze, emerged during the duration of those films.[32]

In chapter 3, I examine the reactions of the Japanese people to Japonisme through their own filmmaking, which also started at the end of the nineteenth century. The emerging Japanese film industry incorporated the unbalanced power structure between Japan and Europe and developed a unique style of cinema.

There has historically been an unequal geopolitical relationship, or an imbalance of power, between Japan and the West since Japan abandoned its locked-door policy in 1854. Yet the relationship has not simply been a binary opposition between cultural dominance and resistance or between center and periphery. Here, focusing on the emerging period of Japanese filmmaking, I aim to further complicate the historian Harry Harootunian's notion of *"doubling"* as "a unique emblem of Japan's modern experience": a fascination with the new uncertainty and resistance to the culture of capitalism.[33] I would stress that the Japanese reaction to the technology of cinema as well as the popularity of Japonisme in Europe was much more complicated than a double bind of fascination and resistance. In particular, in addition to nativized Orientalism, I propose another concept, *internalized* Orientalism, in this chapter in order to depict the complexity. Nativized Orientalism was a conscious pose to cater to the Orientalist fantasy that the Western gaze owned and was mainly for export. I conceive internalized Orientalism to be a conscious act that targeted the domestic audience in Japan. It was a kind of perverse act that a modernizing/Westernizing subject would take when it tried to identify its position with the owner of the Orientalist fantasy. If I use the phrase by the historian Stefan Tanaka, Japan "defined itself in terms of the object" of the Orientalist gaze during the period of its modernization in the late nineteenth century. According to Tanaka, Japan incorporated "parts of the external discourse" of Orientalism from Europe and tried to develop "a voice of its own."[34] We could observe a transition from nativized Orientalism to internalized Orientalism during the process.

The protagonist of this chapter is Shibata Tsunekichi (1867–1929), a Japanese photographer of the Konishi honten camera store who had access to the Cinématographe Lumière when the two French cinematographers came to Japan. Whether the Lumière cinematographers projected their Orientalist fantasy onto Japan or applied their knowledge of the pictorial composition of Japanese ukiyo-e to the films that they made in Japan, Shibata attempted to satisfy both the Orientalist expectations of European spectators and the nationalist goal of the modernizing nation to publicize its ideal cultural image to a European audience. In addition to consciously displaying such exotic-looking Japanese traditional objects as rickshaws and the Imperial Palace, Shibata also documented the streets of Tokyo, which were rapidly Westernizing. Shibata even incorporated the à travers composition in reference to the popular aesthetic discourse of Japonisme. But the significance of Shibata's work went beyond its embodiment of nativized Orientalism and Japan's modernization policy. He also appropriated the Orientalist gaze on the figures of Kabuki actors and geisha, for instance, and used it to confirm the cultural image of Japan for the domestic audience in Japan. When Japanese audiences watched Shibata's work on geisha or Kabuki actors, they identified, consciously or unconsciously, with the foreign gaze toward those Japanese objects. Such a twisted viewpoint toward its own culture worked to formulate Japan's cultural and national identity. In that sense, Shibata's work was an embodiment of invented tradition as well as of internalized Orientalism.

In order to explain the transition from nativized Orientalism to internalized Orientalism in the period of modernization in Japan, I closely analyze the film text and the surrounding discourse of *Momijigari*, the oldest surviving Japanese film, in which Shibata recorded a Kabuki performance by two acclaimed actors of the time, Ichikawa Danjūrō IX and Onoe Kikugorō V. First, referring to the concept of nativized Orientalism, I demonstrate that *Momijigari* was a potential product for export in the midst of the Japonisme wave in Europe. Then I examine the process in which the film began to embody internalized Orientalism, evaluating its own culture through Westernized eyes, especially when it was publicly released after 1903. The film became a representative of traditional Japanese culture and eventually received the honor of an Important Cultural Property (*jūyō bunkazai*) in 2009. Finally, I argue that *Momijigari* existed at the focal point of negotiation among the Orientalist fantasy of Europe, the discourse of Japonisme from Europe, the governmental policy of modernization, and the formation of state nationalism in the nationwide rise of mass media.

This book concludes with an epilogue that discusses the transnational flow of cinema beyond France and Japan. The wave of Japonisme expanded into the United States and played a significant role in the emergence of Hollywood as a film industry. Focusing on the stardom of Aoki Tsuruko, a Japanese female actor, I depict the process of negotiation between the United States and Japan in terms of the Orientalist fantasy, nativized Orientalism, and internalized Orientalism.

In the midst of the age of digital and social media, the question of medium specificity of cinema has been discussed intensely. However, the film historian Weihong Bao claims that "while the question of the medium continues to concern us, even in gestures of its disavowal and overcoming, rarely have these discussions gone beyond the dominant focus of Europe and North America, both in terms of the scope of historical and contemporary instances and critical conceptions." As Bao asks, "What if we shift our viewfinder slightly off center while tracking into the thickness of history?"[35] In the end, what I demonstrate in this book is looking beyond the dominant focus on American and European film theory and engaging the historical questions of geopolitical and transmedial dialogues and negotiations between Europe/America and Japan. I clarify the tension-ridden process of aesthetic, commercial, political, and personal negotiations between French, Japanese, and Hollywood films over the image of Japanese art and culture. By doing so, if I may use Thomas Elsaesser's words, I want to present a trajectory of film history toward "the material and mental 'world' of a community" that would challenge the unwitting yet nonetheless pervasive Eurocentrism and cultural essentialism that insist on reinscribing a divide between the West and the East, even in realms of technological activity that are quite evidently dispersed across cultures today.[36]

The À Travers Cinema

JAPONISME AND THE LUMIÈRE BROTHERS' FILMS

Workers Leaving the Lumière Factory

On March 19, 1895, Louis Lumière set up the Cinématographe Lumière in front of the photochemical factory that his father, Antoine, had built in the district of Monplaisir in Lyon, France, in 1882. By 1892, Antoine Lumière and Sons was the second largest photographic company in the world because of the so-called "blue labels" that Louis had invented to capture images on dry plates with gelatin silver bromide; only Eastman Kodak in the United States was larger. *Sortie d'usine, [1]* (*Workers Leaving the Lumière Factory*) was one of the first films that Louis photographed in 1895.

The film is composed of one long shot. The camera is placed across the street, which is now called Rue du Premier Film, facing the factory exit. The sun is providing plenty of light to capture the scene. A number of female workers exit from the factory. Many of them turn left. Their shadows are clearly visible on the paved street. A man on a bicycle also comes out at a faster speed. Two men come out, dusting each other off with some cloths, and break up toward right and left. We also notice that there is a small door on the wall on the left, and some workers come out of it. A dog also runs out of the door at full speed! But curiously, at least two men go back into it to the blocked, invisible space behind the wall. Last, a carriage is about to appear from the large exit, and the film ends.

Figure 1.1. © Institut Lumière, *Sortie d'usine, [I]* (*Workers Leaving the Lumière Factory*), 1895.

This film is an actuality film that captures the moment of workers' life in Lyon. But if we pay attention to the film's composition, we realize that *Sortie d'usine, [I]* deliberately emphasizes the contrast between the front and the back, as does *Panorama pendant l'ascencion de la tour Eiffel*, that I discussed in the introduction. Indeed, the film historian Noël Burch discusses the existence of at least two separate planes in this film:

> The framing chosen is such that the figures occupy about half the height of the screen when they move towards the frame edge to leave the field of vision. Although a wall occupies half the picture, the sense of space and depth which was to strike all the early spectators of Lumière's films is already present in the contrast between this wall blocking the background to the left and the movement of the crowd emerging from the dark interior on the right, its perspective emphasized by a framing which brings out what seem to be the supports of the roof.[1]

If I may rephrase, the "wall blocking the background" forms the enhanced depth composition rather than a composition of linear perspective. The "contrast" between the first brighter plane in front of the wall and the "dark interior on the right" at the background was, according to Burch, meant to "strike all the early spectators."[2] Especially when the two men go into the blocked, invisible space through the small door on the wall, their movements enhance the contrast between the frontal plane and the background.[3] The contrast between the first plane in front of the wall and the interior on the right at the background, which is enhanced by lighting, leads the eyes of spectators to constantly move between them, in addition to following the movement of the workers leaving the factory.

As I demonstrate later in this chapter in a detailed survey of the Lumière catalog, there are a number of other films with similar composition. *Sortie d'usine, [I]* is an early example of those. The film also indicates that Louis Lumière as a cinematographer was seemingly conscious of a composition with separate planes from the beginning of his filmmaking.[4]

Two Types of Realism in the Nineteenth Century

The film historian Angela Dalle Vacche claims that Louis Lumière was able to "underline spatial depth according to the realist approach of Renaissance perspective."[5] It is true that the Cinématographe Lumière can achieve geometrical perspective because of its lens. In such films as *Sortie d'usine, [I]* and *Panorama pendant l'ascencion de la tour Eiffel*, the lens of the Cinématographe Lumière provides the film with an image in accordance with the method of Renaissance perspective. Yet in these films the contrast between the first and second planes appears too exaggerated to be explained by the realist approach of Renaissance perspective.

Arguably, two types of realism developed in painting and photography throughout the nineteenth century. One was to represent objects in the world in a precise and impartial manner. This type of realism was in accordance with the approach of the Renaissance perspective. According to the cultural anthropologist Thomas Looser,

> In classic Western perspectival space, everything is unified and hierarchized by the single vanishing point; space itself is accordingly homogenous, and everything finds its proper place within that space, including the spectator (drawn into the picture plane via the vanishing point), in accordance with fixed mathematical laws of relation. This yields stable positions of near versus far, subject versus object, and, supposedly, the position and identity of the viewing subject. Again, in a depth model, that now seems almost three-dimensional (but qualitatively homogenous).[6]

As the art historian Oliver Grau claims, Renaissance perspective is not an expression of natural vision but "a technical construction."[7] According to Grau, "Distance between the observer and the object viewed is removed through ubiquitous mathematical analysis of the structure of image space, the totality of its politics of suggestion and strategy of immersion," and the "psychophysical space perceived by the observer as spheroid, a result of the permanent movement of the eyes, had to be abstracted to a flat linear perspective construction."[8] In other words, the Renaissance and the Enlightenment disembodied human vision in the name of precision and impartiality. The precise representation of the exterior world became possible based on a technical and theoretical construction. Camera obscura, which projects light coming into a dark room through a pinhole onto the wall, is an ideal model of perspective as well as disembodied vision because, according to the art historian Jonathan Crary, it transforms the randomness of sensory data into a rational, intellectual vision whose apparatus "corresponds to a single, mathematically definable point, from which the world can be logically deduced by a progressive accumulation and combination of signs."[9] Following camera obscura, daguerreotype, initiated by Louis-Jaques-Mandé Daguerre in 1839, enhanced this impartial representation of the world based on the principle of perspective.[10]

On the other hand, according to the art historian Ishitani Haruhiro, there was another sense of reality, which was "corporeal and subjective."[11] This type of realism emphasized how to represent the world as our bodies actually perceive it. This type of realism developed in conjunction with Romanticism, which developed in the late eighteenth to early nineteenth century to challenge classicism, which "idealized, clear accountability" of the exterior world typified by perspective.[12] Although the human body lost its monopoly on representing the world to the photographic method, a new awareness of the physiological perception of the world and the expression of it using the human body emerged. Ishitani claims that the daguerreotype maintained the mechanism of the camera obscura, which would establish correct proportion and perspective and "represent an object as it was," but in heliography, another photographic process, invented by Joseph Nicéphore Niépce around 1822, a photographer "could control colors and contrasts" in order to achieve the "essence" of an object that the photographer saw.[13] As Ishitani concludes, "The important issue for the artists who were facing the age of mechanical reproduction was not whether they chose between photography and painting but how they interpreted, translated, and constructed an object."[14]

Coexistence of Two Realisms in Lumière Cinema

Extrapolating from Ishitani's conclusive remark, how did the Lumière brothers and their cinematographers interpret, translate, and represent objects in the world? I believe that the two realisms that Ishitani defines coexist in Lumière cinema.

On the one hand, the film is like the daguerreotype in a sense that acute attention to details is presented in the depth of field. The Cinématographe Lumière mechanically acknowledged the exterior world and represented the light and motion in it instantly. The film scholar Mary Ann Doane claims that photography's "means of connecting object and representation—light waves—were literally intangible and greatly reduced the potentially corruptive effects of mediation."[15] Doane continues: "Beyond the inevitable selectivity of framing and angle, the camera always seems to evade the issues of subjectivity, agency and intentionality in the process of an unthought and mechanical recording."[16] Indeed, the prevailing discourse on cinema in the late nineteenth century focused on the fact that the motion picture camera would be technologically capable of extracting instants in continuous movements. In 1896 British film critic O. Winter even called Lumière films nonartistic, based on his thoughts about the camera's eyes, which inhumanely and mechanically capture all the things they see—trivial things, important things, things in close or at a great distance—without any bias and without any selective system such as a human brain:

> The eye of the true impressionist . . . is the Cinematograph's [sic] antithesis. It never permits itself to see everything or to be perplexed by a minute survey of the irrelevant. It picks and chooses from nature as it pleaseth; it is shortsighted, when myopia proves its advantage; it can catch the distant lines, when a reasoned composition demands so far a research. It is artistic, because it is never mechanical, because it expresses a personal bias both in its choice and in its rejection. It looks beyond the foreground and to the larger, more spacious lines of landscape.[17]

In this type of discourse, the Cinématographe Lumière works "as a transparent and incorporeal intermediary between observer and the world," to use Crary's words.[18] Thus, as the film scholar Hase Masato argues, the motion picture camera captures many more things than the intentions of the cinematographers, including such natural phenomena as wind, water, waves, and smoke.[19] "By way of the cinema," Hase continues, "contemporaneous viewers encountered the world in which no human emotion can be felt."[20] Similarly, film historian

Dai Vaughan uses the word *spontaneities* to describe how the Cinématographe Lumière captures nature and human life in the world: "People were startled not so much by the phenomenon of the moving photograph, which its inventors had struggled long to achieve, as by the ability of this to portray spontaneities of which the theatre was not capable."[21]

On the other hand, I would argue that Louis Lumière as well as the cinematographer of *Panorama pendant l'ascencion de la tour Eiffel* were well aware of the physiologically transient nature of their own eyes. Using the extreme contrast between the two layers and the moving camera placed on the elevator, in the case of *Panorama pendant l'ascencion de la tour Eiffel*, the cinematographer was conscious of how to mobilize the eyes of the viewers. In this sense the approach that both this cinematographer and Louis Lumière took when they used the motion picture camera was corporeal. I call this attempt "realism in the eyes of the beholder." In other words, they were the cinematographers-beholders.[22]

Two Realisms, Impressionism, and Japonisme

Preceding Lumière films, the two types of realism already coexisted in impressionism. As the art historian Takashina Shūji claims, impressionism was the "thorough form of Realism" because of its "belief in capturing light within a frame" based on the optical theory of the period.[23] The impressionists did not consider reality to be as static as painters such as Gustave Courbet depicted, but saw it as being incessant transition. In order to capture such motions and instants, according to Takashina, they started to work outside of their studios and develop their techniques, methods, and forms, including "the unique sketching touch."[24] The aesthetician Paul Souriau argues that photographic images are, in a sense, physiologically false; they fail to represent movement as we really see it, for what is lacking is the "real token" of movement: its luminous tracing or visible wake. Thus, the artistic mode that for Souriau is most conducive to the representation of movement is the sketch. It is as if the speed, momentum, and necessary imprecision of the sketch embody all the attributes of our perception of motion.[25] Consequently, the impressionists' thorough pursuit of representation ended up in a different type of realism: the world of the senses, or the world captured by the senses. In other words, impressionists started out from the first sense of reality, or mechanicality, and moved into the second sense of reality, or physiology.

Strategically or not, the impressionists acknowledged the coexistence of the elements of two realisms, mechanicality and physiology, in the Japanese ukiyo-e woodblock prints that arrived in France in the 1860s. The skill of *dessin*, or sketching with quick brushstrokes, in Hokusai's *Manga* drew particular attention.[26] On the one hand, Hokusai's work was significant to the impressionists because of its mechanicality, its precision in capturing the movements in the environment. To their eyes, Hokusai accomplished the first sense of reality, the impartial representation of the world. Théodore Duret, an advocate of impressionism, claimed that the purpose of dessin was naturalism that could "stabilize" the striking conditions of living things and nonliving objects as they were without adding or deleting anything.[27] Duret stated that "Japanese artists, who cannot withdraw once they place their brushes on their canvas, stabilize images with their brushes in their raised arms without a break. Their boldness, easiness, and sureness are out of reach for any Western artists who have other capabilities and skills. Because of their tastes, it is worth noting that Japanese people are the first and the most perfect Impressionists."[28]

On the other hand, Hokusai's work was a high achievement of corporeal reality because of his use of his hands and the swift touch of his brushes.[29] Edgar Degas, who meticulously studied movements in Hokusai's *Manga*, emphasized that artistic forms should be constructed with the hands.[30] Maurice Letouzé, who reviewed the Japanese paintings at the 1900 Exposition Universelle in Paris, claimed that "the best example of how Japanese painters display their masterful techniques with their hands is in their expression of animals. See the two tigers by Ōhashi Suiseki. One of them is resting half of its body and yawns with its mouth wide open. The other tiger, which has just climbed upon a rock, turns around and shows its grin, the grin that characterizes cats."[31]

The project of instantaneity by Claude Monet, whose collection of Japanese woodcuts was unmatched in quality and in quantity by any other painter, was an attempt to identify the physical skill of dessin with mechanicality. Monet's technique is "not that of the *conventional* sketch," argues the art historian Richard Shiff.[32] According to Shiff, Monet employed "a very broad brushstroke," which made "reference to a rapid speed of execution and, by implication, to the spontaneity and lack of deliberation in his own response to nature," like a machine.[33] In Monet's *Boulevard des Capucines* (1873), for instance, pedestrians are depicted in a blurred image with "rhythmic brushstrokes," according to art historian Klaus Berger.[34]

At the same time, according to another art historian, Aaron Scharf, an image such as *Boulevard des Capucines* was not so much a duplication of the human vision but an imitation of the image recorded by "the sluggish mechanisms of early cameras" before the development of more-sensitive plates and faster shutter systems of instantaneous photography.[35] Thus, Monet was trying to identify his brush with the early photographic machine.[36] The 1890–91 series *Les Meules à Giverney* (*Haystacks*) was Monet's attempt at instantaneity in order to represent the exterior world precisely based on his bodily sense of light, using the swift touch of his brush.[37] As a result, poet Emile Verhaeren claimed in 1902 that Monet's eyes and hands became "the photographic gun" and captured objects in midair.[38]

Kinzō-gata-kōzu, chūkei-datsuraku, or en=kin-hō

In close connection to the coexistence of the elements of mechanicality and physiology, which was seen in such work as Monet's *Boulevard des Capucines*, the impressionists focused on the novelty of composition in ukiyo-e. One of the most outstanding compositions that such ukiyo-e artists as Hokusai and Hiroshige used frequently was *kinzō-gata-kōzu*, the term coined by the art historian Naruse Fujio in 1979.[39] It literally translates as the "type of composition with close images." According to Naruse, in kinzō-gata-kōzu objects in the frontal plane are depicted expansively. These objects appear in extreme close-ups while the landscape at the second plane is scaled back. The objects in the close frontal plane often partially block a view of the back. The middle ground is not depicted but often omitted. Two layers, the front and the back, are directly connected, which results in a dramatic composition.[40]

In the realist approach of Renaissance perspective, such a way of connecting the gap between the front and the back would not be recommended, even though in reality, kinzō-gata-kōzu was the Japanese appropriation of the Renaissance perspective that arrived from the West. After the eighth shogun, Tokugawa Yoshimune, relaxed the rules of importing foreign books in 1720, European engravings had found their way to Japan either through China or brought by the Dutch East India Company, which had contact with Japanese artists on the island of Dejima in Nagasaki. Renaissance perspective arrived in Japan along the way. The ukiyo-e painter Okumura Masanobu studied those engravings and adopted Renaissance perspective in a genre called *uki-e* (floating picture) in 1739.[41] In many cases, uki-e applied linear perspective to portray the interior (of Kabuki theaters, etc.) and combined it to the exterior, which was not depicted in the rules of linear perspective but in the style of Japanese scroll paintings that adopted a bird's-eye perspective, or parallel perspective. As such, Okumura used two different modules in a "self-conscious" manner.[42]

Figure 1.2. Okumura Masanobu, *Enjoying the Evening Cool near Ryogoku Bridge* (*Ryōgoku bashi yūsuzumi uki-e*), ca. 1740. Hand-colored woodblock print; beni-e, horizontal o-oban. 44.6 × 65.5 cm. Clarence Buckingham Collection. 1932.1355. The Art Institute of Chicago. Photo Credit: The Arts Institute of Chicago/Art Resource, NY.

Following Okumura's introduction of the uki-e genre, various experiments were conducted by the artists of the so-called *Akita ranga*, in particular. Akita ranga was a short-lived school of painting within the larger Japanese genre of *ranga*, or Dutch-style painting, which lasted roughly from 1773 to 1780.[43] Instead of faithfully following the geometric method of linear perspective and its resulting univocally integrated "homogenous" space, according to the art historian Inaga Shigemi, what the Akita ranga artists emphasized was the distance between front and back that creates a "heterogeneous" and "equivocal" space.[44] Inaga claims that these artists were not satisfied with linear perspective because a truthful application of it would significantly limit the amount of information that could be included in a painting. In order to focus on the details of people or things within the same frame, the frontal plane (detailed) and the back (landscape depicted in perspective) were "segregated."[45] Inaga argues that the idea of *shakkei* (borrowed scenery), or incorporating background landscape into the integral composition of a garden, which originated in China but had been substantially adopted in the Japanese garden, also played a significant role here.⁴⁶ In order to focus more on the contrast between the frontal plane and the back, Inaga rephrases kinzō-gata-kōzu to *chūkei-datsuraku* (omission of the middle ground) or *en=kin-hō* (method of dividing front and back).⁴⁷ Naruse's term, kinzō-gata-kōzu, does not fully capture the extreme gap between the frontal plane and the back that Akita ranga artists initiated.

Hokusai was well acquainted with the concept of Renaissance perspective.⁴⁸ His early watercolors, which were recently discovered, follow linear perspective rather faithfully.⁴⁹ Hokusai intentionally deviated from the realist approach of Renaissance paintings and divided the space within the picture frame into two.⁵⁰ He used it "as one among many modes of spatial organization that could be played with, and even layered over other kinds of space," as Thomas Looser claims.⁵¹ According to Looser, some of Hiroshige's images also often play with two or more viewpoints within the same image, inviting the viewers not so much to reject depth as to layer viewpoints. The media scholar Thomas LaMarre also claims that in these woodblock prints by Hokusai and Hiroshige, "layering takes priority over positioning, which opens the viewpoint to multiplication and distortion, to play and divergence."⁵²

Such multiplication, distortion, play, and divergence of the movements of the eyes are enhanced by impressionists and postimpressionists. They were collectively interested in the composition that Naruse calls kinzō-gata-kōzu and Inaga calls chūkei-datsuraku or en=kin-hō in the midst of their challenge to the dogmatic paradigm of linear perspective and the resulting univocal space, even if ukiyo-e was not their only source of inspiration. Monet, among others, started to incorporate kinzō-gata-kōzu/chūkei-datsuraku/en=kin-hō in his work by the late 1880s, when he was practicing his project of instantaneity.⁵³ The art historian Mabuchi Akiko claims that Monet did not simply emphasize the sense of depth or pursue compositional eccentricity per se.⁵⁴ Instead, what Monet expressed was his awareness of the human eye. Although he followed the relaxation of the rigidity of linear perspective in plein-air painting, led by Jean-Baptiste-Camille Corot, whom he admired, Monet studied ukiyo-e and learned how it shifted viewpoints to make the eye explore the whole visual field.⁵⁵ In works such as *Le Printemps à travers les branches* (*The Banks of the Seine or, Spring through the Trees*, 1889), writes Mabuchi, "Monet seemed to be aware that it was the issue of the focal point [of human eyes] that could not be avoided."⁵⁶ Mabuchi continues: "When we look at a view through things, such as a screen, bamboo trees, and tree leaves, which exist right in front of

Figure 1.3. Claude Monet, *The Banks of the Seine or, Spring through the Trees* (*Le Printemps à travers les branches*), 1878. Huile sur toile, 52 × 63 cm. Credit: Musee Marmottan Monet, Paris/Bridgeman Images.

us, our eyes initially focus on the things that obstruct our vision, and then our focal length switches to the world behind. More strictly speaking, our focal points constantly change in accordance with the distances between us and every single object. In the case of photography, a photographer needs to choose where to be focused whereas a painter can leave it ambiguous because the issue of temporary delay comes in."[57]

Monet attempted to express the physiological sense of vision, which can portray more diverse experiences than the dogma of Renaissance perspective. It is true that the composition of *Le Printemps à travers les branches* is similar to that of Corot's work *Souvenir de Mortefontaine* (*Memory of Mortefontaine*, 1864).[58] Yet Monet did not include anything but the tree leaves in the front plane, whereas Corot painted the entire tree as well as some people on the ground right next to the tree.[59] As a result, Corot's painting follows the conventional linear perspective, whereas Monet's work enhances the distinction

Figure 1.4. Jean-Baptiste-Camille Corot, *Souvenir de Mortefontaine* (*Memory of Mortefontaine*), 1864. Oil on canvas, 65 × 89 cm. MI692bis. Photo: René-Gabriel Ojéda. Musée du Louvre, Paris. © RMN-Grand Palais/Art Resource, NY.

between the front and the back. As such, Monet created "a sense of space by making the eye move actively from one tilted horizontal plane to the next."[60]

À Travers and Physiology in Monet and Cézanne

To describe such mobile and flexible viewpoints in ukiyo-e that Monet recognized, Mabuchi uses the term *à travers*, the sense of vision that "transits or moves from one end of a plane to another."[61] Consequently, with this notion of à travers, Monet did not only express his sense of vision but also attempted to mobilize the gaze of the spectator and invite the eyes to explore the whole visual field within the frame, even to the point of leading the eyes out of the painting.[62] The art historians Virginia Spate and David Bromfield argue that Monet adopted the viewpoint in ukiyo-e to express "the fragmentary, yet dynamic modern experiences of space as the eye plunges into the deep channel of the crowded street."[63]

Speaking of "modern experiences" of "the eye," Monet was clearly aware of the recent developments in physiology. As the art historian Charles F. Stucky writes, "Fascinated by the premises of retinal physiology, Monet selected motifs that draw attention to the distinction between sensation and perception. For example, he favored landscape subjects that are essentially lattices through the interstices of which distant objects appear as little fragments of color comparable to individual retinal sensations. During the later 1870s, he developed several such motifs, as did Pissarro and Cézanne, apparently to stress that vision, in its primitive state, is the awareness of innumerable little stimuli registered on optical nerve fibers."[64]

In the 1850s the German physiologists Johannes Peter Müller and Hermann von Helmholtz perfected the ophthalmoscope and found that the surface of the retina is composed of thousands of minute photoreceptors. Helmholtz wrote the following in *Treatise on Physiological Optics* (1856–66): "It is natural for the attention to be distracted from one thing to another. As soon as the interest in one object has been exhausted, and there is no longer anything new in it to be perceived, it is transferred to something else, even against our will. When we wish to rivet it on an object, we must constantly seek to find something novel about it, and this is especially true when other powerful impressions of the senses are tugging at it and trying to distract it."[65]

Similarly, on the opposite side of the Atlantic the Harvard ophthalmologist B. Joy Jeffries demonstrated in 1871 that sight is not a purely optical phenomenon because the eyes are as muscular as the other bodily organs and "hardly cease motion for an instant."[66] In 1878, based on the work of Müller, Helmholtz, and Jeffries, the French scientist Louis Emile Javal formalized an understanding that vision occurs in terms of short, fast jumps, which he termed "saccadic" movements.[67]

In this sense, as the art historian Norman Bryson claims, in nineteenth-century art forms "there is a considerable intervention of the bodily into the frame—in the visibility of pigment and gesture, in the rise of the sketch, and in bravura styles such as that of Delacroix or of Daumier."[68] Monet's work represented such an "intervention of the bodily into the frame." More specifically, in Monet's project of instantaneity and his attentiveness to the sense of vision, we can detect a connection between the discourse of Japonisme and the development of physiology at that time.

The "intervention of the bodily into the frame" was also observable in the late paintings of postimpressionist Paul Cézanne. Even though Cézanne was not a collector of Japanese prints and did not follow the emergence of Japanese art in Paris stage by stage,[69] he was also aware of the notion of à travers in perceptual experience and engaged with representational practices of it. In *Suspensions of Perception*, Jonathan Crary demonstrates that various works in science, philosophy, psychology, and art in the second half of nineteenth-century Europe revealed how "volatile" the psychological conceptions of "attention" are and how "transitive" the human perception of reality is.[70] In particular, examining *Fontainebleau (Pines and Rocks*, c. 1900), Crary claims that Cézanne disclosed, confronted, and inhabited the "instability of perception."[71] As Crary argues, "The creative discovery [of Cézanne was] that looking at any one thing intently did not lead to a fuller and more inclusive grasp of its presence, its rich immediacy. Rather, it led to its perceptual disintegration and loss, its breakdown as intelligible form. . . . That is, attention was part of a dynamic continuum in which it was always of limited duration, inevitably decomposing into a distracted state or a state incapable of maintaining what had initially seemed like a grip on an object or constellation of objects."[72] To Crary, Cézanne's late work demonstrates the painter's awareness of "the body, its pulsings, its temporalities, and to the intersection of that body with a world of transitions, of events and of becoming."[73]

As Crary claims, "the nonselectivity of the cinema eye" is distinguished from "the texture of a human attentiveness."[74] The motion picture camera has perceptual constancy in principle, but cinematographers' eyes have the discontinuous nature of the visual field. Also, spectators' eyes have the inconsistency of human perception. Cézanne was acutely aware of the difference between the eye of the photographic machine and human eyes. On the one hand, Cézanne did not oppose using photography for landscape painting. In the last years of his life, he argued that "while an artist is at work, his brain should be unencumbered, like a sensitized plate, a recording machine, and no more."[75] On the other hand, Cézanne understood the difference between painting (no matter how realistic) and nature. His brushstroke, or his touch, clearly showed autonomy that distinguished his body from the "sensitized plate." The art historian Hayashi Michio calls this Cézanne's "double bind."[76] Similarly, Crary proposes to think of "a Cézanne who could imagine himself as a 'double-system,' a reservoir of historical and personal traces *and* a blank mechanical apparatus with an implacable functionality."[77]

The À Travers Cinema of the Lumière Brothers

While Cézanne might have tried to turn himself into a "double system," as his critics have suggested, the films of the Lumière brothers, including *Panorama pendant l'ascencion de la tour Eiffel* and *Sortie d'usine, [I]*, had their own double binds. The Lumière brothers configured cinema as a mechanical visual technology that would play with human perception. They shared the notion with

Cézanne that "a stable punctual model of perception is no longer effective or useful."[78] They did not presuppose a static vision or "a vantage-point outside the mobility of duration, in an eternal moment of disclosed presence," but they accepted the fragility of perception and expressed indecisiveness or multiplicity of look.[79] In that sense the Lumière brothers were aware of the multiplicity of perspectives, or what the film historian Jacques Aumont calls the "variable eye" and the "mobilization of gaze."[80]

As the Lumière brothers claimed, "It is found that the eye is attracted whenever the elements of a different nature are gathered on the board and make appearance; that is, whenever there is a contrast, or an *opposition*."[81] Already in 1894, in their article on how to create artistic photography, the Lumière brothers emphasized the importance of unity: "The eye must be struck by a highlighted, principal object, on which the interest must be carried all the way. Then, it must be guided gradually into all other parts in the tableau. That is the principle of unity.... The attention should never be divided equally between two or more subjects. The second rule is that of equilibrium. All planes in a tableau must be compensated. If this principle is not taken into account, the picture will fall into pieces."[82] As such, they were conscious of the mobile physical location of the spectator and the unstable vision of the beholders.

Arguably, the Lumière films such as *Panorama pendant l'ascencion de la tour Eiffel* and *Sortie d'usine, [I]* were experiments that attempted to fully use the "saccadic" movements from one focal point to another. The focus was not on "unity," which they later stressed, but the mobility of the human eye. In Lumière films, events like street scenes unfold beyond the cinematographer's control, but at the same time the cinematographer formulates images for his eyes as well as for the presupposed spectatorial gaze. Viewers with the mobile gaze pick out individual movements from foreground to background and beyond the borders of the frame. In other words, Lumière films expressed the transitive state of perceptual experience, or the physicality of human eyes, in their cinema with the à travers effect. I call their films the à travers cinema.

It is true that the Lumière brothers were industrialists. Their letters of correspondence with various scientists and craftsmen clearly indicate that they were keen to use the best devices created by others and to add new technical solutions to succeed in the photography business. The number of patents that they obtained helped to establish their company.[83] They produced short films "primarily as a means of publicizing the company and its products," according to film historian Richard Abel.[84]

But at the same time, as Noël Burch emphasizes, the Lumière brothers saw themselves throughout their lives as researchers, as scientists.[85] The first known public showing of the Lumière Cinématographe in Paris on March 22, 1895, was at the Société d'Encouragement à l'Industrie Nationale, a conference for the science monthly *La Revue Générale des Sciences*.[86] That was nine months earlier than the famous commercial screening at the Grand Café on December 28, 1895. According to the film historian Tom Gunning, the enthusiasm that the audience of their first exhibition of films expressed about the representation of motion "astonished" the Lumière brothers, who had initially considered the products of their photographic machine to be usable only as scientific evidence.[87] No matter how spellbound the spectator was by the projection of moving images, one should assume that the Lumière brothers maintained their scientific minds. Abel even states that the Lumière Company "took no interest in the commercial exhibition of films."[88]

It is noteworthy that at the conference on March 22, 1895, Louis Lumière presented the Cinématographe side by side with another project of theirs, color photography.[89] As Leon Vidal reported in *Le Moniteur de la photographie*, "The prestige of movement triumphs over that of color,"[90] although I would question the hasty decision about which triumphed over which. Louis's real life's work was color photography, Lumière Autochrome.[91]

Gunning categorizes the first moving images into two broad groups: (1) "most typically those of the Lumière Company," which focus on showing images in the world, like "a new eye suddenly opening onto the world"; (2) such films as the first Edison Kinetoscope films and the Skladanowsky films, which present performers shot against a darkened background and "recall the scientific studies of the body of Muybridge and Marey and other chronophotographers."[92] I would argue that the Lumière films in Gunning's first category are also "scientific studies of the body"[93] but that their attitude toward the human body is different from that of Étienne-Jules Marey, who had less interest in cinema than in analysis of human and animal motion through photographic images. In June 1895, when the Lumière films were screened in Lyon for French photographic club members, Pierre-Jules-César Janssen, a French astronomer and chair of the club, called them "animated photography" in order to distinguish them from the analytical photography of movements explored by Marey.[94] Following Janssen, in 1900 Marey distinguished his work from Lumière films and stated that "animated projection, which has caught the public's interest so greatly, offers but a few advantages from a scientific point of view: in actual fact it does not provide anything that cannot be seen with great precision with the human eye."[95] Marey's physiological focus was on the study of movement that cannot be captured by the human eye, but the Lumière brothers' emphasis was on the study of the movement of the human eye.

For Marey, according to Burch, "animals, and hence men, are machines."[96] As Marey wrote in 1874, "Living beings have been frequently and in every age compared to machines, but it is only in the present day that the bearing and the justice of the comparison are fully comprehensible."[97] Burch concludes that Marey's endeavors of the graphic analysis of animal and human movements with his chronophotography "opened the way to Taylorism," the methodology advocated by Fred W. Taylor in the 1910s, whose main objective was to improve economic efficiency by scientifically managing labor productivity.[98]

For the Lumière brothers, the focus was not to find "a way to subordinate man more closely to the machine."[99] In contrast to that idea, their films experimented with how transient the eyes of the viewers of the world could be. What the Lumière brothers did at the emergence of cinema was a contested negotiation between the two spaces of possibility: active and physical viewers versus passive and incorporeal witnesses.

Examining Marey's work, Mary Ann Doane asks: "Are these two tendencies within modernity—abstraction/rationalization and an emphasis upon the contingent, chance, and the ephemeral—irreconcilable? Do they simply represent two different modalities or attitudes operating independently during the same time period, each undisturbed by the other?"[100] Claiming that contingency "emerges as a form of resistance to rationalization," Doane argues that contingency as the thing that goes beyond intention is unavoidably a part of rationalization.[101] I rephrase Doane's questions: are physicality and mechanicality irreconcilable? The à travers cinema by the Lumière brothers was a practice to reconcile the two and open up "the possibility of visual experience that was intrinsically nonrationalizable, that exceeded any procedures of normalization," as a result of the encounter between the two.[102] Their films were a representation of industrialization and mechanization but simultaneously contained an intention to maintain or restore the physicality of the artist as well as the spectator. In other words, referring to Japonisme, the Lumière brothers tried to combine art (composition) and science (physiology) in their films.[103]

The Lumière brothers' attempt should also be distinguished from the eventual dominant method of filmmaking: narrative. Their work was an attempt to provide meaning and "human control" to an aesthetic representation of contingency, but not by giving it a narrative, as montage or editing did later by manipulating time and space. Doane argues that "the cinema confronts the difficult task of endowing the singular with significance, of manufacturing an event in a medium designed to record, without predilection, all moments. . . . Despite the dominance of the actuality in the first decade of the cinema, despite the extensive fascination with the camera's relation to 'real time' and movement, narrative very quickly becomes its dominant method of structuring time."[104] It is true that the Lumière brothers became interested in exhibiting their films for a fee and started commercially exploiting their equipment developed for scientific ends. However, when they projected their films on the screen, instead of controlling the instability of the human eye like Taylorism, their films sought to find a way to mobilize the eyes of the cinematographer-beholder within the camera frame. Within a frame, using depth composition and object movements, the Lumière films visualized this mechanism of distracted and transit perception. It is true that there is a sense of "manipulation and stimulation" in their project. Their films present specific objects that need attention. Some of their films have stories: clear structures of beginnings and endings. But at the same time there is no concrete arrangement toward establishing a coherent story line that needs to be followed consciously. To use Crary's words, Lumière films were a project of a "continuum," in which "attention and distraction . . . ceaselessly flow into one another."[105]

In *Panorama pendant l'ascencion de la tour Eiffel*, for instance, with the elevator's continuous movement the contrast between the frontal layers and the back layers is much more exaggerated than the kinzō-gata-kōzu/chūkei-datsuraku/en=kin-hō composition in the works of Hokusai, Hiroshige, Rivière, Monet, and Cézanne. Movements are the key. As each metal bar of the Eiffel Tower comes on-screen and offscreen as black shadows, the Palais du Trocadéro, the garden in front, Pont d'Iena, a number of people in the garden and on the bridge as small dots, and eventually the Seine appear and reappear within the frame, slightly changing their sizes and their angles. This game of hide-and-seek creates the à travers effect, which expresses the sense of vision of the anonymous cinematographer who is on the elevator as well as physically mobilizes the eyes of the spectator.

The mandated change of our eyes' focus resulting in the à travers effect is a movement within the frame. In addition, the camera's traveling movement along with the elevator of the Eiffel Tower enhances another compositional motif that Monet, among other impressionists, learned from ukiyo-e. Hiroshige's work often included a motif that Takashina Shūji calls the "*shidare* (weeping form) motif,*"* which displays branches of weeping willows or flowers of weeping cherries or wisterias drooping at the very front plane from the top of the frame. For instance, in Hiroshige's "Yatsumi no hashi" ("Yatsumi Bridge") in *Meisho Edo hyakkei* (*One Hundred Famous Views of Edo*, 1856–58), the trunk of the tree is only partially seen within the same frame.

Figure 1.5. Utagawa Hiroshige I, "Yatsumi Bridge" ("Yatsumi no hashi"), from the series *One Hundred Famous Views of Edo* (*Meisho Edo hyakkei*), 1856–1858. Woodblock print (nishiki-e); ink and color on paper. Vertical ōban; 35.7 × 23 cm (14 1/16 × 9 1/16 in.). Museum of Fine Arts, Boston. William S. and John T. Spaulding Collection. 21.10430.

Takashina confirms that the shidare motif was never used in European art before Monet.[106] In 1909, commenting on his series of water lilies, Monet referred to Japanese art as one of his inspirations and highly valued its "aesthetics of denoting the whole by a part."[107] Takashina argues that the shidare motif further indicates the "continuity between the painted space and the exterior space" and that Japanese art has the "aesthetics of continuity."[108] In addition to the à travers effect, *Panorama pendant l'ascencion de la tour Eiffel* incorporates the shidare motif with the metal bars of the Eiffel Tower drooping from the top of the frame. Furthermore, the traveling shot of the film visualizes this aesthetics of continuity by continuously reframing the view, renewing the configuration between the photographed space and the exterior space (a panoramic effect).

Thus, Lumière films shared the impressionists' concerns about the two types of realism as well as their active engagement with Japonisme. Although the automatism of the camera eye captures the profilmic events in front of it, Louis Lumière, who photographed *Sortie d'usine, [I]*, and the anonymous Lumière cinematographer of *Panorama pendant l'ascencion de la tour Eiffel* placed the camera in order to make the à travers effect happen for the spectatorial eye. They did not have the hand or the touch of the painter any longer, but the duration of the motion picture camera made the project of instantaneity still possible. There, the physicality of the cinematographer as well as that of the spectator was physiologically maintained along with the mechanicality of the camera eye.[109] Thus, Lumière films used the motion picture camera instead of painter's brushes and reclaimed the physicality of human eyes.

Physiological Realism and the À Travers Cinema by the Lumière Brothers

Let me briefly turn to the theories of cinematic realism before discussing other Lumière films in detail. The Lumière brothers had presented their theory of realism even before most film theories came to exist. In his 1945 essay, which was later re-titled "The Ontology of the Photographic Image," the film critic André Bazin argued that "originality in photography as distinct from originality in painting lies in the essentially objective character of photography. For the first time, between the originating object and its reproduction there intervenes only the instrumentality of a nonliving agent. For the first time an image of the world is formed automatically, without the creative intervention of man.... All the arts are based on the presence of man, [but] only photography derives an advantage from his absence."[110]

For Bazin, cinema records the space of objects and between objects automatically and inhumanly.[111] As I have suggested, the attraction of Lumière films is not limited to this phenomenological automatism of the motion picture camera. In addition to the instants captured by the mechanical eye of the camera, the à travers effect in Lumière films incorporated the impressionist project of instantaneity: the artistic intention to reproduce an act involving the physical actions of human eyes and hands. The Lumière brothers did not use their mechanical instruments to produce objective data, as did their contemporary Étienne-Jules Marey.[112] Instead, the Lumière brothers' attempt was to be honest to the eyes of the spectator as well as the cinematographer in accordance with the physiological experiments in subjective vision and uncertain perceptual experience that were also happening in the nineteenth century across a wide range of disciplines.

Bazin claimed that the introduction of the "personality of the photographer" into the production by "automatic means" was limited only to the "selection of the object to be photographed and by way of the purpose he has in mind."[113] Although Bazin did not clearly address what he meant by "the purpose," the film scholar Dudley Andrew claims that it was "clear" for Bazin that "either a filmmaker utilizes empirical reality for his personal ends or else he explores empirical reality for its own sake. In the former case the filmmaker is making of empirical reality a series of signs which point to or create an aesthetics or rhetorical truth, perhaps lofty and noble, perhaps prosaic and debased. In the latter case, however, the filmmaker brings us closer to the events filmed by seeking the significance of a scene somewhere within the unadorned tracings it left on the celluloid."[114]

According to Andrew, the dichotomy can be rephrased as "an opposition between narrative realism and perceptual realism. . . . If perceptual space and time are rendered with honesty, a narrative will lie obscured within the ambiguities of recalcitrant sense data. If, on the other hand, narrative space and time are the object of a film, perceptual space and time will have to be systematically fragmented and manipulated."[115] According to the philosopher Jacques Rancière, these two opposing elements—"perceptual realism" and "narrative realism"—can be also termed the "aesthetic" logic of Romanticism that emphasizes the passivity of the camera and the "representative" idea of art inherited from Aristotle, which makes fiction the arrangement of actions into a unified whole.[116]

It is probably true that Lumière films use empirical reality for particular ends: for "perceptual realism," for "narrative realism," or for both. But I think that they also *explore* empirical reality in their own way. In this sense,

Lumière films search a third type of realism. To be more specific, the reality that Lumière films such as *Panorama pendant l'ascencion de la tour Eiffel* and *Sortie d'usine, [I]* explores is the one of the sense of vision: how transient it can be. The Lumière brothers intervened in the automatism of the motion picture camera in a physiological manner. Lumière films can be called "physiological realism," which is distinguished from either "narrative realism" or "perceptual realism."

Andrew argues further about the Bazin dichotomy by using the terms "*signification via* the world" and "*sense within* the world."[117] As he writes, "We have seen that Bazin believed that the world has a sense, that it speaks to us an ambiguous language if we take care to attend to it, if we silence our own desire to make that world signify what we want it to."[118] Perhaps Lumière films can be called sense *to* the world because they emphasize the sense of vision as the meditative act between sensing the world and creating signs, between "the art of nature" that "comes to us automatically through a photo-chemical process" and the human act of signification out of "aspects of the world which formerly we were unable or unwilling to see."[119] When Bazin speaks of the myth of total cinema, he claims that cinematic realism is "namely an integral realism, a re-creation of the world in its own image, an image unburdened by the freedom of interpretation of the artist or the irreversibility of time."[120] However, Tom Gunning argues for something more:

> At the point of its invention cinema pursued not only the possibility of a complete mimetic presentation of the world but also the creation of an image beyond the manipulations and interpretations of artists, not a particular artist's image of the world, but the "world in its own image." . . . Bazin's myth [of total cinema] moves beyond the subject, envisioning an image of the world not dependent on the expressive role of artistic subjectivity. Bazin may root the origin of the cinema in the obsession of its inventors, but the significance of this ideal cannot be reduced to subjective investment. Rather than subjectivity, Bazin's total cinema strives to achieve "the world in its own image." This unique image seeks precisely to overcome the distinction between subjectivity and objectivity. . . .[121]

There is no need to regard Lumière films as total cinema. But I still want to locate them between the "subjectivity" and "objectivity" that Gunning suggests. Despite Gunning's careful explication, Bazin's notion of the "world in its own image" still remains rather ambiguous. Yet Lumière films and the emphasis on the sense of vision by way of the à travers effect distinguish themselves from both a "mimetic representation of the world" and the "manipulations and interpretations of artists."[122]

In addition, Lumière cinema's à travers effect cannot be confined within 1970s ideological criticism on deep-focus cinematography. Critics of *Cahiers du cinéma* and *Cinéthique* in France not only questioned Bazin's claim about the objectivity of the camera but also criticized the depth of field observed in Lumière cinema. In his 1971 essay "Technique and Ideology," Jean-Louis Comolli, the editor in chief of *Cahiers du cinéma* from 1965 to 1972, regarded the Louis Lumière film *L'Arrivée d'un train en gare de La Ciotat* (*Arrival of a Train at La Ciotat, 1897*) as "a 'primitive' depth of field," which "was produced and regulated outside of any special manipulation by the sole fact of the disposition to make the primitive cinematic lens conform with the 'normal vision of the human eye,'" but "already" in which "the framing, camera angles and 'mise en scène' are overtly determined by the depth of field that allows for the train to arrive at the station, the passengers to wait for it and the spectators to feel fright at and admiration for it."[123] Hence, continued Comolli, "as 'innocent' as it seems (because it is 'automatic' and 'spontaneous'), this inscription of depth also marks its ideological presuppositions and the *calculations* that determine it."[124] The problem for Comolli was that the Lumière films uncritically maintained the Renaissance laws of perspective and bourgeois ideology.[125] As we have already seen, the à travers effect in Lumière cinema was not a naive replication of Renaissance perspective by a motion picture camera. Instead, with constant movements, blockings, and juxtapositions between front and back, it emphasized the physiology of the cinematographer-beholders, in conjunction with the late nineteenth-century discourse on Japonisme among impressionist and postimpressionist painters, printmakers, and photographers as well as the discourses on the physiology of the eyes. With its à travers effect, which emerged as a result of the Lumière cinematographers' engagement with Japonisme, Lumière cinema superseded both the automatism of the motion picture camera and the classical codes of aesthetic representation.

Four Types of the À Travers Cinema in the Lumière Catalog

There are a number of films in the Lumière catalog that use the à travers effect of the kinzō-gata-kōzu/chūkei-datsuraku/en=kin-hō composition with the contrast between the front and the back. It may not be true that all of them were produced under the direct influence of Japonisme, but they still shared a very similar compositional and often physiological strategy. I categorize those films into roughly four categories: (1) films that adopt the kinzō-gata-kōzu/chūkei-datsuraku/en=kin-hō composition, (2) films that create a kinzō-gata-kōzu/chūkei-datsuraku/en=kin-hō composition by the sudden but planned

Figure 1.6. © Institut Lumière, *Mauvaises herbes* (*Weeds*), 1896

appearance of moving objects, (3) films in which the front and the back interact violently, and (4) panoramic films in which the moving camera constantly recreates the kinzō-gata-kōzu/chūkei-datsuraku/en=kin-hō composition.

Type I: Films that adopt the kinzō-gata-kōzu/chūkei-datsuraku /en=kin-hō composition

The kinzō-gata-kōzu/chūkei-datsuraku/en=kin-hō composition was shared by a number of cinematographers of the Lumière Company. In *Mauvaises herbes* (*Weeds*, 1896), for instance, Auguste Lumière depicted female workers burning weeds. Gigantic white smoke created by the burning weeds blocks almost half of the right side of the frame while shadowy tree trunks and branches do the same for the left side of the frame. The bright background is barely seen through the contrasting objects in white and in black. The women keep working in the very frontal plane.

We find other white morphing objects that block the view in *Gros temps en mer* (*Bad Weather on the Sea*), another early film shot in 1896 by an anonymous cinematographer, where huge white waves keep attacking the giant rock in the

Figure 1.7. © Institut Lumière, *Gros temps en mer (Bad Weather on the Sea)*, 1896.

Figure 1.8. Katsushika Hokusai, "The Great Wave off Kanagawa" ("Kanagawa oki nami ura"), from the series *Thirty-Six Views of Mount Fuji (Fugaku sanjūrokkei)*, ca. 1830–1831 (Tenpō 1-2). Woodblock print (nishiki-e); ink and color on paper. Horizontal ōban; 25.2 × 37.7 cm (9 15/16 × 14 13/16 in.). Museum of Fine Arts, Boston. William Sturgis Bigelow Collection. 11.17652.

Figure 1.9. © Institut Lumière, *Laveuses sur la rivière* (*Women Washing on the Riverbanks*), 1897.

frontal plane from the offscreen left and there is a shadowy line of mountains at the back. Intentionally or not, this film compositionally imitates one of the most famous ukiyo-e prints by Hokusai, "Kanagawa oki nami ura" ("The Great Wave off Kanagawa," c. 1829–32) in the *Thirty-Six Views of Mt. Fuji* series. *Gros temps en mer* adds more à travers effect with actual movements of the waves.

Laveuses sur la rivière (*Women Washing on the Riverbanks*), an 1897 film shot by another unknown cinematographer, displays a ukiyo-e-style composition that lacks the middle ground. The sense of a lack of perspective is caused by the film's use of multiple blockings. The horizon is invisible, blocked by the building at the background. The middle ground is completely blocked by the low structure of the laundry platform in front. Instead of depth, the composition of this film looks as if nine belts were compiled one by one from the bottom to the top: (1) the surface of the river shimmering with reflecting lights and the washers' white clothes and skins, (2) the floor of the platform, (3) the shadowy space where nine female washers sit in line, (4) the lower roof over the platform, (5) the blinds, (6) the upper roof of the platform, (7) the fence and the bush, (8) the whitish ground on which three men with straw

Figure 1.10. © Institut Lumière, *Lancement d'un navire* (Launch of a Ship), 1896.

hats stand, and (9) the walls and doors of the building. Seemingly, there is a gap that separates the frontal plane and the background between the sixth and the seventh belt.

Type II: Films that create a kinzō-gata-kōzu/chūkei-datsuraku/en=kin-hō composition by the sudden but planned appearance of moving objects

In *Lancement d'un navire* (Launch of a Ship, 1896), movement of an added object to the screen plays a more significant role. Louis Lumière most likely photographed this film. He forcefully created separate planes as well as the à travers effect of the spectatorial eyes by using movement of a gigantic object. At the beginning, the film appears to have a linear perspective from the front to the background. The crowd shows their back in the front, and there are more people at the far back. All of a sudden, a huge black object invades the frame from the offscreen left, completely blocking the view of the background from the frontal plane. Because of the movement of the big boat, the composition suddenly turns rather two-dimensional. Once the boat starts to move out of the frame to the right, the viewers recognize the separation between the two

Figure 1.11. © Institut Lumière, *L'Arrivée d'un train à La Ciotat* (*Arrival of a Train at La Ciotat*), 1897.

planes. Moreover, when it moves, the boat also cuts off a number of celebratory ribbons and ropes, which fall onto the crowd in front. The danger of the debris adds a shocking effect for the spectatorial eyes.[126]

A famous 1897 film by Louis Lumière, *L'Arrivée d'un train à La Ciotat*, is a variation of *Lancement d'un navire*. The film historian Georges Sadoul pointed out "the incessant change of the viewpoint."[127] According to Sadoul, such changing viewpoints consequently create "a series of transforming images that simulate the continuity editing of today's films" in this single-shot film.[128] At first, this film appears to adopt a linear perspective with its composition at the La Ciotat station. After a man pushes a cart and leaves to the offscreen space on the right, a train enters the frame with a diagonal movement to the frontal left. When the train eventually stops at the station, the black body of the train blocks the background to the left. At first the eyes of the spectator naturally follow the diagonal movement of the moving train. But when the train stops, the film creates a rather two-dimensional composition that separates the background from the frontal plane, where the passengers walk off the train. Compared to *Lancement d'un navire*, the à travers

Figure 1.12. © Institut Lumière, *Plate-forme mobile et train électrique* (Mobile Platform and Electric Train), 1900.

effect is in limited use here, though. The spectatorial eyes do not really go back and forth.

Plate-forme mobile et train électrique (Mobile Platform and Electric Train), a film shot by an anonymous cinematographer at the 1900 Exposition Universelle in Paris, is a complicated version of the train film with a constantly transforming kinzō-gata-kōzu/chūkei-datsuraku/en=kin-hō composition. On the track that is constructed high above the street an electric train approaches from the far left, makes a curve, and leaves out of the frame to the left at the frontal plane. In addition, at the very frontal plane, people on a moving platform pass by the frame from left to right and constantly block the view.

The shocking effects that the sudden but planned appearance of an object cause and the transformation of the composition from a linear perspective to kinzō-gata-kōzu/chūkei-datsuraku/en=kin-hō are often observable not only in the Lumière Company's launch films and train films but also in its military films and in its street films. As for the military films, *Salut dans les vergues* (Salute in the Yards), which Lumière cinematographer Alexandre Promio (1868–1927) photographed in Croatia in April 1898, has a spectacular action that

Figure 1.13. © Institut Lumière, *Salut dans les vergues* (Salute in the Yards), 1898.

enhances the blocking function of the kinzō-gata-kōzu/chūkei-datsuraku/en=kin-hō composition. A crowd of sailors rapidly climbs up two masts of a boat anchored in the frontal plane and opens a number of flags to salute.

Regarding the street films, *Les Pyramides [Vue générale]* (*The Pyramids*), a March 1897 street film photographed by Promio in Egypt, consists of a single, almost-fifty-second shot. As the film scholar Michael Allan points out, the film is clearly divided into three planes. At the far end is the towering pyramid and, in the middle, the Sphinx.[129] These two historic monuments stand still under the bright sunlight. The astonishment happens in the very frontal plane: a row of travelers, rocking back and forth with the steps of their camels, abruptly appears from the offscreen left, moves across the frame, and leaves to the offscreen right. The travelers are rather shadowy figures except for their extremely white indigenous clothes. Compared to *Panorama pendant l'ascencion de la tour Eiffel*, the camera is fixed and the movement within the frame is horizontal. Yet the game of hide-and-seek—the objects at the back come in and out of sight—stays the same. As the film historian Jean-Claude Seguin argues, "This view, which combines strength and richness of composition and movement, is a work of art where the timeless and the temporal come together to offer a reflection on motionless and moving, photography and cinematogra-

Figure 1.14. © Institut Lumière, *Les Pyramides (Vue générale);* (The Pyramids), 1897.

phy."¹³⁰ Similarly, in a recent rerelease of these early Lumière films, Bertrand Tavernier, the French filmmaker and director of the Institut Lumière, notes that "the confrontation between the people on the camels and the Sphinx and the pyramids impressed a lot of directors; an Egyptian director like Youssef Chahine . . . saw that it was very, very modern."¹³¹

Arguably, Promio started consciously using the "modern" effect of the kinzō-gata-kōzu/chūkei-datsuraku/en=kin-hō composition in such films as *Salut dans les vergues* and *Les Pyramides (vue générale)* after he had encountered accidental invasions of the frame by foregrounding objects, which were common to early cinema internationally. In his first international trip in May 1896 as a Lumière cinematographer, Promio visited the Exposition Nationale in Geneva, Switzerland. The recording of tourism occupied a significant part of Lumière cinema. In *Cortège arabe* (Arab Parade), Promio is photographing a street scene in front of the Palais des Fées in a long shot when a group of tourists abruptly enters the frame from the frontal right. Their bodies block the camera vision. When a man accompanying a child tries to do something about this, the film roll comes to an end. Was the man the director of this film, or did he simply notice the camera and come closer to it? In any case, the kinzō-gata-kōzu/chūkei-datsuraku/en=kin-hō composition and the à travers effect

Figure 1.15. © Institut Lumière, *Cortège arabe* (Arab Parade), 1896.

accidentally occur in this film. As Seguin claims, "After having traveled and experienced the games of the multiple perspectives, Alexandre Promio began to apprehend what could be the foundations of a cinematographic art. He was faced with 'documentary' views. All animated images betray a presupposed 'mise en scène' that will only assert itself afterwards."[132]

In these accidental cases it is not appropriate to refer to the influence of Japonisme. Those compositional elements came in because of the technological conditions of filming in natural, uncontrolled surroundings. But once those accidents became controlled and strategically integrated in the films' aesthetic compositions, I argue that those controls and strategies of the cinematographers existed within the widely shared discourse of Japonisme.

Promio started using compositional movements in a strategic manner in 1897–98, as seen in *Salut dans les vergues* and *Les Pyramides (vue générale)*.[133] Promio was an optician before he witnessed the presentation of the Cinématographe Lumière at the Grand Café in Paris and became attracted to the medium. He contacted the Lumière brothers via an old school friend of theirs from La Martinière and started working for the Lumière Company in March 1896.[134] As an experienced optician, Promio must have been familiar with the developments in physiology, including the work of Louis Emile Javal and the "saccadic" movements of human eyes. From October 30, 1898, to March 26, 1899, Promio published a series of twenty-one articles, "Notes on Photography" (Notes sur la photographie), in the journal *Le Progrès illustré* in Lyon. Even though he did not specifically discuss cinematography, it is obvious that his thoughts came from his experiences of filmmaking during the preceding few years. In his first installment, Promio raised a question based on his medical-science background as well as on his experiences of cinematography:

> Is photography an art or a science? It is quite evident that science alone presided over its discovery and that the progress it has made up to the present day has been the result of long scientific studies. But, besides the lack of scientific knowledge that must be possessed by those who practice it (here we speak of amateur photographers), how great is the place occupied by artistic feeling in the composition of an image, in the choice of the subject! . . . Do we not find in photography the same rules of art that preside over the study of painting? Whether it is a canvas or sheet of paper, a porcelain or a glass plate, the rules of the art are the same. In the painter and the photographer it is the same concern for the balance of the painting, the same attention for cleverly arranged lighting gives the subject an artistic relief.[135]

Then, later in the series when he went into more detail on his thoughts on composition, he discussed the relationship between photography and the physiology of the human eye:

> The aim of the composition is to produce a pleasant representation of the subject's forms. For that, the two conditions which must be fulfilled, without, however, harming the truth of the picture depicted, are: unity and balance. The eye must be attracted, restrained by a principal object highlighted, on which the interest must first be directed; then it must be guided gradually in all parts of the image. This is the principle of unity. The balance of a painting is realized whenever the lines are cleverly compensated, that is, if the drawing must have a certain amount of oblique lines along one of the diagonals of the rectangle, it is necessary to arrange so that there is in the image an equal quantity of oblique lines along the other diagonal.[136]

Here, like Louis Lumière, Promio was clearly aware of the arbitrary physiological movements of the eye; he insisted on the importance of unifying and balancing them with the rules of geometry and lines. Even though Promio did not refer to the à travers effect, he was conscious of the transient nature of

Figure 1.16. © Institut Lumière, *I. Avant l'inauguration. Arrivée des souverains* (Before the Inauguration. Arrival of the Sovereigns), 1896.

human vision when he experimented with his cinematography scientifically and artistically.

Promio was not the only Lumière cinematographer who accidentally became aware of the combination effect of the frontal plane and the background and who started cinematographic experiments in composition and movement. Constant Girel (1873–1952), another Lumière cinematographer, who will be one of the protagonists of the following chapter, started to use the kinzō-gata-kōzu/chūkei-datsuraku/en=kin-hō composition in his films of tourism as well as in his street films. Even though Girel was not an optician, he was the son of a pharmacist and had studied science before he joined the Lumière Company.

In one of his first films, *I. Avant l'inauguration. Arrivée des souverains* (Before the Inauguration. Arrival of the Sovereigns), shot in Breslau, Germany, in September 1896 to record the inauguration of the monument erected in honor of Guillaume I, which the German emperor and empress attended, Girel captured the horizontal movements of the people on horses from a slightly high angle. A black top hat of a spectator appears and disappears (in extreme close-ups) several times from the offscreen space on the left and blocks the view.

Figure 1.17. © Institut Lumière, *Chutes du Rhin vues de près* (Rhine Falls Seen from Close Up), 1896.

The invasion of the frame by this foregrounding object accidentally creates a kinzō-gata-kōzu/chūkei-datsuraku/en=kin-hō composition and the à travers effect.[137]

In contrast, in *Chutes du Rhin vues de près* (Rhine Falls Seen from Close Up), a tourist film that Girel shot in Switzerland on September 29, 1896, the frontal plane and the background look more strategically contrasted. An extreme close-up of the waterfall occupies nearly two-thirds of the frame from the bottom while the townscape at the background is seen through smoky splashes (weeping form motif). According to his September 22, 1896, letter to his mother, Girel was already conscious of the contrast between the frontal plane and the background: "Yesterday, the weather was beautiful. I shot 4 beautiful views as I will explain. One view was shot from the boat coming from Coblentz and arriving in Cologne. You see with the shores moving in the background."[138] In *Chutes du Rhin vues de près* the moving target (the splashes and the smoke on the water) in the frontal plane enhances the à travers effect of this film. So we could argue that by late September 1896, Girel had learned the effect of the kinzō-gata-kōzu/chūkei-datsuraku/en=kin-hō composition.[139]

Figure 1.18. © Institut Lumière, *Labourage* (Plowing), 1896.

Type III: Films in which the front and the back interact violently

Deep-space composition is observable in many Lumière films. For instance, *Labourage* (Plowing), a film shot at farms in Normandy for the farmer by an unknown cinematographer in 1896, seemingly imitates Jean-François Millet's paintings in its lighting scheme: the light coming from the frontal left creates strong shadows of the figures diagonally onto the back right. In *Labourage* two lines of cows slowly plow the field from the left side of the background to the frontal right.[140] The focus of films with depth composition is more on smoothing the movement in accordance with a linear perspective.

In contrast, in some of the Lumière films the interaction between the two planes is so abrupt and often violent that the middle plane in the composition is rather ignored or surpassed. The connection of these films to Japonisme may be looser than those films in the other three types, but the sense of chūkei-datsuraku, or omission of the middle ground, is the strongest in this type. In this sense these films still exist in the shared concerns of space and composition with Japonisme.

Concours de boules (Balls competition), an 1896 film photographed in Lyon by an unknown cinematographer, appears to adopt the linear perspective and

Figure 1.19. © Institut Lumière, *Concours de boules* (Balls competition), 1896.

Figure 1.20. © Institut Lumière, *Joueurs de cartes arrosés* (Card Players Watered), 1896.

Figure 1.21. © Institut Lumière, *Duel au pistol (longueur: 12 mètres)* (Duel with pistol [Length: 12 meters]), 1896.

depicts the player and the spectator of a *pétanque* match. But thrown metal balls are flying toward the camera. The balls' rapid movements violently connect the background and the frontal planes.

Joueurs de cartes arrosés (Card Players Watered), another 1896 film photographed in Lyon by an unknown cinematographer, adopted a similar sense of astonishment in one of the earliest examples of a staged comedy. In a composition with depth, two men play cards and end up in a physical fight. Another man who has been watering the garden turns his water hose on the two men so that water is suddenly sprayed to the frontal plane from the background.

Another example is *Duel au pistol (longueur: 12 mètres)* (Duel with Pistol [Length: 12 Meters]), a film shot by Gabriel Veyre (1871–1936), the other protagonist of the following chapter, in Mexico in December 1896. Veyre also studied pharmacy before he was hired by the Lumière Company in January 1896 and traveled to Latin America (Mexico, Cuba, Venezuela, and Colombia) from July 1896 to December 1897. *Duel au pistol (longueur: 12 mètres)* records a duel (most likely staged) between two men: one stands in the frontal plane, the other at the back. The only things that we see in the duel are two lines of smoke coming out of their pistols. It is impossible to see the

Figure 1.22. © Institut Lumière, *Panorama du funiculaire du Mont-Dore* (Panorama of the Mont-Dore Funicular), 1898.

bullets. But the man in front falls as the result of the interaction between the two planes.

Type IV: Panoramic films in which the moving camera constantly recreates the kinzō-gata-kōzu/chūkei-datsuraku/en=kin-hō composition

Panorama pendant l'ascencion de la tour Eiffel is a good example of this type. Although many of the "phantom ride" films in the Lumière catalog maintain the depth of composition of a linear perspective,[141] *Panorama du funiculaire du Mont-Dore* (Panorama of the Mont-Dore Funicular, 1898), cinematographer unknown, is another film in which the moving camera constantly recreates the kinzō-gata-kōzu/chūkei-datsuraku/en=kin-hō composition, as in *Panorama pendant l'ascencion de la tour Eiffel*. This film simultaneously displays both the landscape in the background in bright sunlight and the constant passing of shadowy trees right next to the camera, which blocks the view of the middle ground.[142] The à travers effect is enhanced by the movement of the camera, which is placed at the rear of a cable car that climbs up a mountain. The camera

Figure 1.23. © Institut Lumière, *Namo: panorama pris d'une chaise à porteurs* (Namo: Panorama Taken from a Sedan Chair), 1900.

captures the receding landscape behind the cable car, especially the contrast between the stillness (or very slow change) in the background and the quick and constant replacement of the visible field in the frontal plane.[143]

Last, for *La village de Namo: panorama pris d'une chaise à porteurs* (Namo: Panorama Taken from a Sedan Chair), photographed in the village of Namo in Vietnam in January 1900, cinematographer Gabriel Veyre placed the Cinématographe Lumière on some sort of a cart to achieve a low-position tracking shot. This film begins with a medium-long shot of the people of the village, but as a naked indigenous child smilingly runs right after the camera, the kinzō-gata-kōzu/chūkei-datsuraku/en=kin-hō composition is continuously recreated between the child and the landscape of the village and the people in the background.[144]

These four types of Lumière films demonstrate that many Lumière cinematographers were conscious of how to compositionally reproduce bodily actions with the mechanical eye of the camera. Such awareness occurred in the process of the industrialization of cinema as well as in the midst of the trend of Japonisme. The Lumière brothers and their cinematographers shared their ideas on how to instantly *and* physically capture movement in the outside world with impressionist and postimpressionist painters and printmakers. Ukiyo-e Japanese woodblock prints inspired them with the method of sketching and composition that not only instantly captured moments and movements of the environment but also physically mobilized the eyes of the spectator. The à travers cinema of the Lumière Company was an attempt to reinvent corporeal experiences in representational practices. The endeavor thus communicated not only with the ideas of contemporaneous French painters and printmakers but also with the minds of Japanese artists. The Lumière à travers cinema was a dialogic focal point of Japonisme. In the following chapter we will examine what happened to such dialogues when two Lumière cinematographers, who had been familiar with Japonisme and had already incorporated the concept of the à travers, actually went to Japan to make films in the original Japanese landscape with Japanese people.

Japonisme and Nativized Orientalism

THE LUMIÈRE BROTHERS' "JAPANESE FILMS"

Japonisme and the Lumière Brothers' "Japanese Films"

In January 1897 and October 1898, two prominent cinematographers of the Lumière Company separately traveled to Japan. Their names were Constant Girel and Gabriel Veyre. Their trips to Japan proved that the connection of Lumière films to Japonisme was not limited to the notion of à travers, which dealt with the issues of composition and instantaneity.

The Lumière brothers' film catalog has thirty-three films photographed in Japan. The number itself is noteworthy because no other Lumière film was photographed in any other part of Asia, except French Indochina. A personal connection was probably an important reason. The Lumière brothers had had a Japanese classmate at the La Martinière Institute in Lyon: Inabata Katsutarō (1862-1949). In 1877 Inabata was sent by the Kyoto prefecture on scholarship to study the famous silk industry, the methods of dyeing in particular, in Lyon. He studied chemistry at the La Martinière Institute from 1880 to 1883 and at the University of Lyon in 1884.[1] After he returned to Japan in 1885, Inabata became the leader of the rising silk industry there. Later, Inabata saw the Lumière brothers during his business trip in Europe for his company, Muslin Textile Company (established in 1895).[2] On his way back to Japan, Inabata took a boat, the *Natal*, and Constant Girel was also on board. There is no record, but the two might have had an arrangement to get on the same boat.[3] They arrived in Kobe on January 9, 1897.[4] After his arrival, Girel stayed in a house in Kyoto, the hometown of Inabata.[5] Then Girel and Inabata showed Lumière films at the Nanchi Enbujō Theater in Osaka from February 15 to February 28, 1897, considered to be the first film screenings in Japan. After that, Girel helped with the Cinématographe exhibitions in Kyoto, in Tokyo, and again in Osaka.[6] Gabriel Veyre left France in July 1898, stayed in Canada for two months, and arrived in Yokohama aboard the *Princess India* on October 25, 1898. Because he made some films in Kyoto, Veyre may also have had contact with Inabata, in spite of the lack of official records.

As did other Lumière cinematographers, before and after visiting Japan both Girel and Veyre photographed official events in other countries. Girel photographed the coronation of Russian Tsar Nicholas II and maneuvers of the German Army. Veyre filmed a party of the president of Mexico and an official ceremony of the Cambodian king in French Indochina. But in Japan, neither Girel nor Veyre photographed political events, governmental officials, or anything similar. Girel had a chance to spend some time with the French squadron in Hakodate on Hokkaido, a northern island of Japan, but did not film it.[7] Girel and Veyre contacted the Meiji emperor.[8] Girel wrote in his April 28 letter sent from Kyoto to his family, "Today I will try to do the asking of the Mikado, who is here now, if I can give him a session."[9] By "a session," Girel most likely meant a session that would explain the Cinématographe Lumière to the emperor. The *Otaru shimbun* newspaper reported on July 22, 1897, that Girel "humbly" showed the Cinématographe Lumière to the crown prince and other members of the imperial family.[10] Veyre wrote in his November 12 as well as December 21, 1898, letters that he was preparing for the screening of films at the Imperial Palace.[11] Yet they did not push themselves to photograph the royal family.[12]

Instead, what both Girel and Veyre photographed was the daily lives of ordinary Japanese people. Their films appeared to be actuality films of late nineteenth-century Japan. But if we look closer, we can detect the two cinematographers' Orientalist fantasy about Japan. Japanese people and landscapes were repeatedly placed in premodern spheres in their films. An expression of European hidden pleasure toward a timeless or sensuous Japan was certainly observable there. At the same time we can observe their attempts to apply their knowledge of Japonisme to Japanese people and landscapes. The two cinematographers, familiar with Japonisme, attempted to rearticulate or authenticize the ukiyo-e–style, high-contrast composition in the original Japanese landscape with Japanese people. That is, those films were the result of transmedial efforts to reproduce impressionist paintings' animated forms. So, the vogue of Japonisme that enhanced the attractive image of Japan among

French people was another important reason for the exceptional number of the Lumière "Japanese films."[13]

But what I want to particularly focus on in this chapter is not the reasons behind the production of those "Japanese films" but the process and the result of it. Because of the innate status of cinema as a medium with duration, the "Japanese films" of the Lumière Company recorded, often in an unintended manner, the moments of interaction between the Lumière cinematographers' Orientalist fantasy and the actual Japanese people in front of their camera.[14] A one-directional subject-object relationship could not be maintained any longer; the relationship turned dialogic. Some Japanese people became aware of the technology of cinema as well as of the cinematographers' Orientalist fantasy. In order to cater to that fantasy they seemed to start consciously playing the roles of imaginary Orientals. Borrowing the term coined by the art historian Norman Bryson, I am calling the actions of those Japanese people "nativized Orientalism." Discussing the work of Osman Hamdi Bey, an Ottoman administrator and painter of the late nineteenth century, Bryson writes the following:

> While the French master [Jean-Léon Gérôme] made mistakes in detail when he depicted the world of Islam [in his Orientalist paintings], Osman Hamdi Bey corrected them based on careful research and reconstructed the landscape of the Ottoman empire in the past. The attraction that Gérôme gave exclusively to the imaginary Orient was adapted by Bey and transformed into a new type of art, which is an Ottoman national painting. In fact, Bey's painting appeared when the Ottoman nation abandoned its multilingual and multiethnic empire and reconstructed itself as a nation state. It was a painting that should be called "nativized Orientalism," where negative aspects of the Orient included in Gérôme's case were excluded. The people who had been living in an imaginary world turned into the ones with intelligence, civilization, and philosophy.[15]

In his short essay, Bryson does not fully articulate his concept of "nativized Orientalism." For instance, his analysis does not answer such questions as who the target audience of Bey's work was and exactly how Bey's painting worked to "reconstruct" a nation-state. I use the term *nativized Orientalism* to specifically describe conscious acts of self-exoticization of non-European people for the foreign gaze. Such acts of nativized Orientalism were revealed throughout the duration of some of the Lumière Company's "Japanese films." As I discuss in the following pages, the target audience of their acts was the Lumière cinematographers behind the camera as well as the European people who had an Orientalist fantasy about Japan.

In addition to nativized Orientalism, I will propose another term, *internalized Orientalism*, in chapter 3 in order to describe the relationship between some of the Lumière Company's "Japanese films" and the Japanese government's modernization policy of constructing Japan as a nation-state. When I use these notions, nativized Orientalism and internalized Orientalism, I am certainly inspired by the concept of "strategic essentialism" that the literary theorist Gayatri Chakravorty Spivak introduced in the context of feminism in 1984.[16] According to Spivak, there are times when nationalities, national groups, or minority groups, including herself, need temporarily to adopt essentialized images of themselves in order to support their identity in their political actions and social practices.[17] Since then, Spivak has repudiated the idea of strategic essentialism mainly because it had been deployed in nationalist enterprises that promote essentialism itself. As she commented in a 1989 interview, which was published later in her 1993 book,

> The strategic use of an essence as a mobilizing slogan or masterword like women or worker or the name of a nation is, ideally, self-conscious for all mobilized. This is the impossible risk of a lasting strategy. Can there be such a thing? At any rate, the critique of the "fetish-character" (so to speak) of the masterword has to be persistent all along the way, even when it seems that to remind oneself of it is counterproductive. Otherwise the strategy freezes into something like what you call an essentialist position, when the situation that calls forth the strategy is seemingly resolved.... If one is considering strategy, one has to look at where the group—the person, the persons, or the movement—is situated when one makes claims for or against essentialism. A strategy suits a situation.[18]

I still think Spivak's idea is valid and useful in a historically specific analysis of "a situation." In this chapter and the next I closely analyze situations in which the Lumière Brothers' "Japanese Films" were photographed in order to clarify who essentialized whom—when, how, and for what purposes—and delineate at least two types of strategies: nativized and internalized Orientalism.

Constant Girel and Yokohama Photographs

Constant Girel photographed eighteen films in Japan with the Cinématographe Lumière between January 9 and December 26, 1897. In addition, Girel collected seventy-seven photographs during his stay. Those photographs displayed an interesting mix of geographical records, exotic-looking sceneries, and portraits. Those photographs were compiled in an album with a sophisticated lacquerware cover, on which is carved a geisha in a rickshaw on a run in front of the Mt. Fuji and Kyoto temples.[19] His films apparently depicted the daily scenes of Japan in a documentary style, but these photographs in the album clearly indicated Girel's Orientalist fantasy about Japan as well as his knowledge of the discourse of Japonisme.

The lacquerware cover indicated that it was a typical custom-made album of so-called Yokohama photographs (*Yokohama shashin*). Many of the photographs inside Girel's album look quite similar to the general repertoire of such images. Yokohama photographs, produced by many studios at the port of Yokohama in the 1870-90s, were mainly targeted to globe-trotters who visited Japan. Large quantities of Yokohama photographs were exported to Europe via the UK and Hong Kong as well as to the US, especially during the last decade of the nineteenth century. More than 4,000 photos per year were exported from Yokohama between 1890 and 1901; the peak years were between 1896 (24,007) and 1899 (20,242), presumably because of extra orders from the US.[20] Girel's visit to Japan occurred during these peak years of Yokohama photographs.

In general, there were three subjects identified in the Yokohama photographs: (1) natural landscapes (Mt. Fuji, etc.); (2) historical architecture (shrines and temples in Nikkō, Kyoto, etc.); and (3) portraits of Japanese people, mostly staged in studios.[21] Even though these photographs appeared to document the actuality of places and people in Japan, they were carefully selected, composed, or staged to satisfy the foreign gaze.

The art historian Satō Morihiro locates Yokohama photographs in the context of the "picturesque" style, which arose in the eighteenth century and had spread to the urban popular audience by the mid-nineteenth century. Satō defines the original picturesque as the paintings that captured "rugged rock surface, scraggy cliffs, chaotic trees, ancient ruins, poor farmers, meandering rivers, and winding roads" in "rough touches with asymmetrical compositions."[22] Then he argues that the notion of the picturesque presupposed a "distance" between the viewing subject and the viewed object.[23] Sublime natural landscapes in picturesque paintings were spatially separated from urban spectators. Historical architecture and ruins were temporarily separated from contemporary viewers. Poor farmers or indigenous people in European colonies were separated from the colonizers in terms of class, race, and ethnicity. In other words, Satō claims, picturesque paintings and photographs turned nature and people into "a spectacle to be viewed and appreciated that would never endanger the viewing subject."[24] Referring to the art historian W. J. T. Mitchell's argument on the ideology of landscape that presents artificially created scenes as if they were naturally given ("Landscape is a natural scene mediated by culture"),[25] Satō concludes that the notion of picturesque was based on the "mechanism that symbolically controls various Others by confining them in an [agreeable] image."[26]

Moreover, according to the film historian Giorgio Bertellini, despite the original association with distant landscape, the picturesque style became closely connected to colonialism. Bertellini argues that the picturesque style, which was originally adopted by Northern European elites "to render their cultural experience of Mediterranean Europe," eventually "translated into imaginative and comforting views of distant landscape and exotic characters" and obtained "racial significance."[27] In other words, as the art historian Linda Nochlin argues, the picturesque style legitimized the Western concept of Orientalism.[28] If we combine the arguments by Satō, Bertellini, and Nochlin, Yokohama photographs could be seen as a racialized spectacle of the picturesque style. They catered to the expectations of their consumers—that is, the Orientalist fantasy of the West.

The seventy-seven photographs in Girel's album followed the three types of Yokohama photographs and their picturesque style: (1) apparent geographical documents of Japanese landscape (including a landscape photo of Mt. Fuji and the river in front of it, where a woman in kimono washes clothes while a man awaits a boat, carrying something on his head; and a landscape photo of Mt. Fuji with two rickshaws on a wooden bridge between pine trees); (2) archetypal capture of the architecture of Japan (including a staged photo of five geishas posing on a wooden deck over a river, most likely the River Kamo in Kyoto, playing music with a *shamisen* and a drum, making tea, and showing off their kimonos; two different architecture photos of the Golden Temple in Kyoto; and an architecture photo of the great pagoda of a castle); and (3) specific portraits of working people (including a portrait of a man walking with a heavy load of goods on his shoulder; a photo of boats leaving for fishing; a bird's-eye-view photo of a business port; a photo of Japanese man pulling a cart loaded with seven bags of rice and a Japanese man, possibly his supervisor, with a Western coat and a Western straw hat; and a portrait of Girel's interpreter). These images certainly catered to Girel's Orientalist fantasy about Japan.

A noteworthy difference in Girel's album from a typical one with Yokohama photographs was that it included photographs of European people, including himself. The inclusion of these photos not only indicated Girel's connection to a certain group of people from whom he received aid during his stay in Japan but also implied his shared sensibility with the colonialist and Orientalist thoughts that regarded non-Western space and people as enlightened.[29] In fact, the first photograph in the album is of the Church of Foreign Missions,[30]

Figure 2.1. © Institut Lumière, "Groupe de geishas prenant le thé" (Group of geishas having tea).

Figure 2.2. © Institut Lumière, "Rivière avec barque à voile devant le Mont Fuji" (River with sailing boat in front of Mt. Fuji).

Figure 2.3. © Institut Lumière, "Église d'une Mission Étrangère" (Church of Foreign Missions).

which stood on a mountainside. Curiously, the photograph also captures an old and untidy Japanese house made of wood. Some laundry hangs on the side fence. There is also a Japanese man in kimono standing on the street right next to the church. The whiteness and the height of the church are clearly contrasted as an enlightening existence of the space. Another photograph also indicates such a sense of enlightenment, or Westernization under the supervision of Westerners. The priest stands right next to two Japanese women in kimonos sitting on a bench. Contrary to the festive geisha in typical Yokohama photographs, these two women are in plain kimonos and pose penitently in front of the priest.

These two photographs were most likely taken by Girel. If some of the photographs in the album had not been purchased but had been taken by Girel or by his assistants, they did not only indicate Girel's Orientalist thoughts but also became evidence of the application of his knowledge of Japonisme to authentic Japanese people and landscapes. Girel's album has one landscape photo titled "Torii et cerisiers en fleurs" (Torii and Cherry Blossoms). This is anything but a simple record of Japan even though it captures an actual view of the Yokohama harbor. Compositionally, this photo adopts the kinzō-gata-kōzu/

Figure 2.4. © Institut Lumière, "Japonais posant devant leur maison" (Japanese posing in front of their house).

chūkei-datsuraku/en=kin-hō, the ukiyo-e–inspired composition that was already well-known in Europe, as I discussed in the previous chapter. Branches of a cherry blossom tree in full bloom and a *torii* shrine gate supposedly on a hilltop occupy the close frontal plane, whereas the Yokohama harbor is depicted farther back, and there is almost no middle plane within the frame. In fact, among three thousand color Yokohama photographs preserved at Yokohama Kaikō Shiryōkan (the Yokohama Archives of History), we find exactly the same photo, which is titled "Iseyama kara Kitanakadōri 6-chōme o miru" (A View of Kitanakadōri 6-chōme from Mt. Ise).[31] The photo captures a view of the Yokohama harbor seen over the gate of a shrine at Mt. Ise. A temporary lighthouse, which was built in 1874 and would be replaced by an octagonal lighthouse in 1900, is observable in the left corner of the photo. There is no record of the photographer of this photo. Another photograph that captures the same torii and the view of the harbor was taken presumably before 1882 by Usui Shūzaburo, who was one of the Yokohama photographers after he opened his studio in 1875.[32] Yet the composition of Usui's photograph is different from the one in Girel's album, which uses the kinzō-gata-kōzu/chūkei-datsuraku/en=kin-hō composition in a more explicit manner to put more emphasis on the torii and the cherry blossoms.[33]

Figure 2.5. © Institut Lumière, "Torii et cerisiers en fleurs" (Torii and Cherry Blossoms).

There is a strong possibility that Girel was the photographer of "Iseyama kara Kitanakadōri 6-chōme o miru." His April 28 letter indicated that "Mr. Favre Brand" lent him a small camera to take some photos in Yokohama.[34] According to the letter, Girel photographed cherry blossoms in bloom and enclosed the photos of them with the letter.[35] If that had been the case, Girel was involved with the production of Yokohama photographs. He applied the well-known composition of Japonisme to his photographs taken in Japan. Even if this photo was not taken by Girel, it is still evidence of the fact that he purchased at least one Yokohama photograph that fully used the kinzō-gata-kōzu/chūkei-datsuraku/en=kin-hō composition.

The eighteen Lumière films that Girel made in Japan should be cross-examined with these photographs in his souvenir album. Those films depicted the everyday lives of Japanese people in a documentary style, but they also reflected Girel's Orientalist fantasy about Japan, including his sense of enlightenment. In fact, most of Girel's films could be categorized in the three types of Yokohama photographs: (1) natural landscapes, (2) archetypal historical architecture, and (3) staged portraits of working people.

Eight films out of the eighteen are staged portraits of Japanese people engaging in exotic-looking traditional activities (Type III). Four films involve

Figure 2.6. © Institut Lumière, *Acteurs japonais: bataille au sabre* (Japanese Actors: Battle with the Sword), 1897.

Kabuki actors; one shows geisha of the Gion-Shinchi area in Kyoto; two demonstrate practices of *kendō*, a Japanese martial art using bamboo swords and protective armor; and one documents a religious activity. The sense of "staging" stands out in the films that depict Kabuki actors and kendō practices because those films were photographed in exterior locations. Kabuki and kendō are usually acted or practiced inside.

In *Acteurs japonais: exercice de la perruque* (Japanese Actors: Exercise of the Wig, 1897), the actor Nakamura Ganjirō I practices the lion dance from the Kabuki play *Shin Shakkyō* while costumed in an extremely long white mane.[36] In *Une scène au théâtre japonais* (A Scene at the Japanese Theater, 1897), six Kabuki actors, one of whom is an *onnagata* (female impersonator), dances. In *Acteurs japonais: danse d'homme* (Japanese Actors: Dance of Men, 1897), an actor with a tall hat dances in front of a white curtain with the design of the Japanese flag.[37] In *Danseuses japonaises* (*Japanese Dancers*, 1897), four geisha sit on a platform in front of a temple-like building and two pine trees. These four play the shamisen while another four geisha dance in perfect order. The pine trees look similar to the backdrop drawing of pine trees in Kabuki theaters. In *Lutteurs japonais* (Japanese Fighters, 1897), which was filmed in front of the Hakuran

Kaikan Building near the Heian Jingū Shrine in Kyoto, two men demonstrate a kendō match in front of a building with eight Japanese flags.[38] *Escrime au sabre japonais Japanese Saber Fencing* (Fencing with Japanese Saber, 1897) displays a free practice of kendō in front of a big drum. In *Danceuses: la danse des éventails* (Dancers: The Dance of Fans, 1897), a number of women in religious white dresses with black collars dance a ritualistic dance, striking fans that they hold above their heads. In *Acteurs japonais: bataille au sabre* (Japanese Actors: Battle with the Sword, 1897), the Kabuki actor Ichikawa Sadanji I performs a sequence supposedly from *Maruhashi Chūya*, brandishing his sword at other samurai armed with *naginata* (pole weapons).[39] The sense of "staging" becomes clear when Sadanji I hesitates when his act ends and he retakes the final pose once more. Most likely, the film roll had not reached the end, and Girel wanted to keep the action going in order to avoid wasting it.[40]

Any one frame from these eight films could have been used as a Yokohama photograph. In other words, Girel made eight animated Yokohama photographs with the Cinématographe Lumière.

Six other films, which apparently documented daily activities on the streets in Japan, mixed all three types of Yokohama photographs. These films replicated the settings and compositions of Lumière street films set in France, but Girel emphasized exotic-looking elements in the scenes: the parapet of the bridge, the old wooden buildings of Kyoto, and a young woman in kimono who stops right in front of the camera in *Un Pont à Kyoto* (A Bridge in Kyoto, 1897); *happi* coats that Japanese workers and craftsmen traditionally wear in *Déchargement dans un port* (Unloading at a Port, 1897); Shinto costumes that gathered people wore in *Procession shintoïste* (Shinto Procession, 1897); and a number of people in kimono in *Arrivée d'un train* (Arrival of a Train, 1897).

Une rue à Tokyo (A Street in Tokyo, 1897) explicitly emphasizes performed traditionality. In the diagonal composition of the street that many Lumière films adopted, a rickshaw comes running toward the camera, stops as if the driver is showing off the exotic appearance of his vehicle, drops off a customer who wears kimono, makes a turn, and moves away in the opposite direction. Such movement could not have happened coincidentally right in front of the camera. Curiously, the customer in kimono walks along with the rickshaw from which he had just descended. His unnatural behavior is evidence that the movement of the rickshaw was staged for this film.

Girel thus attempted to make Orientalist fantasy authentic with the use of actual Japanese landscape and people. Moreover, he sometimes incorporated the kinzō-gata-kōzu/chūkei-datsuraku/en=kin-hō composition. By doing so, Girel animated the discourse of Japonisme that he had already been familiar

Figure 2.7. © Institut Lumière, *Une rue à Tokyo* (A Street in Tokyo), 1897.

Figure 2.8. © Institut Lumière, *Sortie d'un temple shintoïste* (Exit from a Shinto Shrine), 1897.

with by using the Cinématographe Lumière in Japan. In *Sortie d'un temple shintoïste* (Exit from a Shinto Shrine, 1897), a thick column of a torii shrine gate occupies the frontal left part of the composition, and a shrine gate building through which a number of people are walking stands in the layer at the back. Girel clearly contrasted the two layers in the film's composition and made it look like an animated ukiyo-e.

In addition to the issues of Girel's Orientalist fantasy and his knowledge of the ukiyo-e style, two films by Girel are noteworthy because they display his Orientalist sense of enlightenment in a unique manner. During his stay in Japan, Girel made two trips to Hakodate, a port city in Hokkaido, a northern island of Japan, in August and October 1897. During his second trip to Hakodate, he photographed two films of the Ainu, an indigenous people in Hokkaido.

I wonder why Girel made these trips to Hokkaido. At that time, it took days to get there from Kyoto. From a business perspective, he had already made sufficient numbers of "Japanese films" in Kyoto and in Yokohama for the Lumière Company and did not need to go to the northern island. So Girel must have had a special reason for his trips. In fact, Girel had an uncle, Father Alexandre Berlioz, a member of the Paris Foreign Mission Society, who became the bishop in Hakodate in June 1891.[41] Most likely, the fathers at the Seminary of Foreign Missions aided his trips to Hokkaido. Girel mentioned the name "Father Aurientis" several times in his letters to his family.[42] Father P. Aurientis was the leading figure at the Seminary of Foreign Missions in Kyoto and stayed there for thirty years.[43] He and Bishop Berlioz must have known each other. Girel wrote in his August 16 letter to his mother that he was at "one of the mission's properties, close to the sea" near Hakodate and participated in "the ordination of a Trappist priest by the uncle."[44] According to Girel's October 18 letter, he also met "the brave Father Râyou, the local missionary" in Sapporo, the capital city of Hokkaido.[45] The Lumière brothers might have chosen Girel for the Japan trip in the first place because of his family connection to the missionary in Japan.

It is not clear exactly in which Ainu village Girel made his films, but it was located near the city of Muroran. Girel wrote about the location in his October 18 letter: "So it is in fact Mororan [sic] that we reached the evening of our departure from Hakodate. We traveled twenty leagues [approximately seventy miles] by train through the virgin forest. Then we arrived at a station and traveled eighteen more leagues on horseback to reach the village in question."[46] Bishop Berlioz was the one who established a church in Muroran in 1891 in order to mission to the Ainu.[47] The first three names in the list of people who

Figure 2.9. © Institut Lumière, *Les Aïnos à Yeso, I* (*Ainos at Yeso, I*), 1897.

were evangelized by Bishop Berlioz in Muroran were Ainu.[48] The three Ainu people baptized by Bishop Berlioz were from Etomo village near Muroran.[49] So the Ainu village where Girel made his two films might have been Etomo. Etomo and the center of Muroran are only a mile apart, but Hakodate and Muroran are approximately 120 miles apart, which fits Girel's description.

In *Les Aïnos à Yeso, I* (*Ainos at Yeso, I*, 1897), one of the two Ainu films by Girel, four Ainu men wearing their traditional-looking costumes dance a "warrior dance," according to Girel's October 18 letter, in front of a house made of wood.[50] They make a small circle to fit their movements within a camera frame. In *Les Aïnos à Yeso, II* (*Ainos at Yeso, II*, 1897), seven women of the Ainu in plain kimonos dance a "bird dance," according to Girel's letter.[51] They made a diagonal line from the frontal right to the back left to fit within the camera frame.

Girel photographed these two films of the Ainu in October 1897, less than two years before the Meiji government of Japan officially announced Hokkaido kyūdojin hogo hō, or the Hokkaido Former Natives Protection Law, which was designed to achieve the assimilation of the Ainu population, on March 1, 1899. Girel's films could have functioned in various ways under these specific sociopolitical conditions.

Figure 2.10. © Institut Lumière, *Les Aïnos à Yeso, II* (*Ainos at Yeso, II*), 1897.

First, Girel's films catered to the "salvage paradigm" among European ethnologists and globe-trotters. The salvage paradigm is an anthropological term that developed in the late nineteenth century and described the belief that practices and folklore of certain indigenous cultures must be preserved and recorded before being destroyed or extinct. Especially after Russia's expansion into Eastern Siberia starting in the early eighteenth century, detailed reports on the Ainu reached Europe. "With the rise of the Rousseauian creed of the 'noble savage,'" argues the art historian Luke Gartlan, "European travelers reimagined the Ainu as a resilient people living in harmony with nature."[52] Ethnographic studies of them, accompanied by a number of photographs, proliferated in Europe and enhanced the salvage paradigm. Girel apparently shared this paradigm when he photographed the Ainu. In the October 18 letter, Girel wrote that he had "happiness" when he was "in these wild places."[53] Girel and his interpreter offered fruit, potatoes, and cakes in return for photographing the Ainu.[54] Girel wrote about the date of departure from the Ainu village: "The next day, we heavy-heartedly left those beautiful men, proud and dignified, who are disappearing little by little, but proudly yield to the Japanese race. It is a real struggle for life where education and civilization annihilate savages."[55]

Girel thus lamented the destructive nature of civilization over natural life, which corresponded to the contemporaneous discourse on modernity.⁵⁶

Second, Girel's films of the Ainu could serve for the nationalizing projects of the Meiji government, which regarded the camera as a key technology.⁵⁷ The position of the Meiji government was a colonizing force within Japan. From the beginning of the Meiji era in 1868, Japanese emigrants settled on the island "Ezo" (the land of barbarians) or "Ainu Moshir" (homeland of the indigenous Ainu), which the Meiji government renamed "Hokkaido" in 1869. In that same year the Meiji government established Kaitakushi (the Hokkaido Development Agency) to assert Japan's sovereignty over the island in order to counter the perceived threat of Russian encroachment. Internally speaking, according to the literary critic Komori Yōichi, the development of Hokkaido was at the heart of an employment scheme for former samurai whose previous privileges were rescinded through the process of abolishing feudal domains.⁵⁸ The development agency supported those former samurai to become farmers. At the same time, argues Komori, the development agency carried out "blatant assimilation policies, issuing most notably an order that strictly abolished 'customs' that were deeply rooted in Ainu livelihood."⁵⁹ Whereas Ainu livelihood had relied primarily on hunting and fishing, those open areas were expropriated as land for Japanese settlers. Rituals related to Ainu traditional views on life and death were forbidden.⁶⁰ The development agency sent photographers to topographically document the modernization of the island initiated by the agency as well as to capture images of the Ainu from anthropological and archeological perspectives in order to promote the assimilation policies.⁶¹ The enforcement of the Hokkaido Former Natives Protection Law of 1899 finalized the assimilation policies by turning the Ainu into "citizens" through the phrase "former natives."⁶² According to Komori, the livelihood of the Ainu, which was fundamentally rooted in nature, was destroyed by this process.⁶³

The Meiji government obviously shared with Europe the Orientalist enlightening viewpoint toward the premodern culture of the Ainu. The hiring of Baron Raimund von Stillfried by the Colonization Agency in 1872 to photograph the Ainu clearly indicated this viewpoint: Stillfried was a prolific Yokohama photographer from 1868 to 1881. Far from spontaneous records of a Japan soon to disappear amid the realities of the modern world, Stillfried's studio-based Yokohama photographs eliminated the signs of modernity, adding impeccable grooming, attire, and painted backdrops with iconic images of Japan, such as Mt. Fuji, and demanded his models' absolute compliance to his direction.⁶⁴ According to Luke Gartlan, instead of subscribing to the salvage paradigm, Stillfried presented "an idyllic notion of 'old Nippon'" in his studio portraits, featuring models decorated as "traditional" Japanese types (and not as individual personalities).⁶⁵ The Meiji government thus wanted to treat the Ainu as an "idyllic notion of 'old Nippon'" in order to distinguish them from the modernizing and Europeanizing Japan.

"Without a doubt," argues Komori, "one of the goals of the Hokkaido Former Natives Protection Law was to extricate Ainu from the educational and medical activism of foreigners and to place them under the auspices of the state then called the Greater Japanese Empire."⁶⁶ If that was the case, the positions of Stillfried and Girel were conflicted between the "activism of foreigners" and service for the Meiji government's assimilation policies. Girel was not officially hired by the Japanese government to photograph the Ainu.⁶⁷ But he seemed entangled within the nation-building agenda and politics of the Meiji government: the "administration of those 'minorities' within the expanding boundaries of the nation-state" that Gartlan suggests.⁶⁸ Girel explicitly described the Meiji government's "colonization" effort of Hokkaido in his letter, comparing a road from Sapporo to Otaru to one in the French Riviera: "Sapporo, at the heart of the virgin forest was established there and built a few years ago by imperial decree. It is crossed by perpendicular streets in the American style, oriented from North to South, and from East to West. It is the center of the colonization of the large island that stretches from Hakodate to the Kouriles and Kamchatka. Then we veered toward Otaru and thus reached the East coast. What a beautiful road. This stretch of coastline totally reminded me of the coast road from San Remo to Cannes."⁶⁹ For the Meiji government, Girel's films would work as another anthropological and archaeological record of the customs of the "former natives."

Thus, *Les Aïnos à Yeso, I* and *Les Aïnos à Yeso, II* are not simple records of the daily lives of the Ainu. They are products of a religiously, culturally, and politically complicated condition. Considering this condition, it is difficult to certify that the Ainu dances depicted in those two films are authentic ones based on their rituals. In *Les Aïnos à Yeso, II*, the viewers cannot help noticing that there is one man in a traditional-looking costume circling around the dancing women, as if he were monitoring their movements. He could have been a director of their traditional-looking dance. These women are not wearing traditional costumes but plain kimonos. If their dance had been one of their rituals, they should have performed in authentic costumes. By 1897, the people of Ainu were probably aware of the European salvage paradigm regarding them because of their encounters with tourists and photographers. If so, they could have easily performed to satisfy the expectations of foreigners such as Girel. Moreover, by 1897, because of the Meiji government's assimilation policies and the consequential acts of violence against their livelihood, the Ainu had already been suffering and needed protection. Then, in either case, their "warrior dance" and "bird dance" might not have been based on authentic rituals but could have been representations of an invented tradition to cater to the salvage paradigm as well as to desperately ask for protection. If that was the case, the Ainu's acts in these two films were those of self-replicating nativized Orientalism, conscious acts of self-exoticization to cater to the foreign gaze. The "foreign" for the Ainu involved both European and Japanese people. I will come back to discuss this notion of nativized Orientalism in more detail later in this chapter.

Many of the films made in Japan by Girel were not screened in Japan. But *Les Aïnos à Yeso, I*, *Les Aïnos à Yeso, II*, or both were screened in Nagoya on July 1, 1899, as well as in Lyon on January 9, 1898.[70] Although many of the films made in Japan did not look appealing (or were too quotidian) to a Japanese audience, the films about the Ainu looked appealing to mainland Japanese viewers, who were ready to distinguish themselves from the Ainu. The Japanese title that was given to *Les Aïnos à Yeso, I* was *Hokkaido dojin Aino no kuma odori*, literally translates as "The Bear Dance of the Ainu, the Indigenous People in Hokkaido": not a "warrior" dance but a "bear" dance. If it had not been an authentic but an invented-traditional dance, then the name could have been anything. More importantly, the Ainu were called "dojin" in the title and were clearly distinguished from Japanese people even when the Ainu had already been turned into Japanese citizens. In other words, when they watched the Ainu films by Girel, those Japanese spectators identified themselves with the European Orientalist viewpoint while they participated in the Meiji government's imperialist modernization policy to construct Japan as a modern nation-state. I discuss this issue in greater detail in the next chapter when I define the concept of internalized Orientalism.

Gabriel Veyre and Geisha

Gabriel Veyre, another Lumière cinematographer, photographed ten films in Japan during his stay there between October 28, 1898, and March 2, 1899. Veyre shared with Constant Girel the Orientalist fantasy and knowledge of Japonisme. Veyre was more eloquent than Girel about the salvage paradigm, lamenting the "traditions" vanishing as a result of modernization and Westernization. As Veyre wrote in his notes on Japan, "Whenever I go through a city, I see too many vulgar derby hats. They abandon the beautiful unique hairstyle that they have learned from their ancestors and are imitating Western

Figure 2.11. © Institut Lumière, *Récolte du riz* (Harvesting rice), 1898–1899.

hats. There are policemen wearing Western-style uniforms that do not fit. There still are delicate and beautiful wooden houses, but many of them are on the verge of being replaced by unstylish and gigantic concrete buildings."[71] Whereas Girel's films were inclined to the sense of enlightenment probably because of his family/religious background, the films that Veyre photographed in Japan more explicitly incorporated certain trends in Japonisme: the pictorial composition and the motif of geisha.

When Veyre represented Japanese people at work in his films, his goal did not seem anthropological or archeological. For instance, the emphasis of his two films about Japanese farmers, *Récolte du riz* (Harvesting Rice, 1898–99) and *Moulin à homme pour l'arrosage des rizières* (Mill Man for Watering Rice Fields, 1898–99), was clearly their pictorial compositions. *Récolte du riz* and its minimal movements of farmers whose heads are covered with cloth or straw hats rather faithfully recreate the painting *Des glaneuses* (*The Gleaners*, 1857) by Jean-François Millet. Millet once testified to the results of the study of Japanese art, and many of his best effects of atmosphere and light are attributed to Japanese suggestion.[72] As in *Des glaneuses*, the extreme long shot is composed of white sky (approximately one-fourth of the top part of the frame) and the field (three-fourths of the frame at the bottom). A line of trees delineates the two

Figure 2.12. © Institut Lumière, *Moulin à homme pour l'arrosage des rizières* (Mill Man for Watering Rice Fields), 1898–1899.

areas. The field is divided into two colored areas. In *Récolte du riz*, the left side reflects water; all the rice plants have been mowed. Farmers (four in the front and two at the far back) bend their backs and are slowly working in the middle. In *Des glaneuses* the bottom half of the field is in darker colors where most of the stray stalks of wheat have been gleaned while three peasant women bend their backs and work in the middle ground.

Moulin à homme pour l'arrosage des rizières noticeably adopts the kinzō-gata-kōzu/chūkei-datsuraku/en=kin-hō composition of Japonisme. In this film a farmer gives a glance at the camera and starts watering the rice field by stepping on a waterwheel. The farmer and the waterwheel occupy the close frontal plane on the right, and the rice field is seen at a farther layer. Two small houses and a utility pole at the far end emphasize the contrast between the front and the back. Again, the movement of the farmer is so minimal that the pictorial quality of the film is emphasized. The farmers display their routine (thereby "authentic") work in a conventional manner, even though we can point out that the watering action by the Japanese farmer in *Moulin à homme pour l'arrosage des rizières* does not seem necessary.[73] All the rice plants in the field look to have already been mowed; the farmer most likely did his routine work only for the camera. If there is a pictorial quality in these two films, it is created by the compositions that Veyre selected from the discourse of Japonisme.[74]

Other than these two films, Veyre's object of interest was focused: geisha.[75] He made eight films about geisha. The geisha fantasy was clearly a part of the Orientalist imagination that created a gendered hierarchy between the West (dominant and masculine) and the East (obedient and feminine). The connection between the images of geisha and those of Japan was popularized in the discourse of Japonisme. Geisha had been a popular subject of ukiyo-e since the Edo period, but images of geisha first appeared in the published journals and diaries of Europeans who traveled to Japan in the mid-nineteenth century, including those by a Swiss assemblyman, Aimé Humbert (*Le Japon illustré*, 1870), and a French industrialist, Émile Guimet (*Promenades Japonaises*, 1878). In these writings, geisha were introduced as one of many Japanese cultural entities whose historical roots in female entertainers went back to the seventh century (the *Saburuko*) or to the thirteenth century (the *Shirabyōshi*). Geisha were artists/entertainers and different from the courtesans/prostitutes of the pleasure quarters that were built in the sixteenth century and flourished in the eighteenth century. Their role was to divert brothel patrons while they waited for their appointed courtesan to become available. Despite that fact, the image of geisha was still connected to the pleasure quarter. When the images of geisha were found in ukiyo-e that arrived in Europe around the same time as those travelogues, they naturally caught the eyes of an audience that had never visited Japan but was looking for the sensual attractions of Orientalist paintings. Even when the artists stayed in Japan and depicted the details of Japanese lives, they tended to turn Japanese people and landscapes into mythic and ideal objects based on Orientalist fantasies. The details obtained from firsthand experiences in Japan by people who lived there enhanced the sense of authenticity of fantastic images. Examples were the illustrations of geisha by Charles Wirgman, an English sketch artist and correspondent for the *Illustrated London News*, who resided in Japan from 1861 until his death in 1891; illustrations by Georges Bigot, a French cartoonist who arrived in Japan in 1882 and married a Japanese wife in 1895; and colored photographs of geisha by Felice Beato, a Venetian photographer who stayed in Japan from 1863 to 1884.[76] The roles that photography (and, later, cinema) played were not small when they captured the real bodies of Japanese people and actual spaces in Japan.[77] With the popularity of Gilbert and Sullivan's *The Mikado; or, The Town of Titipu* (1885), Sidney Jones's British musical comedy *The Geisha* (1896), and Puccini's *Madama Butterfly* (1904, modeled on Pierre Loti's 1887 novel, *Madame Chrysanthème*, John Luther Long's 1898 novella, and David Belasco's 1900 play

Madame Butterfly), the image of geisha as obedient women who were trained to be agreeable to men and sensual courtesans who were victims of the Japanese system of legalized prostitution became widely popularized in the West.[78] It was true that European artists, including Veyre when he made *Moulin à homme pour l'arrosage des rizières*, closely studied the aesthetic compositions of ukiyo-e and incorporated them in their work. There was a communication or negotiation process there as I have discussed in the previous chapter. But when it came to geisha, the dialogic nature of Japonisme was surpassed by the one-directional imagination of Orientalism.

Although Veyre observed the depleted social status of Japanese women from a kind of anthropological perspective, he maintained his geisha fantasy, which existed in the discourse of Japonisme. On the one hand, Veyre stated the following:

> The moral debasement of the woman [in Japan] is a result of the Buddhist idea that the woman does not have a soul. The woman is a "thing" for her husband or her father. . . . The husband divorces his wife when he does not like her any longer. Even if the father does not sell off his daughter, he loans her to people. To his eyes, his daughter is nothing but a commodity whose value depends on beauty and intelligence. The inferior social status and the tyranny of men are surely the reasons for the appeal of the obedient and little frail woman of Japan, which is often compared to a bird in a birdcage.[79]

Then, on the other hand, Veyre defined Japanese women in a rather archetypal, dichotomized manner: "In order to fully understand the social status of Japanese women, we need to completely wipe out the sense of Western morality from our minds. . . . Japanese girls are extremely attractive because they combine decency and indecency, obedience and obscenity."[80] His films apparently reflected his geisha fantasy strengthened by his firsthand observation of the status of women in Japan.

Danse japonaise: I. Kappore (Japanese Dance: I. Kappore, 1898–99) and *Danse japonaise: V. Gocho Garama* (Japanese Dance: V. Gocho Garama, 1898–99) were apparently staged, even though these films were shot outdoors: a water pond in front reflected shimmering lights. These two films, which shared the same setting and were most likely photographed on the same date, clearly followed Girel's *Danseuses japonaises* in terms of the theatrical composition in extreme long shots. Four geishas on a platform dance with fans while one geisha plays the shamisen.

Danse japonaise: III. Geishas en jinrikisha (Japanese Dance: III. Geishas on a Rickshaw, 1898–99) shares a premise with Girel's *Une rue à Tokyo*, the street

Figure 2.13. © Institut Lumière, *Danse japonaise: I. Kappore* (Japanese Dance: I. Kappore), 1898–1899.

Figure 2.14. © Institut Lumière, *Danse japonaise: V. Gocho Garama* (Japanese Dance: V. Gocho Garama), 1898–1899.

Figure 2.15. © Institut Lumière, *Danse japonaise: III. Geishas en jinrikisha* (Japanese Dance: III. Geishas on a Rickshaw), 1898–1899.

film with the staged performance of a rickshaw driver. This film may be called a documentation of the everyday activities at the entrance of a geisha house, but again it was clearly staged. The camera was placed in front of a geisha house. As soon as a geisha and her caretaker appear from the far right, a rickshaw arrives from the offscreen left. The driver momentarily glances at the camera and drives out of the frame to the right. Then a similar action is repeated with a different geisha and a different rickshaw driver. Like many of Girel's films, any one frame of these films with geisha could be used as a Yokohama photograph and would cater to the fantasy of Orientalism (the motif of sensuous non-Western women) or, in this case, to that of Japonisme (the theme of obedient but sensuous geisha).

Dialogic Moments and Nativized Orientalism

As we have seen, the "Japanese films" by Girel and Veyre represented their Orientalist fantasy while they also represented authentic Japanese landscapes and the daily lives of Japanese people in a pictorial form that sometimes appropriated the aesthetic composition of ukiyo-e. Yet there were times when cinema's innate status as a medium of duration could put the coherence of Girel and Veyre's acts of materializing their Orientalist fantasy into question. In some of their films the Cinématographe Lumière captured dialogic moments between the French cinematographers and the Japanese people in front of the camera. I must say that the dialogues between the photographers and the photographed occurred rather accidentally. Those dialogues were different in nature from the aesthetic communication between the European and Japanese arts that happened when those cinematographers consciously used the kinzō-gata-kōzu/chūkei-datsuraku/en=kin-hō composition in their films. Neither Girel nor Veyre intended to have such dialogues with the Japanese people in front of their cameras. Nor did they even apparently notice that such dialogues had happened. But the mechanical eye of the motion picture camera recorded those moments.

Two films among eighteen by Girel, which I have not discussed yet, captured such moments. In a film titled *Repas en famille* (*Family Meal*, 1897), Girel photographed Inabata Katsutarō, who implemented the first film screening in Japan in 1897 with Girel, and his family (his first daughter, Kiku; his second daughter, Mari; his niece Natsu; and the maid of the house, whose name is not known).[81] The film was photographed at an *engawa*, a narrow wooden deck of a Japanese house. The camera was placed outside of the house. *Shōji* sliding doors behind the five people separated this limited space from the interior of the house. All family members were in kimono, and the two adult women's hairstyles were done properly in a traditional manner. In a long shot, Inabata takes out a cigarette, puts it into a Japanese-style pipe, lights up the pipe from a brazier placed in front of him, smokes a little bit, receives a teacup from the maid, respectfully bows to her (the maid also bows), and sips some tea. An infant held by an adult woman is forced by her to drink some tea as well.

From an anthropological or ethnographic perspective, what was recorded in this film appears to be a scene of everyday life in Japan: wearing kimono, sitting on the floor, having tea in a ceremonial manner, etc. This film nicely fit into the salvage paradigm in nineteenth-century photography. Luke Gartlan suggests that nineteenth-century imperial photographers were tasked with the documentation of "traditional" societies, including Japan, before the tide of modernization and Westernization erased their presence.[82] Gartlan quotes a critic at the photo exhibition by Austrian photographers Baron Raimund von Stillfried and Hermann Andersen in London in 1877: "From Japan comes quite a gallery of Japanese landscapes, subjects and objects, technically excellent but specially interesting as illustrating the costumes and peculiarities of old

Figure 2.16. © Institut Lumière, *Repas en famille (Family Meal)*, 1897.

Nippon, now so rapidly passing away. Messrs. Stillfried and Andersen, it is to be hoped, may still continue their field of researches."[83] *Repas en famille* could be regarded as one such project of preservation: to document "traditional" daily life in Japan before its inevitable demise caused by modernity. It was certainly a part of the Orientalist imagination that presupposed a dichotomy between the modernized West and the premodern East.

However, if *Repas en famille* had been screened for the contemporaneous Japanese audience (it was not), they should have noticed a number of strange elements in the film. For instance, Inabata's kimono, the black *haori* with family crests, as well as the two infants' flashy garments and the women's traditional hairstyles, are too formal for a daily scene. Inabata receives a teacup from the woman at the left and deeply bows to her. The woman is a maid; thus, it is not appropriate for the master of the house to respectfully bow to her. Also, curiously, the title of the film, *Repas en famille*, indicates that the film is about a family meal. However, nobody in this film eats anything at all. As the art historian Kinoshita Naoyuki points out, no Japanese filmmaker would title this film "A family meal."[84]

Figure 2.17. "A Scene of a Family" in *Le Japon illustré*.

It was Girel who wanted to include the ritualistic behavior of bowing by Japanese people in this film.[85] Most likely, he intended to document the "Japanese family meal," whose image had already been known in the visual archive of Japan (paintings, drawings, and photographs). Kinoshita suggests that by the end of the nineteenth century, the image of the "Japanese family meal" existed in Europe in the forms of paintings and photography.[86] For instance, an 1873 photograph, *Gozen—Meal Time* (Gozen—Shokuji no jikan), appeared in the English journal *The Far East*. In the photo, young parents (or a mother and an older brother) are giving a meal to a baby. Kinoshita argues that this was a staged photograph from a European perspective on Japan because the motif of a "family meal" in art did not exist in Japan at that time. The notions of "modern family," "home," and "family dining" had barely emerged in the era of modernity.[87] Perhaps it was one of the Yokohama photographs. Similarly, an illustration titled "A Scene of a Family" was published in *Le Japon illustré* by Aimé Humbert. In the illustration a Japanese man in kimono is sitting on a floor, being served sake by one of his children. The other child, who is on the lap of the Japanese man, supposedly his father, holds a cup for him. The caption states that this illustration was based on a photograph. The original photo, possibly another Yokohama photograph, must have been a staged one

Figure 2.18. © Institut Lumière, "Constant Girel: Mes deux esclaves et mon interprète à Kyoto" (Constant Girel: My Two Servants and My Interpreter in Kyoto).

because small children were not supposed to serve sake to their fathers in the usual family environment in Japan.[88]

Kinoshita also points out that some Yokohama photographs depict "family meals." "Eating at Home" depicts two women at the meal, served by two other women. Another photo, with no title, shows a man, a woman, and a child eating noodles on an engawa platform and being served sake by a young woman.[89] Under these conditions of invented-traditional images of Japan in Yokohama photographs that had been circulated in Europe during the period of Japonisme, Girel already had formulas of images that he could apply to the actual landscape and the people in Japan.

Indeed, a photograph in Girel's photo album has a setting that is quite similar to that of *Repas en famille*. In "Constant Girel: Mes deux esclaves et mon interprète à Kyoto" (Constant Girel: My two servants and my interpreter in Kyoto), Girel's interpreter, Muramatsu, is sitting on the *tatami* mat with two young boys and serving tea. Like *Repas en famille*, this snapshot appears to freeze a moment of everyday life in Japan. But this photograph also contains strange artificiality: Muramatsu is in a kimono with his family crest on it, an outfit too formal for a daily scene. Also, among the three, he is obviously the master of the house, yet he is the one who is serving tea for the two children. This would not have happened in Japan during the Meiji period, when patriarchy ruled.

Another film by Girel titled *Dîner japonais* (Japanese Dinner, 1897) also depicted Japanese people having a meal. This film could be situated within the context of the same visual archive of Japan. For instance, in 1883 Georges Bigot, a French painter and cartoonist, published a lithography album, *Asa* (Morning), that mainly depicted images of Japanese people of various professions. Like Yokohama photographs, the album's main target was European tourists. At the very end of the album, Bigot included a shadow-picture cartoon titled *Dîner japonais*. The cartoon is composed of seventeen successive images and depicts a politician, a high-class bureaucrat, and a merchant, who hosts them as they visit a restaurant. The three enjoy geisha's songs and dances. On their way home, the merchant tries to bring a geisha into bed while the politician and the bureaucrat peek at the couple.[90] Bigot published a drawing titled *Une petit fête à la maison de thé* (A Little Party at the Tea House), which basically repeats the story of *Dîner japonais*, in the June 28, 1890, issue of the popular Paris magazine *Le Chat Noir*.[91]

To a viewer familiar with Bigot's cartoon and drawing, Girel's *Dîner japonais* looks almost exactly like them, but in motion and with actual Japanese people in play. In an extreme long shot, three women in kimono, supposedly geisha, are playing the shamisen, two women by their sides are singing, two women are serving cups of sake to two men at the table, and two more women are drinking with the two men. This film was clearly photographed in exterior under the sunlight, but a Japanese-style *goza* mat on the ground and a Japanese screen at the back function to imitate an interior space in a Japanese house. So it was staged like a Yokohama photograph. The imagination that formulated this film was based solely on the Orientalist fantasy. But because of the location in Japan and the appearance of Japanese people, as in a Yokohama photograph, the entire scene looks like an everyday Japanese practice. Setting aside the fact that this was not a normal daily dinner practice in Japan but a scene of entertainment with geisha, the scene was still not authentic: no food should have been placed in front of the geishas, the sake cup should not have moved around so rapidly among the people at the table, and one man was supposed to be the main guest of the table, so he should not have served himself rice (the other man who acted comically was the so-called *hōkan*, a middleman between the guest and the geisha). No matter how authentic this film looks with the presence of actual Japanese bodies, it is not even as realistic as Bigot's cartoon, which at least depicts the restaurant space and its details correctly. Bigot must have visited the place and made sketches.

Figure 2.19. © Institut Lumière, *Dîner japonais* (Japanese Dinner), 1897.

Inabata should have known better when he appeared in *Repas en famille*. He must have noticed that there were too many inaccurate depictions of Japanese daily life in the film. Then why did he agree to appear? Inabata understood Girel's conscious or unconscious desire to materialize what he thought of everyday life in Japan with authentic Japanese places and people. Inabata was aware of the Orientalist gaze that the Lumière Company possessed. Inabata also knew what the Cinématographe Lumière was. When he placed himself in front of it, he was clearly aware of the movie camera that was filming him. During the short duration of *Repas en famille*, Inabata turns to his left and looks directly toward the camera at least three times: once after he had placed a cigarette in his pipe, another time after he smoked, and the last time after he sipped tea. When he turns to the camera, Inabata is conscious of how the filming is going. Most likely, using his eyes, he is trying to communicate with Girel, who was behind the camera. He is probably asking Girel with his eyes if he had behaved as Girel had wished even if the cinematographer did not realize Inabata's intention. For the contemporary European audience, including Girel, the returning gazes by Inabata should not have mattered much. On many occasions, the people who were captured by the Cinématographe Lumière during their everyday activities directly looked into the camera or turned their gazes to the cinematographer, mostly out of curiosity.

Considering Inabata's awareness of the Orientalist gaze and the act of filmmaking, we could conclude that the film *Repas en famille* captured a dialogic moment between the photographer and the photographed even when this conversation, or negotiation, was recorded accidentally. Girel did not intend it to happen and was not even fully aware that it had occurred. Yet Inabata acted out an image of "traditional" Japan to cater to the Orientalist fantasy that the Lumière Company's "Japanese films" contained. Thus, during the film's duration, *Repas en famille* revealed Inabata's embodiment of nativized Orientalism, a self-conscious performance of the exotic Other.

This mechanism is similar to what happened between Girel and the Ainu in *Les Aïnos à Yeso, I* and *Les Aïnos à Yeso, II*, as well as between Girel and the man at the dinner table in *Dîner japonais*. Yet the Ainu probably did not know about movie cameras even if they had already been familiar with photography. They might have danced out their invented traditions in front of the camera, but no dialogic moment was captured accidentally during the duration of those two films. So even if the Ainu consciously embodied nativized Orientalism, it was not revealed within the two films' diegetic spaces alone. Only when viewers take the sociopolitical context of the historical moment into consideration can they think about the possibility of the invented tradition in the photographed dances.

In the case of *Dîner japonais*, there were certain recorded dialogic moments between Girel and a person in the film. During the duration of the film, the man at the dinner table looks toward the camera three times when he serves himself rice.[92] Like that of Inabata in *Repas en famille*, this behavior of the man in this film is as if he were asking Girel, "Am I doing OK here?" Contrary to Inabata, however, this man probably did not know what the Cinématographe Lumière was or fully understand what was going on. Returning gazes might have been his expression of dismay. Also, there was no way to see if this man was aware of the Orientalist fantasy that the French cinematographer had. If so, unlike Ianabata's case, the man was not consciously engaging with nativized Orientalism. There was a possibility that Inabata was also at the filming location and instructed the man to act out the Japanese dinner party. There is no evidence that Inabata was there, but he was present at the filming of another film by Girel, *Acteurs japonais: exercice de la perruque*, that I mentioned earlier. Girel's letter from Kyoto to his family on September 21 stated that he and Inabata would go pick up an actor before the filming.[93] Inabata's biography also noted that the photographing of the film with the Kabuki actor

Nakamura Ganjirō I took a whole day at Gion in Kyoto.[94] If Inabata was at the filming of *Dîner japonais*, the man in the film could have communicated with both Inabata and Girel with his eyes. Then again, it was Inabata who embodied nativized Orientalism from behind the camera.

Discussing *Nihonjinron* (theory of Japaneseness) and *Zhōngguórénlùn* (theory of Chineseness), the linguist Edward McDonald considers "nativised Orientalism" in a negative manner: "Both kinds of discourse would, paradoxically perhaps, count as types of 'orientalism' in Said's terms, since although they are being produced by the 'natives' rather than by the 'foreigners,' their roots lie in the historical pressures on the native sense of self in these countries."[95] Inabata might have performed an expected image of a Japanese man having a family meal in *Repas en famille* because of the "pressures" from Girel the foreigner and the Lumière Company. But considering his souvenir album and his other films, it was unlikely that Girel realized that what he saw in *Repas en famille* was not an authentic scene of "everyday life" in Japan. Thus, it was Inabata who chose to demonstrate the invented tradition for the camera. If that was the case, the initial power structure of the owner of the gaze and the object of the gaze became questionable. Inabata was no longer a passive object of the controlling gaze. He empowered himself during the duration of a shot. This is the mechanism of nativized Orientalism revealed in *Repas en famille*: the film became possible only in the context of Japonisme.

If Orientalism unconsciously constructs a Western self through an ostensible focus on its "Oriental" other, what does nativized Orientalism do? First, as we have seen in Inabata's case, it is a conscious act. The gaze from the West is always on the mind of the people who embody nativized Orientalism. Second, the focus is still on "Oriental" otherness. But now it is the other who constructs itself as the other. The binary between the Western self and the non-Western other is maintained, but the latter is no longer the former's fantastical possession. So nativized Orientalism constructs a non-Western other by the other. Third, nativized Orientalism is a rebellious act, albeit with certain limits. It recuperates the power of cultural-image formation to non-Western people. In the case of Inabata, he maintained the status of an object for a foreign gaze, but he simultaneously became a producer of his cultural image. Eventually, there appeared Japanese people who created their own works similar to Lumière's "Japanese films" to export them to the West. In the field of Yokohama photographs, for instance, recent research on the pioneer Japanese photographer Shimooka Renjō demonstrated that there were acts of nativized Orientalism within Yokohama photographs. Shimooka learned his skills from foreign visitors to Japan in the 1850s; took over a studio in

Figure 2.20. © Institut Lumière, *Chanteuse japonaise* (Japanese Singer), 1898–1899.

Yokohama from an American photographer, John Wilson, in 1862; and became a producer of Yokohama photographs.[96] According to the historian Ozawa Takeshi, Shimooka "accommodated the exoticism of customers from abroad so that he used a Japanese girl as an accompaniment, let his customers put on kimono, *hakama*, and samurai armor, changed the setup of his studio to a *zashiki* room with tatami mats, placed a stone lantern [which is not an interior object] right next to *byobu* screens."[97] Shimooka's words, documented in his biography, indicate that he was fully aware that his souvenir photographs caused misunderstandings of Japanese culture and customs.[98] In the following chapter I examine the work of the cinematographer Shibata Tsunekichi as a creator of "Japanese films" of his own. Moreover, as I demonstrate, Shibata's work often went beyond nativized Orientalism and indicated what I call internalized Orientalism.

A Fantastic Image and an Authentic Smile

In a film titled *Chanteuse japonaise* (Japanese Singer, 1898–99) by Gabriel Veyre, a Japanese woman in kimono also turned her gaze to the cinematographer behind the camera. Unlike Inabata, she most likely did not know about the Cinématographe Lumière. She probably did not know what was going on when

Figure 2.21. © Institut Lumière, *Danse japonaise: II. Harusame* (Japanese Dance: II. Spring Rain), 1898–1899.

she was being filmed. But she did what Inabata did not do: she smiled at the camera. That was another dialogic moment between the photographer and the photographed accidentally captured by the movie camera.

Chanteuse japonaise was one of three geisha films in which Veyre photographed geisha's dances in medium long shots. In the other two, *Danse japonaise: II. Harusame* (Japanese Dance: II. Spring Rain, 1898–99) and *Danse japonaise: IV. Jinku* (Japanese Dance: IV. Lively Dance, 1898–99), a couple of geisha dance with fans (in the former) and with umbrellas (in the latter). What we cannot help noticing in these two films is how bad their dances are. The two women's dance movements are rough and unsynchronized in *Danse japonaise: II. Harusame*. An apparently drunk man, who looks like the man in *Dîner japonais*, is dancing with the women in *Danse japonaise: IV. Jinku*. One geisha cannot even open the umbrella that is essential to her performance. Such amateurishness could be surprising to European viewers with the Orientalist fantasy. To them, geisha were supposed to be accomplished traditional performers of premodern Japan. It would take many months of training to become a professional geisha. But the moments of contingency, or of reality, depicted in these two films could destroy the timeless image of Japan.

Figure 2.22. © Institut Lumière, *Danse japonaise: IV. Jinku* (Japanese Dance: IV. Lively Dance), 1898–99.

The case was more subversive in *Chanteuse japonaise*. One of the women who appear in *Danse japonaise: II. Harusame* and *Danse japonaise: IV. Jinku* plays the shamisen in a medium long shot. After a while, she looks into the camera and shows a "hesitant" smile, the word that Kinoshita Naoyuki used to describe the film.[99] Kinoshita argues that such an unexpected "hesitant" smile could be captured only by cinema and reveals the "reality of geisha" as "a human being."[100]

Closely examining one of Stillfried's untitled studio portraits (a Yokohama photograph), in which a Japanese woman is playing the shamisen, Gartlan argues that "throughout Stillfried's practice, the sitter's averted gaze became a signature aspect of his genre work.... Given the meteoric rise of photography in Japan, the association of an averted, absent-minded gaze with notions of cultural authenticity was certainly not politically neutral. Stillfried's retrospective notion of a feminized authenticity presents a society amenable to the foreign photographer's operations—of compliant sitters who avert their eyes from the camera in symbolic obeisance to his visual control."[101]

Contrary to Stillfried's Yokohama photographs, in *Chanteuse japonaise* the Cinématographe Lumière recorded the geisha's un-averted gaze. Based on his

Orientalist fantasy about Japan, Veyre most likely intended to formulate "a feminized authenticity" with the actual body of the geisha. Yet the smile of the young woman at the camera—as well as the amateurish uncontrolled dances in *Danse japonaise: II. Harusame* and *Danse japonaise: IV. Jinku*—moved away from Veyre's "visual control." Compared to Inabata's conscious act of inventing tradition in *Repas en famille*, these women's behaviors were more spontaneous and unconscious. They did not embody nativized Orientalism. Still, the movie camera captured moments of negotiation between the Orientalist fantasy of geisha in European minds and the reality of geisha as human beings. These dialogues could happen in the context of Japonisme only when the Lumière Company decided to send out its cinematographers to Japan.

I want to further interpret what happened in *Chanteuse japonaise*. My focus is more on the action after the woman showed the "hesitant smile." The rest of the film captured her continuing to play the shamisen and singing after the initial smile. She kept looking toward the camera. Even though she did not understand moviemaking, she was clearly aware of the gaze of a foreigner.

In a 1995 essay the film theorist Livio Belloï convincingly rearticulates the relationship between operator and filmed subjects in Lumière films based on the sociological notion of "interaction . . . the reciprocal influence of individuals upon one another's action in one another's immediate physical presence."[102] Belloï defines "the on-looker" as the one who has "the tendency to look at street curiosities and to contemplate its 'natural' attractions" and the "observer" as the one "renouncing motion, focusing on a fixed point in space" and "singularizing himself," and then argues, "Once the cameraman distances and institutes himself as observer, the on-looker's attitude is transformed as well. From distracted, mobile and open as his glance was, the on-looker's glance now *stops*, focusing on the observer and his machine, which have become genuine poles of attraction, indeed centers of visual attention."[103] Closely examining *Lyon: débarquement d'une mouche* (Lyon: Coming Ashore from a Boat, 1896), Belloï notes three categories of reactions from "the on-looker" when he or she "becomes conscious of the observer and his machine."[104] The first one is "an indirect recognition of the camera," with which the onlooker "tries to catch a glimpse of his presumed object" in a "*reversed* look."[105] The second category is "a negative recognition of the camera": a lady dressed in black quickly masks her face with her left arm and disappears from the camera frame, which shows an attitude that expresses "defiance."[106] The third category "supposes a *look*, presented quite openly to the camera."[107] Belloï adds a "leftover" of these three categories: one character in *Lyon: débarquement d'une mouche* offers "an exaggerated look" and makes a gesture of greeting "ostentatiously" to the observer

Figure 2.23. © Institut Lumière, *Lyon: débarquement d'une mouche* (Lyon: Coming Ashore from a Boat), 1896.

behind the camera.[108] As Belloï argues, "His behavior is neither interrogation (the intrigued look) or shyness (the concealed look given by the lady in black)," which is "a question of addressing, ostensibly, a gesture of connivance."[109]

The reaction of the young Japanese woman in *Chanteuse japonaise* could belong to the second category because she hesitantly smiled. Her initial smile could have been caused by the sense of loss in front of the recording machine that she was not familiar with. Her unexpected smile captured her in reality. The film showed the moment when she revealed her real self with an authentic human body no matter how powerfully the cinematographer tried to reflect his geisha fantasy on her. But her action after that moment of dismay signified that she ended up playing the role of a cheerful and obedient geisha for the male gaze. In other words, her reaction changed to "an exaggerated look" after she returned her gaze and continued her performance as a geisha. She started to address, ostensibly the observer, with gestures: playing the shamisen and singing. Her continuous performance indicated her acknowledgment of the gaze of the observer and her response of catering to that gaze as a geisha.

Contrary to Inabata's act, her behavior as a geisha was so naive, or so professional, that it should not have been called an embodiment of nativized

Orientalism. She did not consciously exoticize herself for the foreign gaze. There certainly existed a gendered power relation between the two, but that was more economic: between a geisha and a customer. Such a capitalist negotiation around the reality of—not the image of—geisha was also recorded in *Chanteuse japonaise*. Still, the duration of the film captured the moments in which she deviated from a fantastic image of an obedient and sensual geisha to a human being who had emotion, and finally to a more active subject who consciously catered to a specific expectation of her.[110]

Japonisme and Internalized Orientalism

CINEMATOGRAPHER SHIBATA TSUNEKICHI AND THE BIRTH OF CINEMA IN JAPAN

The Earliest Surviving Japanese Film

It was in November 1899, less than five months before the opening of the Exposition Universelle in Paris in 1900. At the Kabukiza Theater in Tokyo, two acclaimed Kabuki actors, Ichikawa Danjurō IX and Onoe Kikugorō V, were performing *Momijigari* (*Maple Viewing*), a popular repertoire that originated in a Noh play turned into a Kabuki dance. In it, Danjurō IX had appeared as the princess Sarashinahime for the first time in October 1887. Now he was back in that role, and Onoe Kikugorō V was playing the samurai Taira no Koremochi.[1] In the play the samurai is invited by beautiful women, including Sarashinahime, to a maple-viewing party at Mt. Togakushi. He enjoys sake while watching the women dance. When he falls asleep, a god appears in his dream. The god reveals to Koremochi that the women are in fact monsters in disguise and leaves him a sacred sword. Koremochi wakes up and exterminates the monsters with the sword.

On the morning of November 28, cinematographer Shibata Tsunekichi (1867–1929) used a Gaumont camera and about two hundred feet of film to quickly photograph *Momijigari* and the two illustrious actors.[2] The shooting of *Momijigari* did not occur inside of the Kabukiza Theater but in the backyard in order to secure sufficient light. As Shibata recalled,

It was a sunny morning, but the wind was strong. We set up a backdrop outside, in front of Umebayashi, the teahouse for the Kabuki audience, which was located behind the Kabukiza Theater. We built a stage in front of the backdrop. All supporting actors held the backdrop to prevent it from being blown away by the wind, hoping that Danjurō IX would not change his mind.... When he performed as Sarashinahime with two fans, Danjurō IX dropped one of them because of a gust of wind. For such an accomplished actor, it was a mistake of a lifetime. But we did not retake the shot. In retrospect, it turned out to be a charming mistake.[3]

The extant 35mm print, preserved at the National Film Archive of Japan, is composed of five fixed long shots, following the opening credits.[4] In the first two shots, lasting approximately 136 seconds combined (there is a noticeable film roll change after seventy seconds or so), Sarashinahime (Danjurō IX) performs a fan dance wearing a dark-colored *furisode*, a kimono with long sleeves. Behind him is the trunk of a huge pine tree, with two thinner trees placed diagonally as props in front of a backdrop, onto which trees and a stone garden have been painted. There is also a *kuroko* stagehand, who dresses all in black, sitting beside the trunk of the pine tree. He helps Danjurō IX when he drops a fan in the first shot. In the third shot, which lasts approximately sixty-two seconds, the Mountain God, played by young Onoe Kikugorō VI, dances with a sacred pole while Koremochi (Kikugorō V) is asleep on the right of the frame. In the fourth shot, which lasts only twenty seconds, Koremochi wakes up, prepares his sword, and holds a *mie* pose, a signature attitude struck by a Kabuki actor, who freezes for a moment to express his enhanced emotion. In the fifth shot, which lasts approximately fifty-seven seconds, with the same props and backdrop, Koremochi and a monster with dark long hair (Danjurō IX) perform a sword-fighting dance together. The stagehand comes forward once to pick up some things dropped on the stage by the actors. Midway through the shot, the actors momentarily pause and look toward the camera, Koremochi raising his sword and the monster holding a *mie* pose. Then they resume their dance. The monster starts swirling her long hair until the shot fades out.

Despite the mistake by Danjurō IX, the Japanese Ministry of Education, Culture, Sports, Science, and Technology designated *Momijigari* to be an Important Cultural Property (*jūyō bunkazai*) in 2009, under the nation's Law for the Protection of Cultural Properties, making it the first film to receive the designation. As such, *Momijigari* is officially considered to be the earliest surviving Japanese film.

However, *Momijigari* was not actually the earliest Japanese film made.[5] As the film curator Irie Yoshirō articulates, filmmaking in Japan had already

Figure 3.1. *Momijigari (Maple Viewing)*, 1899. Collection of National Film Archive of Japan.

Figure 3.2. *Momijigari (Maple Viewing)*, 1899. Collection of National Film Archive of Japan.

started in 1897.⁶ Konishi honten (later Konishiroku shashin kōgyō, now Konica Minolta), the photo-material merchant, imported a motion picture camera (presumably from the British camera manufacturer Baxter & Wray) in 1897 and started filming and developing motion pictures with its cameraman Asano Shirō.⁷ Shibata Tsunekichi joined the filmmaking at Konishi around 1898.⁸ The earliest films by Asano and Shibata were publicly screened in June and July 1899 by Hiromeya, the advertising agency that had initiated an exhibition of Vitascope in Japan earlier. This is considered to be the first exhibition of Japanese-made films in Japan. Irie meticulously examined newspaper articles, advertisements, memoirs, and frame captures from nonextant films that have been published in various forms to show that Konishi was steadily producing films and increasing its number of titles and that Hiromeya constantly exhibited the Konishi films.⁹

Momijigari was photographed during that period, but the film was not produced by Konishi. Considering the rare opportunity of the two great actors performing together, Inoue Takejirō, the head of exhibition at the Kabukiza Theater at that time, asked Danjurō IX to take photographs of them making some special *kata* (poses) as a record for future generations (Inoue did not even mention that it would be a motion picture recording).¹⁰ Matsumoto Kōshirō VII, a disciple of Danjurō IX, claimed that the actor agreed to be photographed "only for the pedagogical purpose" of instructing future Kabuki performers.¹¹ The film historian Ueda Manabu suggests that no retake was done to correct Danjurō IX's mistake during the filming because the recording of *Momijigari* was not meant for exhibition to the general public.¹² Indeed, *Momijigari* was not publicly screened in a theater until July 7, 1903, four years after the recording of the performance.¹³ The only exception was a private screening at Danjurō IX's residence in Tsukiji, Tokyo, on the evening of November 7, 1900.

Yet was Inoue Takejirō thinking only of the pedagogical purpose when he asked Danjurō IX about the filming? For the successful exhibitor of Kabuki, wasn't the appearance of the two prominent actors too good an opportunity to pass up?

In this chapter, mainly focusing on the career of the film's cinematographer, Shibata Tsunekichi, I demonstrate that *Momijigari* is not only the earliest surviving Japanese film but also one of the earliest films intended for export to Europe. I argue that *Momijigari* might have been meant for non-Japanese viewers in order to cater to their fantasy about Japan: another example of nativized Orientalism. Then, when the film was publicly released in 1903 for the domestic audience as the first Japanese-produced film, it started to be recognized as representative of Japanese culture. The 2009 designation of the film as an Important Cultural Property was a recent recognition of it. In other words, the film about a traditional art form that was originally prepared for the foreign gaze was translated into the formation of a national culture. As I discuss in detail later in this chapter, this was a process of internalizing Orientalism. Again, all this happened as a dialogic negotiation over the image of Japan during the period of Japonisme. As such, I conclude that Japanese filmmaking emerged in close connection with Japonisme.

The Earliest Surviving Japanese Film for Export?

The Kabuki scholar Kamiyama Akira speculated that the filming of *Momijigari* was meant for the 1900 Paris Exposition Universelle.[14] Kamiyama said that he gave up on that idea because he was not able to find any empirical proof.[15] But I have found a piece of supporting evidence: Kawaura Kenichi, the head of Yoshizawa shōten, which was responsible for the first public screening of *Momijigari* in 1903, recalled that "Inoue Takejirō, the head of the Kabukiza Theater, and I discussed and told Shibata to photograph *Momijigari* for export."[16] According to Kawaura, the people who were responsible for photographing *Momijigari* were indeed thinking of European audiences.

When Shibata filmed *Momijigari* in November 1899, the Japanese government was finalizing the selection of products to be exported for the 1900 Paris Exposition Universelle, which occurred in the midst of the Japonisme trend. The Japanese government received an official invitation to the exposition from the French government in January 1896. The head office for the exposition was established under the minister of agriculture and commerce on May 9. The head office quickly came up with a specific policy about how to select products to be exhibited. In short, their ideas were (1) the World Exposition was "a place for competition of a number of industrial technologies" so that the selected products needed to be "competitive enough" but would "not interfere with future trade in any way," and (2) all selected products would "formulate the image of the nation to the outside world and publicize its national spirit."[17] It is clear from this policy that the desire of the Japanese government was to publicize how Japan had become a modernized nation whose products were sufficiently competitive in international trade. In other words, the government boasted about the Japanese national identity and addressed the "dream of export."[18] As examples, the head office listed three particular things to be selected: "regular merchandise that was worth trading and had competitive status as trading goods, or if not competitive enough at this point, ones that had the potential to expand the market in the future; art objects that represented the unique Japanese grace and taste and demonstrated the original characteristics of Japanese art; machine tools and related things that had adopted European and American technologies but would simultaneously demonstrate new devices and improvements."[19]

Momijigari could be a perfect fit. It could become an excellent example of the use of "machine tools and related things that had adopted European and American technologies but would simultaneously demonstrate new devices and improvements." *Momijigari* used a motion picture camera and film stock, among other European and American technologies, in an innovative manner: edited shots that enhanced the spectacle of the transformation from a woman/ *onnagata* to a long-haired monster.

At the same time, *Momijigari* would satisfy the governmental policy of selection because it embodied "the unique Japanese grace and taste and demonstrated the original characteristics of Japanese art." Recent studies in art history indicate that the image of *Momijigari* had already been introduced to a large number of European spectators in 1876. In that year, Claude Monet exhibited his painting *La Japonaise* (*Camille Monet in Japanese Costume*) at the Second Impressionist Exhibition in Paris. Monet completed this large-scale oil painting in the midst of the Japonisme vogue. In the painting Monet's wife poses in a vividly red kimono in front of a wall filled with a number of Japanese fans. The kimono that Camille wears is identified as an *uchikake*, a formal style worn by brides of the rich merchant class or by high-class geisha during the Edo period, as well as in Kabuki stage performances. The major motif of the kimono is a fierce-looking samurai, who is about to draw his sword. On the red kimono we also see a number of maple leaves floating above the samurai's figure.

According to the art historian Yokoyama Akio, the design of the kimono in *La Japonaise* was most likely based on *Momijigari*. Yokoyama suggests that the story of *Momijigari* had been a traditional source for ukiyo-e woodblock print motifs since the early nineteenth century, including such works as *Taira no Koremochi* (1830s) and *Buyū gi Genji: Momijiga, Taira no Koremochi* (Brave Genji: Celebrating Maple, Taira no Koremochi, 1840s), both by Utagawa Kuniyoshi. Especially in *Buyū gi Genji*, as Yokoyama points out, the samurai's posture as well as the composition of the maple leaves around him look very similar to those in *La Japonaise*. Even though Monet did not own this particular piece, he did own twenty-three other works by Kuniyoshi, so there was a chance that he was familiar with *Momijigari* motifs as well.[20]

Figure 3.3. Claude Monet, *La Japonaise* (*Camille Monet in Japanese Costume*), 1876. Oil on canvas. 231.8 × 142.3 cm (91 1/4 × 56 in.). Museum of Fine Arts, Boston. 1951 Purchase Fund. 56.147.

Figure 3.4. Tsukioka Yoshitoshi, *Taira Koremochi Conquering the Devil Woman on Mount Togakushi* (*Taira no Koremochi Togakushiyama kijo taiji no zu*), 1887. Color woodblock print; oban diptych. 75 × 26 cm. Frederick W. Gookin Collection. RX22839/03. The Art Institute of Chicago. Photo Credit: The Art Institute of Chicago / Art Resource, NY.

Figure 3.5. © Institut Lumière, *Une rue à Tokyo [I]* (A Street in Tokyo I), 1898.

Moreover, *Momijigari* was a continuously popular source for ukiyo-e throughout the late nineteenth and early twentieth centuries. Tsukioka Yoshitoshi, only one year older than Monet, was a disciple of Kuniyoshi and completed a work on *Momijigari*, titled *Taira no Koremochi Togakushiyama kijo taiji no zu* (*Taira Koremochi Conquering the Devil Woman on Mount Togakushi*), in 1887. In this work, not only is the posture of the samurai almost exactly the same as in Monet's *La Japonaise*, but the colors of the samurai's dress (the blue-green kimono and the blue *hakama*) are similarly contrasted with the vivid red dress of the woman behind him. It is not known whether Yoshitoshi was familiar with *La Japonaise*, but the resemblance seems too striking to be accidental. Like Kuniyoshi's work, Yoshitoshi's ukiyo-e attracted European spectators.[21]

Even if Monet was not familiar with the play and the ukiyo-e of *Momijigari*, it is certain that he saw a kimono with the samurai motif. Quite a number of kimonos used by geisha were exported to France during the period of Japonisme, and motifs from *Momijigari* presumably came with them. The art historian Geneviève Lacambre points out that the kimono Monet painted was probably owned by merchant Philippe Sichel, who purchased various objets d'art in Japan in 1874.[22] According to another art historian, Mabuchi Akiko,

Monet talked about *La Japonaise* to an art dealer and said, "I had a chance to look at an excellent dress and was recommended to paint it. Embroidery is done with golden threads, and some parts are as thick as a few inches."[23] Monet had a great chance to familiarize himself with the motif of *Momijigari* without even knowing it. Then he made European spectators aware of the motif by his famous painting. In such a context it was logical for the Japanese government to consider including a film that recorded famous Kabuki actors' performance of *Momijigari* in the list of products for the 1900 Paris Exposition Universelle. They would have regarded such a film as an embodiment of "the unique Japanese grace and taste and [demonstration of] the original characteristics of Japanese art."[24]

Nativized Orientalism and Representation of Modernization in the Work of Shibata Tsunekichi

The film *Momijigari* could also have been seen as appropriate for the 1900 Paris Exposition Universelle because it was photographed by Shibata Tsunekichi. Shibata's work could cater to the expectations of European audiences toward Japan while it would simultaneously comply with the Japanese government's modernization policy.

Curiously, according to the Lumière catalog, five films were photographed between Girel's departure in December 1897 and before Veyre's arrival on October 25, 1898. According to the film historian Koga Futoshi, a building seen in one of those films, *Une rue à Tokyo [I]* (A Street in Tokyo I, 1898), was a temporary structure in the Imperial Palace built for the thirtieth anniversary of Tokyo as the capital of Japan.[25] The anniversary festival was held on April 10, 1898, when neither Girel nor Veyre was in Japan. There is no record of any other Lumière cinematographer being sent to Japan. According to Koga, another film historian Komatsu Hiroshi confirmed that there were only two Japanese technicians who could operate motion picture cameras at that time, the above-mentioned Asano Shirō and Shibata Tsunekichi of Konishi honten, and that Shibata was the one who was able to make films using the Cinématographe Lumière in April 1898.[26] Indeed, Konishi had a business relationship with the Lumière Company. Because I have not found further evidence, my argument in this chapter relies on Komatsu's confirmation that Shibata was the cinematographer of the Lumière films that were photographed during the absence of Girel and Veyre.[27]

As opposed to the films by Girel and Veyre, which basically attempted to reconfigure Japan within the exotic image of an atemporal Orientalist space, the

Figure 3.6. © Institut Lumière, *Une rue à Tokyo [II]* (A Street in Tokyo II), 1898.

Lumière films that were presumably photographed by Shibata did not explicitly show geisha or other exotic objects per se. Instead, those films juxtaposed those exotic images with scenes of a modernizing and Westernizing nation. In other words, two different senses of time—the atemporal/imaginary past and the modernizing present—were expressed simultaneously in Shibata's films.

For instance, *Une rue à Tokyo [II]* depicts a row of three-story Western-style buildings on a Ginza street. One of them has the name of a store written in the Western alphabet: Hattori (now the Seiko Watch Corporation). Japanese people in Western dress and/or with Western-style black umbrellas are clearly visible in this film. Similarly, in *Station du chemin de fer de Tokyo* (Tokyo Railway Station, 1898), a number of trams run along the streets of Shinbashi under electricity service poles. Shibata thus included in his films the modernized elements in Japanese urban landscapes as a reality of Japanese daily life. Girel and Veyre avoided these scenes because they display a transforming Japan. They focused on exotic and atemporal space. As we discussed in the previous chapter, the focus of Girel's version of *Une rue à Tokyo* was clearly on the exotic appearance of a rickshaw in an obviously staged setting, even though we see a couple of Japanese people wearing European-style derby hats.

Figure 3.7. © Institut Lumière, *Station du chemin de fer de Tokyo* (Tokyo Railway Station), 1898.

Figure 3.8. © Institut Lumière, *Une rue à Tokyo* (A Street in Tokyo), 1897.

Figure 3.9. © Institut Lumière, *Une avenue à Tokyo* (An Avenue in Tokyo), 1898.

Yet Shibata's films did not simply document the Westernizing streets of Japan. Like Inabata Katsutarō, who embodied nativized Orientalism in Girel's *Repas en famille*, Shibata understood the European expectations of exoticism. In Shibata's *Une rue à Tokyo [I]*, one of the buildings at the Imperial Palace, with its traditional architecture and some snow on the roof, is visible at the far end while a tall man in a dark, Western suit is clearly noticeable in the front. In *Une avenue à Tokyo* (An Avenue in Tokyo, 1898), the cherry trees—the Japanese national tree—are in full bloom on the riverbank with rickshaws running under them, even as crowds of Western-style umbrellas and derby hats worn by men in kimonos create strong contrasts between the white blossoms and black objects.

Moreover, Shibata was not only careful about what he would photograph but also conscious of how it should be presented. He was clearly aware of the trend of Japonisme in Europe. By the time Shibata made his films, it was widely known among Japanese intellectuals that impressionism and postimpressionism were influenced by ukiyo-e. As the critic Kume Keiichirō wrote in his 1911 essay in the Japanese magazine *Taiyō* (*The Sun*), "Shin-Inshōha no eikyō" (The Influence of Postimpressionism), "Doubtlessly, the modern paintings, which have flat appearances, reexamine perspective and beams of light, and abandon shades of colors, have been tremendously influenced by Japanese drawings, especially Japanese prints."[28] To be more specific, Shibata incorporated the kinzō-gata-kōzu/chūkei-datsuraku/en=kin-hō composition that Lumière films often used. In some of his films, Shibata exaggerated the contrast between the movements in the front and the stillness in the background. Both *Une rue à Tokyo [I]* and *Une rue à Tokyo [II]* emphasized three separate layers within a frame. In *Une rue à Tokyo [I]*, the Imperial Palace exists at the back without moving, crowds of people barely move in the second layer, and in the front plane, people move in and out of the frame at some speed. Some of them stop at the center of the screen, aware of the camera. With this film alone, Shibata seemed to use the kinzō-gata-kōzu/chūkei-datsuraku/en=kin-hō composition in order to enhance the Orientalistic contrast between a traditional atemporal space (background) and a modern space with movement (front). Yet he complicated such a Eurocentric binary view in another film while maintaining the compositional (front and back) and thematic (tradition and modern) contrasts. In *Une rue à Tokyo [II]*, the disparity between the static background and the speedy movement in the front is more drastically presented. But the rickshaws that pass by at full speed in the frontal layer look traditional. The rows of stores, some of which look Westernized, stood still at the back. Thus, Shibata cleverly combined exoticism and modernization in terms of both content and style.

Similarly, in the film *Momijigari* Shibata depicted the exotic-looking motif of *Momijigari* in kimono or in ukiyo-e, which had been adopted and popularized in the Japonisme vogue by Monet, by mechanically re-presenting it in the recorded form of a Kabuki performance. The long-haired monster's dance in *Momijigari* could also remind the viewers of Girel's 1897 film *Acteurs japonais: exercice de la perruque*, which I discussed in chapter 2. In that film, following Yokohama photographs with Kabuki actors, Girel staged Nakamura Ganjirō I, who practiced the lion dance, costumed in an extremely long white mane, in an exterior setting in Kyoto.

Thus, in Shibata's films the traditional and the modern are constantly in dialogue or in negotiation. As noted earlier, this balancing act between tradition and modernization was what the Japanese government was trying to adopt when it prepared for the 1900 Paris Exposition Universelle. The Lumière films by Shibata, which were made for the European audience within the Japonisme vogue, embody nativized Orientalism on the one hand and publicity of Japan's modernization on the other. So does *Momijigari*, if the film was indeed meant for the 1900 Paris Exposition Universelle.

Internalized Orientalism in the Work of Shibata Tsunekichi

It is noteworthy that Shibata also photographed geisha, the main target of the Orientalist fantasy about Japan within the Japonisme vogue, in a certain number of films from the very beginning of his film career. Arguably, one of the very first films photographed, developed, and printed by Japanese filmmakers—in this case Shibata and Asano Shirō—was a film about geisha: *Geisha no teodori* (Geisha's Dance, 1897). The print of this film no longer exists, but an illustration of this film is seen in an 1899 flyer of the film exhibition, which is preserved at the Tsubouchi Memorial Theater Library of Waseda University.[29] The flyer has ten illustrations of Japanese-made films, and six of them depict singing and dancing by geisha. One of these illustrations is presumably from *Geisha no teodori*.

It is also noteworthy that one of the illustrations, titled "Sukoburu hijō naru Hamamachi Okada enkai" (Very Unusual Dinner at Hamamachi Okada), in which two men sitting on the tatami floor have food and sake with a couple of geisha, looks very similar to Girel's *Dîner japonais* in terms of its motif and composition. Similarly, the other five illustrations with geisha resemble five films by Veyre: *Danse japonaise: I. Kappore; Danse japonaise: II. Harusame; Danse Japonaise: IV. Jinku; Danse japonaise: V. Gocho Garama;* and *Chanteuse japonaise*. In fact, one of the illustrations has a caption that includes the word "Kappore." Because the flyer also includes an illustration of an apparent Lumière film, *Baignade en mer* (*Swimming in the Sea*, 1895), with the title "Futsukoku saidai kaisui yokujō" (The Biggest Beach in France), it is possible that the "Kappore" illustration depicted the Veyre film *Danse japonaise: I. Kappore*.[30]

Why did Shibata and Asano choose geisha as the topic of their first films? Were they thinking from the very beginning about exporting their films to cater to the Orientalist fantasy? Asano recalls the situation around 1899: "Those of you who are familiar with the conditions of the mid-Meiji period can understand why the exhibitors requested geisha's dances to be filmed. The popularity of geisha represented the era. The bestselling postcards were those of geisha. That was why we photographed geisha's dances at the restaurant Kagetsu in Shinbashi."[31] Geisha was already one of the popular motifs in ukiyo-e of the Edo period, but the critic Saeki Junko distinguishes geisha in ukiyo-e from those in commercial postcards and motion pictures in the modern era. She argues that Japanese men, especially intellectuals and highly trained technicians such as cinematographers, were learning to identify their gaze with the Western male gaze: they tried to use the image of geisha as the emblem of a premodern sensibility that needed to be overcome. As Saeki puts it, "By defining women in sexual terms, Japanese men [in the Meiji period] tried to identify

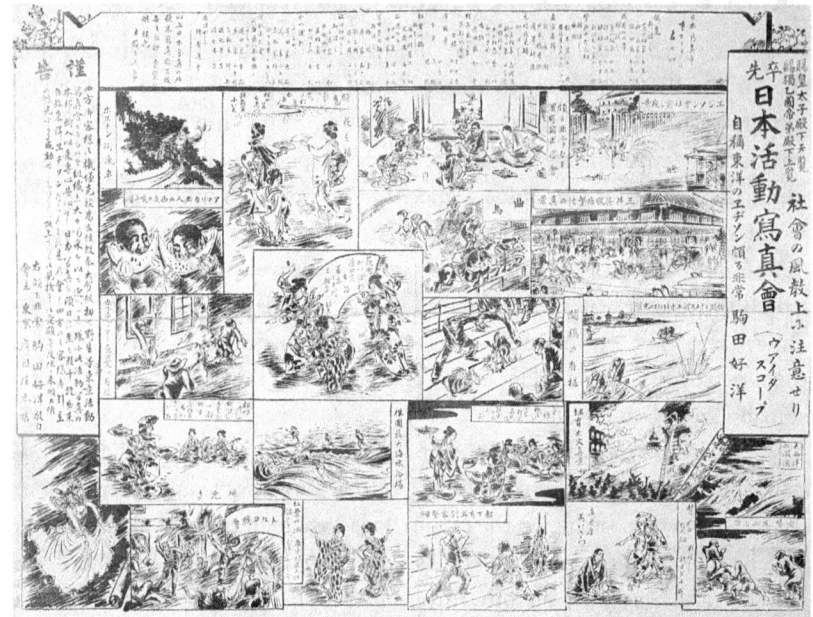

Figure 3.10. Flyer of 1899 film exhibition by Sossen Nihon katsudō shashin kai. 06265 "Vitascope niyoru 'Nihon shashin' kōgyō no tsuji bira." Collection of Tsubouchi Memorial Theater Museum of Waseda University.

themselves with the 'Western male,' place themselves in a superior position to the 'Japanese female,' confirm themselves as transnational male subjects, exclude 'savage sexuality' as characteristic of the 'Other,' and obtain a 'civilized' national image."[32]

If we follow Saeki's argument, the geisha films that Asano and Shibata made for the Japanese domestic audience can be regarded as examples of what I call *internalized* Orientalism. Like nativized Orientalism, internalized Orientalism could emerge only when the European Orientalist fantasy about Japan arrived in Japan within the context of Japonisme. Whereas nativized Orientalism was a conscious pose for the Western gaze and mainly for export, internalized Orientalism was a conscious act targeting the domestic audience in Japan. People like Shibata acknowledged exotic-looking objects, such as the geisha, within Japan and looked at them from the position of the modernizing/Westernizing self. They presented those objects as being exotic to themselves. In other words, people like Shibata were aware that such exotic-looking objects were representatives of the premodern Japan that needed to be overcome or even imaginary entities that only existed in the Orientalist fantasy. But at the same time, they consciously formulated a cultural image of Japan by way of the Orientalist viewpoint. They distributed it not only to foreign viewers (nativized Orientalism) but also to domestic mass audiences in Japan (internalized Orientalism).[33] What they did was an ambivalent act of a modernizing/Westernizing subject that identified its position with the owner of the Orientalist fantasy.

Even before becoming a cinematographer, Shibata had contributed to the formation of internalized Orientalism in the rising mass media as a photographer. After working at a photo studio in Tokyo, he entered the photography department of the Hakubunkan publishing company. In January 1895, in the midst of the First Sino-Japanese War, Hakubunkan launched arguably the first general-interest magazine in Japan, *Taiyō* (*The Sun*), for which Shibata played a significant role.

Before the publication of *Taiyō*, most magazines and journals in Japan were more specialized and much smaller in number of pages.[34] In contrast, the target of *Taiyō*, with its massive 200-plus pages and inexpensive price (one-fourth of the price of an approximately 50-page magazine), was the entire population of Japan. The literary scholar Suzuki Sadami argues that Hakubunkan's magazines were "clearly characterized by the company's cultural policy to contribute to formulating the general education for the Japanese people as a whole, based on the notion of *kokumin kokka shugi* (state nationalism)."[35] Indeed, Ōhashi Shintarō, who established Hakubunkan with his father, Ōhashi Sahei, stated in the opening remarks of the inaugural issue of *Taiyō* that the goal of the magazine would be "to start making our nation shine in the world."[36] With Ōhashi's effort, *Taiyō* circulated nationwide, whereas most newspapers were read locally (*Yorozu Chōhō* in Tokyo and *Osaka Asahi Shinbun* in Kansai).[37] As a result, the circulation of *Taiyō* went up to 100,000 per issue during the first years (1895–99).[38] *Taiyō* initiated the age of mass media in the entire nation of Japan.

One of the innovations of *Taiyō* was its substantial incorporation of photography as its major content. Hakubunkan was confident about this move toward a visual photographic magazine because of the success of its 1894 publication, *Nisshin senso jikki* (Report of the First Sino-Japanese War), which fully incorporated copperplate photography in the printing.[39] The inaugural issue of *Taiyō* not only listed the titles of illustrations (mostly photographs) in the issue on its cover without mentioning any essay titles or any author names; it also published an anonymous report titled "Shashin jutsu ōyō no hattatsu" (The Development of How to Apply the Technology of Photography). What the report stressed was the effects of photography in the modern world: "It has become an indispensable technology in such areas as politics, military, science, art, and industry.... They say that in London daily photo-journals have been published one after another.... The advances and effects of photography are tremendous."[40] Speaking of the "advances," by 1895 various technological advancements, including the advent of the dry plate, had made it much easier for amateur photographers to take photographs.[41] *Taiyō* started a photo competition for amateur photographers in 1902, and these amateur photos eventually formed the core of the photography pages of the magazine.[42]

As the anonymous report in the inaugural issue indicated, the focus of the photography pages in *Taiyō* was photojournalism. For that purpose, the amateur photo contests in *Taiyō* clearly prioritized transparency over pictorialism. It was Shibata Tsunekichi who served as a judge for the contest and published a report titled "Kenshō shashin no shinsa" (Evaluation of the Contest Photos) in the March 1, 1905, issue of *Taiyō*. In the report, Shibata highly valued the transparency of photography: "It is very regrettable that there are so many works with the hazy style and easy tricks that deviate from the legitimate trajectory of photography."[43] He continued: "Primarily, the best photography most clearly presents the object to be photographed and makes its theme and composition easy to appreciate." Shibata even called it "cowardly" if a photographer "displays only a part of the main object and obscures the other parts."[44] In other words, *Taiyō* published photographs with viewpoints clearly visible and understandable to the magazine's nationwide readers.[45]

Landscape photographs, both foreign and Japanese, occupied many pages of *Taiyō*, at least two to three pages per issue (several different photographs were often included on one page). According to the literary studies scholar Hibi Yoshitaka, foreign landscape photos in *Taiyō* were categorized into two types: representatives of "civilized" and "advanced" nations, such as the architecture of Italy, and objects for "ethnographic study," including the customs of Siberian natives.[46] A sense of adoration was implied in the former type, but a Western-style colonial gaze was identifiable in the latter. As Hibi argues, such dichotomy in foreign landscape photos in *Taiyō* "embodied the thoughts of ontological hierarchy" among cultures.[47] Because of the transparency that *Taiyō* emphasized, such dichotomy forced general readers in Japan to unconsciously participate in the colonial structure. The photographs of Taiwan, Burma, and Sakhalin, in particular, were connected to the Japanese colonial policy. The "ethnographic" photographs of those locations helped form Japan's own Orientalist fantasy.

Along the same lines, *Taiyō* published a number of landscape photos of famous places in Japan: the Itsukushima Shrine and its famous torii gate standing in the ocean, the Tōshōgu Shrine in Nikkō, the temples in Kyoto, Shinto festivals with royal families (e.g., the thirty-year commemorative event in 1897 of Emperor Kōmei's death), and so forth. These photos were not far from Yokohama photographs, which consciously presented Japanese landscape and people for the foreign gaze. In essence, they presented archetypal images of Japan (with the exception of news photos of natural calamities). For instance, a photograph titled "Kyoto Shijōgawara nōryō" (Summer Evening on the Shijō River, Kyoto) was published in the inaugural issue.[48] It displayed six Japanese women in kimono, presumably geisha, sitting on a deck that faces the River Kamo. Satō Morihiro assumes that this photo was printed from a glass negative of a Yokohama photograph.[49] There was a very similar photo in Constant Girel's album as well. A photograph like this published in *Taiyō* fits perfectly into what the literary critic Karatani Kōjin calls the "discovery of landscape," by which he describes the nineteenth-century Japanese discovery of a national self, or the construction of internality based on the experience of externality.[50] After abandoning the locked-door policy of the Tokugawa shogunate in the 1850s, the Meiji government adopted official policies of *bunmei kaika* (civilization and enlightenment) and *fukoku kyōhei* (wealth and military strength of a country) in order to raise the status of Japan to be competitive with colonial powers. Such policies resulted in the substantial Westernization of Japan by the late 1890s. The dominant trend during this period was to reject things Japanese and embrace thoughts, systems, and technologies from Europe and the United States. A return of national pride and the resurrection of pre-Meiji "tradition" came only after this period of fervent Westernization and a victory in the First Sino-Japanese War (1894–95). As the film historian Aaron Gerow claims, "Formulations of the idea of a pure *kokutai* (national polity) . . . were inevitably based on the presence of those foreign things that were supposedly being excluded from the pure nation."[51] As a result, the pre-Meiji past and the Japanese landscape started to be viewed from Westernized eyes. In other words, they became objects of an "invented tradition" by way of internalized Orientalism.[52]

The landscape photographs in *Taiyō* formulated the images of Japan based on (1) the colonialist dichotomized view between the modern and the traditional, and (2) the exoticism-seeking gaze toward Japan, modeling Yokohama photographs. This time the target was not foreign tourists but domestic general readers in Japan. As such, we could argue that the Japanese landscape

Figure 3.11. Shibata Tsunekichi, "Fujisan chōbō" (View of Mt. Fuji), *Taiyō* 4, no. 7 (April 5, 1898).

photographs in *Taiyō* were not only examples of an invented tradition but also embodiments of internalized Orientalism. By circulating such an internally Orientalized view on Japan and its potential colonies to nationwide viewers, *Taiyō* contributed to the formation of the image of Japan as a nation.

Shibata was in the midst of *Taiyō*'s project of internalized Orientalism. In addition to serving as a judge of the amateur photo contests, he contributed at least ten works of Japanese landscape photos to *Taiyō* during the period between April 1898 and May 1905. Even though he emphasized the value of transparency in his 1905 "Evaluation of Contest Photos," Shibata also understood the significance of pictorialism in photography. In fact, in 1907 he joined Tokyo shashin kenkyūkai (the Tokyo Photographic Research Society), which was devoted to artistic photographs, as a supporting member.[53] His photographs are characterized by the combination of transparency and pictorialism. Above all, Shibata was obsessed with the image of Mt. Fuji. Five works among the ten capture this scene: "Fujisan chōbō" (View of Mt. Fuji) (April 5, 1898), "Gotenba yori nozomu yuki no Fujisan" (Snow-Clad Fuji from Gotenba) (August 20, 1898), "Suruga Gotenba no yuki no Fujisan" (Winter View of Mt. Fuji from Gotemba, Suruga) (September 5, 1898), "Yuki no Fuji" (Snowy Fuji) (April 1, 1905), and "Bōen renzu nite satsuei seshi yuki no Fuji" (The Snow-

Figure 3.12. Shibata Tsunekichi, "Gotenba yori nozomu yuki no Fujisan" (Snow-Clad Fuji from Gotenba), *Taiyō* 4, no. 17 (August 20, 1898).

Clad Fuji Sketched by a Telephoto) (May 1, 1905).[54] It was as if Shibata had been creating his version of Hokusai's popular series of ukiyo-e prints, *Fugaku sanjūrokkei* (*Thirty-Six Views of Mt. Fuji*, c. 1830). It is coincidental that, as I mentioned in chapter 1, when Shibata was publishing a series of photos of Mt. Fuji, Henri Rivière was creating *Les trente-six vues de la tour Eiffel* from 1888 throughout the 1890s, being inspired by Hokusai. It is doubtful that Shibata was familiar with Rivière's work at that time. But it is certain that Shibata was aware of the trend of Japonisme in Europe, in which Mt. Fuji played a significant role in formulating the archetypal image of Japan. In all five photographs of Mt. Fuji by Shibata, even though none of them were published in winter months, the mountain is covered and/or surrounded by snow, which obviously enhances the sense of exoticism. Moreover, four of them (except the last one, which was photographed with a telephoto lens) display Japanese country houses with thatched roofs as well as rice paddy fields. As such, these photographs look much closer to Yokohama photographs.[55]

Moreover, another photograph by Shibata, titled "Suishōsekai (Honnen ichigatsu yōka no asageshiki)" (The Crystal World: The Morning View on January 8 of This Year), incorporated the kinzō-gata-kōzu/chūkei-datsuraku/en=kin-hō composition.[56] A wooden support of a tree crossed diagonally

Figure 3.13. Shibata Tsunekichi, "Suruga Gotenba no yuki no Fujisan" (Winter View of Mt. Fuji from Gotemba, Suruga), *Taiyō* 4, no. 18 (September 5, 1898).

Figure 3.14. Shibata Tsunekichi, "Yuki no Fuji" (Snowy Fuji), *Taiyō* 11, no. 5 (April 1, 1905).

Figure 3.15. Shibata Tsunekichi, "Bōen renzu nite satsuei seshi yuki no Fuji" (The Snow-Clad Fuji Sketched by a Telephoto), *Taiyō* 11. no. 7 (May 1, 1905).

Figure 3.16. Shibata Tsunekichi, "Suishōsekai (Honnen ichigatsu yōka no asageshiki)" (The Crystal World: The Morning View on January 8 of This Year), *Taiyō* 8, no. 2 (February 5, 1902).

Figure 3.17. Shibata Tsunekichi, "Hachigatsu nijūsan nichi yoru no denkō" (The Lightning in the Stormy Night of August 23), *Taiyō* 4, no. 18 (September 5, 1898).

within the frame at the very frontal plane and blocked the view, whereas a Japanese-style wooden bridge occupied the plane in the background. The overall composition was similar to an ukiyo-e by Hokusai or Hiroshige.

The remaining work (a juxtaposition of two photos), titled "Hachigatsu nijūsan nichi yoru no denkō" (The Lightning in the Stormy Night of August 23), should be examined in terms of ukiyo-e as well.[57] On the surface the work looks like a science photograph in the manner of photojournalism. The priority was seemingly on the precise representation of a natural phenomenon captured instantly by the camera. However, if we juxtapose this photo with Hokusai's "Sanka hakuu" (Rainstorm beneath the Summit, 1830–33), one from *Fugaku sanjūrokkei*, Shibata's focus on pictorialism becomes clear. In "Sanka hakuu," Hokusai depicted thunderbolts at the skirts of Mt. Fuji. Although the sky above the mountain is still blue, the plains at the foot of the mountain are in pitch black, on the verge of a summer storm. "Sanka hakuu" is often called "Kuro Fuji" (Black Mt. Fuji) because of the darkness. The overall appearance of Shibata's photo was quite dark because of the low-key lighting. But the brightness and the zigzag shape of the lighting stand out. Even though no Mt. Fuji is captured in this photo, we could argue that Shibata thought about Hokusai's famous ukiyo-e. He contributed the above-mentioned photo, "Suruga Gotenba

Figure 3.18. Katsushika Hokusai, "Sanka haku-u" (Rainstorm beneath the Summit), from the series *Thirty-Six Views of Mount Fuji* (*Fugaku sanjūrokkei*), ca. 1831 (Tenpō 2). Woodblock print (nishiki-e); ink and color on paper. Horizontal ōban; 26.2 × 38.2 cm (10 5/16 × 15 1/16 in.). Museum of Fine Arts, Boston. William Sturgis Bigelow Collection. 11.25222.

no yuki no Fujisan" (Winter View of Mt. Fuji from Gotemba, Suruga), in the same issue of *Taiyō* (September 5, 1898).

The film *Momijigari* needs to be located within this context. Was Shibata considering the film to be a project of nativized Orientalism for European spectators as well as that of internalized Orientalism for domestic audiences? If the producers of the film, Inoue Takejirō, the head of the Kabukiza Theater, and Kawaura Kenichi, the head of Yoshizawa shōten, were serious about exporting this film to Europe, Shibata would not have said no to their idea. Even if Danjurō IX did not want this film to be screened publicly, Shibata might have thought about Japanese viewers, who would appreciate a traditional art form.

In the end, *Momijigari* was not sent to Paris in 1900. But, as noted earlier, the film was screened publicly in a theater in Japan on July 7, 1903.[58] That screening was only a substitute for a canceled live performance by Danjurō IX and Kikugorō V at the fifth Domestic Industrial Exposition (Naikoku Kangyō Hakurankai) in Osaka, but the film was rereleased widely in Tokyo, Osaka, Yokohama, Nagoya, Kyoto, and Kobe by a new film company, Yokota shōkai, in 1908.⁵⁹ During its rerelease, *Momijigari* became a film that embodied internalized Orientalism, whether Shibata had anticipated that or not. When the domestic audience in Japan looked at the film, they most likely identified themselves with a foreign gaze toward the film.

When *Momijigari* was screened at the Kinkikan Theater in Tokyo on May 8–31, 1908, it was one of only three films photographed in Japan. Eleven other films were the ones produced by Pathé.⁶⁰ The three films photographed in Japan were *Momijigari*, *Kyoto dentō hatsudensho no kaji* (The Fire at Kyoto Electric Company), and *Shimabara tayū no dōchū* (A Geisha's Walk). The Japanese titles of the eleven Pathé films were *Karadaru no gyōretsu* (The March of Empty Barrels), *Shiutome katagi* (The Mother-in-Law Character), *Shinan hikōki* (The Newly Invented Airplane), *Kettō daishōri* (The Great Victory in the Duel), *Kakan nai koi* (The Cowardly Love), *Kachiku dorobō no chie* (The Knowledge of the Cattle Thief), *Ikita dōzō* (A Living Statue), *Kiki kaikai jidō ryōri* (Mysterious Automatic Cooking), *Shittatsuri no akiregao* (The Bailiff's Stunned Face), *Fushigi no kagami* (The Mysterious Mirror), and *Gama no yōjutsu* (The Toad's Witchcraft).⁶¹ *Kyoto dentō hatsudensho no kaji* was screened between two Pathé films. It was supposedly a spectacular disaster film with news value, so it can be assumed that issues of nationality or cultural specificity were not very significant. The film could have easily blended in with other non-Japanese films. *Shimabara tayū no dōchū* is a geisha film, which could easily cater to the Orientalist fantasy of non-Japanese viewers. According to a May 8 advertisement for the Kinkikan Theater, *Shimabara tayū no dōchū* was "photographed by a cinematographer from the Pathé Company of France."⁶² Moreover, we have also discussed that the popularity of geisha films among Japanese men would indicate internalized Orientalism. Screened back-to-back with the geisha film, Sarashinahime's dance in *Momijigari* could be juxtaposed with a geisha dance, especially in a long shot of the onnagata, played by Danjurō IX in a long-sleeved kimono. *Momijigari* thus blended in with films shot by European cinematographers. Most of the viewers at the theater could have thought it was a foreign film. In fact, when the print of *Momijigari* was discovered in 1928 after being lost during the Great Kantō Earthquake in 1923, newspapers claimed that the film was "photographed by a foreigner."⁶³ The information was later corrected, but such a mistake indicated the general view toward the film, at least between 1908 and 1928. Just as the geisha film was enjoyed by those viewers as a depiction of an exotic-looking traditional culture within themselves, the Kabuki performance in *Momijigari* could have worked as reconfirmation of a traditional art form of Japan by way of the foreign viewpoint, especially when many people in the audience of the theater were no longer familiar with the Kabuki art of Danjurō IX and Kikugorō V.⁶⁴

The screening at the Fujikan Theater (August 28–October 3) was equally striking in this respect. According to Ueda Manabu, at least eleven films were screened under the program title "Tour of Japan by Foreigners." The titles alongside *Momijigari* included *Osaka Dōtonbori no nigiwai* (The Crowd of Osaka Dōtonbori), *Okayama Kōrakuen, Kyoto Chionin, Nara no Kasuga* (Okayama Kōrakuen, Kyoto Chionin, and Kasuga of Nara), *Gifu no hanagasa seizō* (Flower-Umbrella Making in Gifu), *Yokohama shi gunjin kangei kai* (Military Reception in the City of Yokohama), *Nihonbashi uogashi* (Fish Market in Nihonbashi), *Asakusa kōen* (Asakusa Park), *Onna kamiyui no ie* (The House of a Female Hairdresser), and *Geisha no odori* (Geisha's Dance).⁶⁵ It was not clear who photographed those films, Japanese cinematographers or non-Japanese ones. Either way, the entire program of the Fujikan Theater, which included *Momijigari*, could have been packaged and exported to any world fair as a set of Yokohama photograph-style films. At the same time, as the title of the program indicated, Japanese domestic audiences enjoyed these films by way of the foreign viewpoint.

Momijigari, photographed by Shibata Tsunekichi, could have been one of the earliest films for export to Europe, and it catered to the Orientalist fantasy about Japan. Even though it was not sent to the 1900 Paris Exposition Universelle, the film's producers were well aware of the foreign gaze. Such awareness probably made it easy to include this film in a program that emphasized the sense of foreignness rather than that of domesticity when the film was publicly released in Japan for the first time. As a result, it became a representative of traditional Japanese culture during the period of the modernization policy by the Japanese government. As such, *Momijigari* was a combination of two processes: exporting goods that European buyers expected and viewing its own culture through Westernized eyes.

In other words, the production and the exhibition of the film *Momijigari* were the sites of dialogic negotiation over the image of Japan within the Orientalist fantasy of Europe, the discourse of Japonisme from Europe, the governmental policy of modernization, and the formation of state nationalism in the rising nationwide mass media. *Momijigari* embodied Shibata Tsunekichi's reactions to Japonisme in Japan, which went beyond the double bind of fascination with and resistance to the technology of cinema. The film was not only a product of nativized Orientalism, a conscious pose to cater to the Orientalist fantasy, but also an enactment of internalized Orientalism, a conscious act that targeted domestic audiences in Japan. What Shibata attempted was to satisfy both the Orientalist expectations of European spectators and the nationalist goal of the modernizing nation to publicize its ideal cultural image to the domestic audience. The Japanese viewers of *Momijigari* of 1908 and later were invited to identify with the foreign gaze toward Japanese culture no matter how warped such a viewpoint was regarding its own culture.

EPILOGUE

Japonisme and the Birth of a Female Film Star in Hollywood and in Japan

Japonisme at the 1900 Paris Exposition Universelle

The year was 1900. The city of Paris hosted the Exposition Universelle from April 15 to November 12. Both Lumière cinema and Japonisme played significant roles there.

Five years had passed since the Lumière Company first projected motion pictures to thirty-three Parisian audiences at the Salon Indien du Grand Café on December 28, 1895. The Lumière brothers knew that they had to offer something spectacular to the sensation-seeking fair audience. According to the film historian Emmanuelle Toulet, the 1900 Exposition Universelle offered cinema "an opportunity for official and international recognition" that would go beyond the initial "curiosity" of the French public.[1] In addition to the official installation of its machines, supplies, and film stock in "Class 12: Photography" on the first floor of the Palace of Education on the Champs-de-Mars and specialized events at the International Congress of Photography held at the Palaces of Social Economy and of Congress,[2] the Lumière Company set up the Cinématographe Géant, a giant screen that measured twenty-one by eighteen meters, in the immense Festival Hall (fifteen thousand seats) of the Gallery of Machines, a spectacular building itself made of glass and iron.[3] Screenings of a program lasting twenty-five minutes, which included fifteen films (titles were changed regularly) and the projection of fifteen color photographs, were given free of charge to demonstrate in a spectacular manner what the company had filmed with its equipment.⁴ A total of 326 screenings were held from May 15 to November 12, and the audience averaged around 5,000 per screening, approximately 1,400,000 in total.⁵ With their exotic as well as aesthetic appeal, the films that were inspired by Japonisme and used the kinzō-gata-kōzu/chūkei-datsuraku/en=kin-hō composition, as well as the "Japanese films" photographed by Constant Girel, Gabriel Veyre, and presumably Shibata Tsunekichi, most likely had a huge impact on the exposition audience when they were exhibited on the gigantic screen.

Just a few blocks from the exposition site, at the theater of Loie Fuller on rue de Paris, a spectacular marble architecture designed by Henri Sauvage that replicated Fuller's famous butterfly dance, Sadayakko, the first female actor in modern Japanese theater, and her husband and actor Kawakami Otojirō performed a Japanese dance in an Orientalist work, *La Geisha et le Chevalier* (*The Geisha and the Knight*), that made them Parisian sensations. Her death scenes were favorably compared to those of Sarah Bernhardt. This was ironic because Kawakami's theater specialized in political satire and social criticism, most famously in the stage song "Oppekepē," about depression, poverty, and the vulgar behaviors of the nouveau riche in 1890s Japan. Moreover, according to the historian Ayako Kano, in Japan Kawakami's troupe had embodied the idea of "straight theater" (*seigeki*) that demanded the elimination of stylized song and dance as well as all-male performance of Kabuki in favor of realism.⁶ In Paris, Sadayakko and her husband became famous because of the non-straight elements (stylized song and dance of geisha) even when Sadayakko, a female actor, performed on stage. However, perhaps this kind of critique of contemporary Japanese society was not what a non-Japanese audience expected. Their Orientalist fantasy about Japan had been enhanced during the Japonisme vogue. They wanted to see geisha instead of a modernized image of the country. In fact, at the World Tour Panorama Pavilion (Panorama du tour du monde), a number of geisha from Tokyo sang and danced in front of paintings of Japanese scenery. This exhibition was not an official one planned by the Japanese government but by Messageries Maritimes, a French merchant shipping company, without approval of the Japanese Head Office for the exposition.⁷ Kawakami's troupe needed first to meet the expectations of the French spectators who were familiar with the discourse of Japonisme in order to show what it really wanted to show. As Kawakami recalled in 1901, "For foreigners, we must show something different with beautiful costumes. It must be a period piece with dances. We must do it quickly and cannot let them wait. That is what they want. Otherwise, they do not watch Japanese plays at all."⁸ As I have discussed in chapter 3, such a balancing act was necessitated when the Japanese government finalized the list of Japanese products to be introduced at the exposition. We can call the dancing act of Kawakami and Sadayakko in Paris another embodiment of nativized Orientalism.

Japonisme in America: *Madame Butterfly* and Aoki Tsuruko's Stardom in Hollywood

The preceding US tour of the Kawakami troupe had some success, but not consistently. Two actors of the troupe became ill and died. Kawakami fell sick. The couple had to leave their niece, Tsuruko, in San Francisco, where she was adopted by a Japanese painter, Aoki Toshio. This girl, Aoki Tsuruko (1891–1961), would become the first Japanese female film actor and star. There was no relationship between the Lumière Company and Aoki's career, which was established in the early period of the Hollywood film industry. But Japonisme played a significant role in the process there as well.

Aoki, now generally remembered only as the wife of Sessue Hayakawa, a Japanese actor and Hollywood superstar of the silent era, was a Hollywood star preceding Hayakawa. After the Japanese painter who adopted her died, a female journalist at the *Los Angeles Examiner* raised Aoki. Aoki studied at the Egan Dramatic School in Los Angeles before she started her film career playing supporting characters in Fred Mace's comedy films in the early 1910s.[9] Then she played a leading role in a Majestic film, *The Oath of O Tsuru San* (director unknown, 1913), the film that was as "dainty and attractive as Madame Butterfly," according to the film trade journal *Moving Picture World*.[10] After the success of the film, Aoki starred in numerous films about Japan developed by the New York Motion Picture Company (NYMPC) by Thomas H. Ince, one of the first influential producers in the early Hollywood film industry.[11] In 1913–14, *Reel Life*, the promotional magazine for films distributed by Mutual Film Corporation, placed a still photo of Aoki on its cover at least three times.[12]

By the time Aoki started her acting career, Japonisme as the European vogue in art had been fascinating people in the United States. After the Centennial Exhibition of 1876 in Philadelphia, when many Americans made their first contact with Japanese art and culture, the penetration of Japanese goods into the American market brought about a "Japan craze."[13] Because they were imports of European vogue, Japanese works of art were considered high art in the US.

The popularization of Japonisme in the US was aided by an image of geisha, a sensual but obedient female, and by the advent of cinema. In early American films the idea of geisha was connected to a more specific character:

Cio-Cio-San in *Madame Butterfly*, especially because of the success of Puccini's opera at the Metropolitan Opera in 1907 starring Geraldine Farrar. According to one research study, fully half of the films that were released in the US from 1909 to 1915 portraying cross-cultural relations took the form of ill-fated romance, a reworking of *Madame Butterfly*'s narrative of doomed romance between a Japanese woman and an American man.[14]

Aoki's stardom was possible because of the popularity of *Madame Butterfly* within the Japonisme vogue in the US. Or, conversely, Aoki's appearance in early American cinema played a significant role in the popularization of Japonisme in the American mind. Either way, Aoki's Japanese physique functioned to provide credibility to the Orientalist fantasy about Japan.

A typical example of the provision of authenticity to the *Madame Butterfly* narrative is found in an Aoki star vehicle, *The Wrath of the Gods* (aka *The Destruction of Sakurajima*, Reginald Barker, 1914). Thomas H. Ince, the producer of this big production, turned to the Japonisme vogue in order to cater to the newly cultivated middle-class audience of cinema. Ince hired Aoki to make his cinematic version of *Madame Butterfly* more authentic than its precedents.

First of all, Ince emphasized the authenticity of the casting of Aoki in this film in its publicity by using her biography. As a report in the *Moving Picture World* noted,

> It so happens that Miss Aoki is a native of the Island of Sakura, which was practically destroyed by the eruption of the volcano Sakura-Jima. Miss Aoki, having lost practically all her relatives in this eruption, was inconsolable and Mr. Ince thought that he was due to lose her, that she would have to go back home. But in consoling her, he induced her to work in conjunction with him on a thrilling and powerful heart interest story, entitled "The Wrath of the Gods," a four-reel Domino feature, evolving around Japanese legend and depicting the scenes and actions of her countrymen during the eruption, so that she could show the world the sufferings of her people.[15]

In real life, Aoki was not from "the Island of Sakura." She was born, as Obara Tsuruko, in Fukuoka prefecture, which is located about 180 miles north of Sakurajima. Indeed, on January 12, 1914, a volcano erupted on the island of Sakurajima. It was one of the largest disasters in the nation's history. Obviously, the biographical narrative made Aoki into a melodramatic heroine by Western standards. But at the same time, the biographical-style publicity added both physical and psychological authenticity to the character that Aoki played in *The Wrath of the Gods*.

The biographical style was continuously adopted in order to add authenticity to the formation of Aoki's star image as the physical embodiment of *Madame Butterfly*. An article in the *New York Clipper* noted particularly that Aoki had studied piano and vocal music at a convent in Pasadena, California, before she entered the film business.[16] In real life there is no record that Aoki went to the convent before she joined Fred Mace's company or Ince's company.[17] The convent episode in Aoki's fictionalized biography functions to emphasize not the literal but the symbolic conversion of the Japanese woman to Christianity.

Conversion to Christianity is a significant motif in *Madame Butterfly* that normalizes the hierarchical relationship between civilized and masculine America and primitive and feminine Japan. Using Christianity as its enlightening force to save and protect a Japanese woman from a primitive religion, *Madame Butterfly* justified the ideological aspect of US foreign policy: expansion and annexation in the name of enlightenment. Moreover, it functioned to safely contain the imminent horror of the "yellow peril." When Puccini's opera opened in the US in 1906, Japan had defeated Russia in the Russo-Japanese War and created an imminent threat to other colonial powers. The period from the 1910s to the 1920s witnessed a rapid increase of anti-Japanese sentiment against Japan's militarily and politically growing power. Puccini's opera dramatizes the break in the sacred order when the outraged priest (Cio-Cio-San's uncle) interrupts the wedding ceremony, condemns Cio-Cio-San's deceitful renunciation of the community and "her true religion," and curses her with "eternal damnation."[18] The biographical style in Aoki's star publicity provided authenticity to this archetypal tale of a religious collision.

First and foremost, *The Wrath of the Gods* is an archetypal fable pitting the civilized West, embodied by an American sailor, against the primitive East, embodied by a Japanese woman, told as a religious battle between Buddhism and Christianity. The film displays a Japanese village as a primitive community bound by a superstitious tradition and Toya-San (Aoki) as its victim. According to an old local legend of Sakurajima, Buddha has cursed Toya-San's family. If Toya-San marries, it would displease Buddha and the long-inactive volcano, Sakurajima, would erupt. But Tom Wilson, an American sailor (Frank Borzage), appears as embodying the opposite religious belief. Tom gives Toya-San a cross-shaped necklace, saying that this represents the "god of justice." The cross is displayed in a close-up. Embraced by Tom, here Toya-San symbolically converts to Christianity.

The Wrath of the Gods uses *Madame Butterfly*'s narrative in a distorted manner in order to construct Aoki's persona as an obedient Japanese woman like Cio-Cio-San and at the same time as a satisfactorily Americanized woman and

Hollywood star. Even though it is a story of interracial romance between an American man and a Japanese woman, the Japanese woman is not ill-fated like Cio-Cio-San. The American man and the Japanese woman sail to America, the land of freedom, and live happily ever after. Yamaki, Toya-San's father, played by Sessue Hayakawa, takes up the role of Cio-Cio-San. Yamaki sacrifices himself to cut Toya-San's ties with Japan. He leaves his child to the American man. Toya-San, on the other hand, replaces the innocent baby boy in *Madame Butterfly*, who would be protected by an American and raised as an American. Playing out the narrative of *Madame Butterfly* in a twisted manner in cinema, Aoki thus physically embodied an ideal image of a Japanese woman who is obedient to both Japan and Christianity.[19]

Nativized Orientalism in *The Dragon Painter* (1919)

Aoki married Sessue Hayakawa after the shooting of *The Wrath of the Gods*. When Hayakawa became an overnight sensation with *The Cheat* (Cecil B. DeMille, 1915), Aoki's career as a star came to an end. Aoki stopped playing leading roles after *The Beckoning Flame* (Charles Swickard, 1916). Yet she continued embodying the Orientalist fantasy—that is, *Madame Butterfly*.

Certain constraints were placed upon Aoki in defining her role in off-screen space. Aoki's screen image, publicized in fan magazines, became the one that represented archetypal Japanese femininity in the modern American middle-class domestic setting.[20] As the film scholar Sara Ross suggests, while Aoki visually represented a "quaint" woman, often pictured in kimono in her publicity photos, in US print magazines she was described "as behaving as a modern woman" and going against her "Eastern appearance."[21] In other words the image of Aoki in real life turned into that of Cio-Cio-San serving her American husband, if Cio-Cio-San had decided to come to the US as an enlightened Japanese woman. A publicity photo attached to an article in a film fan magazine, *Picture-Play*, emphasized the domesticated role that Aoki played, a reminder of *Madame Butterfly*'s gender relations even between the Japanese husband and wife.[22] In the photo, Hayakawa, in a Western suit, is lighting a cigarette and being served tea by Aoki, in a kimono. The photo clearly displays a Japanese woman faithfully serving her American(ized) husband.[23]

Also on the screen, Aoki continued playing Cio-Cio-San type characters in supporting roles. *The Dragon Painter* (William Worthington, 1919), a Hayakawa star vehicle, was a perfect example of Aoki as a Japanese woman providing authenticity to the Orientalist fantasy of *Madame Butterfly*. The film was based on a 1906 story written by Mary McNeil Fenollosa, the wife of an American art historian, Ernest Fenollosa, who had taught art in Japan from 1878 to 1890. His Japanese art collection became the basis of the Japanese art collection at the Boston Museum of Fine Arts, where he headed the Oriental Department. Fenollosa had an influential role in introducing the Japonisme vogue to middle-class Americans. His wife's novel was written in this trend.

The Dragon Painter was publicized as if it showed authentic Japanese landscapes, costumes, and characters. US film trade journals reported that The Dragon Painter successfully reproduced an "authentic" Japanese atmosphere. Margaret I. MacDonald of Moving Picture World wrote that "one of the especially fine features of the production is the laboratory work, mountain locations of extreme beauty, chosen for the purpose of imitating Japanese scenery, and supplying Japanese atmosphere, are enhanced by the splendid results accomplished, in the work of developing and toning."[24] However, the Japanese landscapes and characters of The Dragon Painter stressed the Orientalist fantasy about Japan. In fact, Kinema Junpo, a Japanese film magazine, pointed out that The Dragon Painter "did not show either contemporary or actual Japan."[25] The Dragon Painter displayed the imaginary, exotic, and picturesque Japan that many non-Japanese audiences had been accustomed to within the Japonisme vogue.

In fact, The Dragon Painter is filled with objects of the Orientalist fantasy about Japan. The opening shot, an extreme long shot of Hanake, where Tatsu lives, artificially combines the actual location of Yosemite Valley and exotic-looking objects, such as a torii and a straw-thatched hut. Moreover, the room of the heroine Umeko, played by Aoki, is filled with typical objects found in the Japonisme vogue: a Japanese garden with a gate, a stream, a small bridge, stone lanterns, and a peacock in front of a small shrine; a room with tatami mats, *fusuma* (Japanese sliding doors), and *shōji* (Japanese wooden screen doors with translucent paper); paintings of Mt. Fuji and a dragon; and paper lanterns. Umeko wears a luxurious kimono and the beautiful hairstyle of an unmarried woman, *shimada*. After making up in front of a Japanese-style mirror table, she dances a Japanese dance with a silver fan in front of flowers arranged in a Japanese style, while her housemaid plays the shamisen and Japanese drums. She sits beside a shōji window under the beautiful moon. Even after the wedding, Umeko keeps wearing her long-sleeved kimono, which married women traditionally do not wear, and her shimada hairstyle, which should have changed to the less showy *marumage* of married women. Umeko even shows her extremely obedient and self-sacrificial nature as a stereotypical Japanese woman. In order to save her husband's talent, she attempts suicide, as did Cio-Cio-San.[26]

Figure E.1. Umeko (Aoki Tsuruko) in *The Dragon Painter* (1919).

In addition to its display of Orientalist objects, *The Dragon Painter* is a conscious reflection of the Japonisme vogue. It is a story about a young painter, Tatsu, played by Hayakawa. He madly seeks a dragon princess who, he believes, is hiding under the surface of a mountain lake. Kano Indara, whose name is a clear reference to the Kanō school, the longest lived and most influential famous schools of Japanese painting, is impressed by Tatsu's paintings and invites him to become his disciple. The exhibition of his work is appreciated most by European viewers. Moreover, near the opening of the film are at least two shots that incorporate the kinzō-gata-kōzu/chūkei-datsuraku/en=kin-hō composition. In the scene where Tatsu looks for a particular landscape for his work, a shot emphasizes the contrast between two trunks of tall trees in the frontal layer and faraway mountains at the back. Similarly, in a high-angle shot of the following sequence when Tatsu paints near a waterfall, the waterfall in the frontal layer is so gigantic and white that the contrast between this and the forest landscape at the back where Tatsu sits and paints is astonishingly strong.

It should be noted that *The Dragon Painter* was produced at Haworth Pictures Corporation, Hayakawa's own film production company, which was established in March 1918. Already in 1916, only one year after his sensational

Figure E.2. Tatsu (Sessue Hayakawa) and the kinzō-gata-kōzu/chūkei-datsuraku/en=kin-hō composition in *The Dragon Painter*.

Figure E.3. Tatsu at the waterfall in *The Dragon Painter*.

rise to stardom, Hayakawa told a fan magazine that he was not satisfied with his roles in the films in which he had already appeared: "Such roles [in *The Wrath of the Gods* and *The Cheat*] are not true to our Japanese nature.... They are false and give people a wrong idea of us. I wish to make a characterization which shall reveal us as we really are."[27] If he meant what he said, at his own company Hayakawa could have displayed a more authentic image of Japanese people to satisfy Japanese communities in the US, which had been frustrated by the stereotypical images of Japan constructed in mainstream media. However, as Hayakawa confessed later, at Haworth "I was not about to change away from the type of picture which had earned me my fame and following."[28] Like Sadayakko at the 1900 Exposition Universelle, Hayakawa pragmatically realized that too faithful an adherence to modernized Japanese realities alone would not be pleasingly exotic to non-Japanese audiences. The strategy that Hayakawa and Aoki adopted at Haworth was that of nativized Orientalism.[29]

Internalizing the Orientalism of *Madame Butterfly* and the Birth of Female Film Stardom in Japan

The characterization of a Japanese woman as an obedient and self-sacrificial wife and mother did not contradict the Japanese gender politics of the time: "*ryōsai kenbo*" (good wife, wise mother). In fact, Japanese popular publications highly praised the characterization of Cio-Cio-San. Terada Shirō of *Fujin Kōron*, a popular women's magazine, considered Cio-Cio-San not to be "shameful" but "favorable" for her loyalty to her husband.[30] Next, primarily young intellectuals, ranging from film critics and filmmakers to government officials, appropriated Aoki's stardom, which was built upon the image of *Madame Butterfly*, for their own purposes. First, they identified with Hollywood's gaze toward Japanese women in order to maintain the gender relations of Japan. Second, they used her Hollywood stardom in order to modernize Japanese cinema. It was a conscious act of internalizing Orientalism. During that process, a template of the female star in Japanese cinema emerged.

First, as a star in "Western" cinema, Aoki appeared to embody a rebelliously independent "modern girl," or *moga* (the abbreviated term in Japan), who would not be contained in the ideal image of Japanese womanhood: "good wife, wise mother." Aoki's professional status could be seen as subversive to Japan's supposed national unity, which was based on a patriarchal family system whose top position was occupied by the emperor. However, especially after Hayakawa obtained star status with the help of Aoki and her obedient offscreen image, many articles in Japanese magazines focusing solely on Aoki started to appear. No matter how Westernized her lifestyle was, those articles eventually emphasized how devoted Aoki was to her husband, as ideal Japanese wives are. There were several reports from those who visited the Hayakawas in Hollywood. These people expressed pleasant surprise: the Hayakawas' house appeared very Western from the outside, but once inside, they were entertained in a Japanese-style room with Japanese food prepared by Aoki.[31] For them, Aoki was a perfect combination of a modernized/Americanized appearance and an ideal Japanese housewife who was faithfully supporting her husband. As Shigeno Yukiyoshi, an editor of the film magazine *Katsudō Kurabu*, claimed, "Hayakawa's fame is not accidental but owes a lot to his wife Tsuruko.... She is a faithful wife who devotes herself to improving her husband's position."[32] This process was similar to what Ayako Kano calls "wifing," which confined a transgressing Japanese woman to the role of tamed "wife" consistent with the ideology of "good wife, wise mother."[33]

It is noteworthy that in the same period, another Japanese performer who became famous on the international stage playing Cio-Cio-San was severely criticized for her transgressive attitude as a moga. After her debut in London in *Madame Butterfly* in 1915, Miura Tamaki (1884–1946) became the first Japanese opera singer to attain international acclaim. As Aoki did in Ince films, with her Japanese body Miura appealed to foreign spectators as if she were authentically embodying an Orientalist fantasy of the obedient Japanese femininity of Cio-Cio-San.[34] Miura had an image that was the opposite of Aoki's with regard to the discourse on Japanese womanhood. Miura divorced her first husband in 1909 and had an affair with an Italian composer during her international tour, while her second husband was waiting in Japan. As early as 1911, Miura insisted in *Chūō Kōron* magazine, "Gone are the days when wives were called *okusama* [married women who should stay at home] and women distanced themselves from associating with men.... [T]oday, we women must possess 'dignity' and actresses must 'face the world with divine dignity' and faithfully pursue art."[35] Japanese magazines reported that Miura often visited Aoki and Hayakawa in their home in Hollywood when she toured the US, but they also included Aoki's comments about Miura's lifestyle in a somewhat ironic tone and contrasted the two internationally acclaimed Japanese women. Aoki is quoted as saying, "Shibata [Miura] Tamaki's reputation is great. Her lifestyle is very colorful and wonderful."[36] In contrasting Miura and Aoki, two modern girls, Japanese media formulated an authentic image of Japanese womanhood as an obedient housewife like Cio-Cio-San. This was an act of inventing tradition and internalizing Orientalism.

Second, aside from formulating the image of ideal Japanese womanhood around Cio-Cio-San, Aoki's star image as an authentic *Madame Butterfly* had a tremendous impact on the discourse of modernization of cinema in Japan. In the early 1910s, primarily young intellectuals began to criticize mainstream commercial films in Japan. They decried films made in Japan as slavish reproductions of Japanese theatrical works. They promoted a reform of motion pictures in Japan through the production of "modern" and "purely cinematic" films. Their writings and subsequent experimental filmmaking are often noted as *jun'eigageki undō*, or the pure film movement. According to the film historian Joanne Bernardi, one of the goals of the pure film advocates was "the attainment of an internationally viable level of narrational clarity for films also endowed with a comprehensible and distinct national and cultural identity."[37]

The pure film advocates criticized mainstream commercial Japanese motion pictures for being "uncinematic" because, for the most part, they were merely reproducing stage repertories of Kabuki, most typified by the use of onnagata for female roles. In Japan, female motion picture actors did not appear until as late as 1918, when Hanayagi Harumi starred in *Sei no kagayaki* (*The Glory of Life*), a product of the film modernization movement. Before this film, the majority of female characters in motion pictures were played by onnagata, with the exception of a few female actors, including Nakamura Kasen, who appeared in serial *rensageki*, a mixture of film and stage drama.[38] Even in 1919, only three films out of about one hundred fifty films released in Japan used female actors for female roles.[39]

The pure film advocates eventually intended to export Japanese-made films to foreign markets.[40] For example, film theorist Kaeriyama Norimasa referred to *The Wrath of the Gods* and claimed, "Isn't it a huge loss that Japanese producers do not make any films for export and have all the greatly unique landscape of Japan stolen by foreigners?"[41] Aaron Gerow has argued that the presence of foreign-made movies set in Japan in the 1910s motivated the pure film advocates in Japan to produce films for export, not necessarily opposing those films' inaccurate and Orientalist depictions of Japan but displacing the crime of "theft": Japanese films that had been made by non-Japanese people.[42] Aoki and Hayakawa's films were ideal products for the reformists because they used "cinematic" forms and techniques to tell Japanese stories, no matter how strong the represented image of Japan reflected their Orientalist fantasy. In other words, the filmmakers wanted to produce *Madame Butterfly* in Japan to cater to the international film market. Here, the project of modernization of Japanese cinema went hand in hand with an attitude of nativized Orientalism.

When Aoki's stardom was being formulated in Hollywood, such "cinematic" techniques as close-up, artificial three-point lighting, and soft focus were used for film stars both in their films and publicity photos in order to emphasize the actors' physical characteristics and to convey sensual attraction. While serving for narrative clarity and consistency on the one hand, these photographic techniques could also enhance the viewers' sensory perceptions of materiality. Kabuki's use of onnagata was unnatural and inappropriate to cinema because its gender existed as a performance, in which femininity was not defined by actual sexual bodies of actors but by their techniques of displaying ideal feminine behaviors. Critics and fans ascribed to cinema "an imperative towards naturalness and reality, especially because of its mechanical properties, its ability to change framing, and its emphasis on photographic reproduction in the medium."[43]

As opposed to the onnagata, Aoki's novelty to the Japanese spectator was based on an image of physical sexuality, whose physical characteristics were enhanced by photographic technologies. As the film historian Hideaki Fujiki indicates, the March 1917 issue of the film magazine *Katsudō Gahō* juxtaposes a still photo of Tachibana Teijirō, a very popular onnagata at Nikkatsu Mukōjima studio, in a *shinpa* (Kabuki-influenced modern drama) film, *Futari Shizuka* (The Quiet Pair, Oguchi Tadashi, 1917), and a portrait of Myrtle Gonzalez, a Blue Bird film star. The latter is a sensual close-up of the female actor's face and naked shoulders in low-key lighting, dramatically highlighted with sidelight from the left, but the former, a typical portrayal of a shinpa-style film of the time, is a flat-lighted long shot.[44] Even though it is not clear how faithfully this still photo represents the actual scene in the film, this example among many implies how the mise-en-scène of the shinpa-style film emphasizes visibility of the theatrical tableaux in diffused lighting rather than dramatically enhancing fragmented body parts or anything within the frame via spot lighting.[45] Originally a type of political drama associated with *Jiyū minken undō*, the Freedom and People's Rights Movement of the 1880s initiated by Kawakami Otojirō (Aoki's uncle), shinpa dealt with contemporary social issues and Western ideas; however, stylistically it did not completely cut off its ties to native theatrical traditions and made liberal use of many Kabuki conventions, including the onnagata. According to Fujiki, shinpa onnagata express their emotions in the movement of their entire bodies or in special configuration with other actors and the surrounding décor, and wide shots and flat lighting are more suitable to display their performance than close-ups and spot lighting.[46]

More than anything else, it was Aoki's physical body that Japanese critics and fans highly valued. As *Kinema Record* noted, "She owns a good body. Her acting and her body are as good as European and American people."[47] The film magazine *Katsudō Shashin Zasshi* placed a portrait of Aoki in its photo gallery

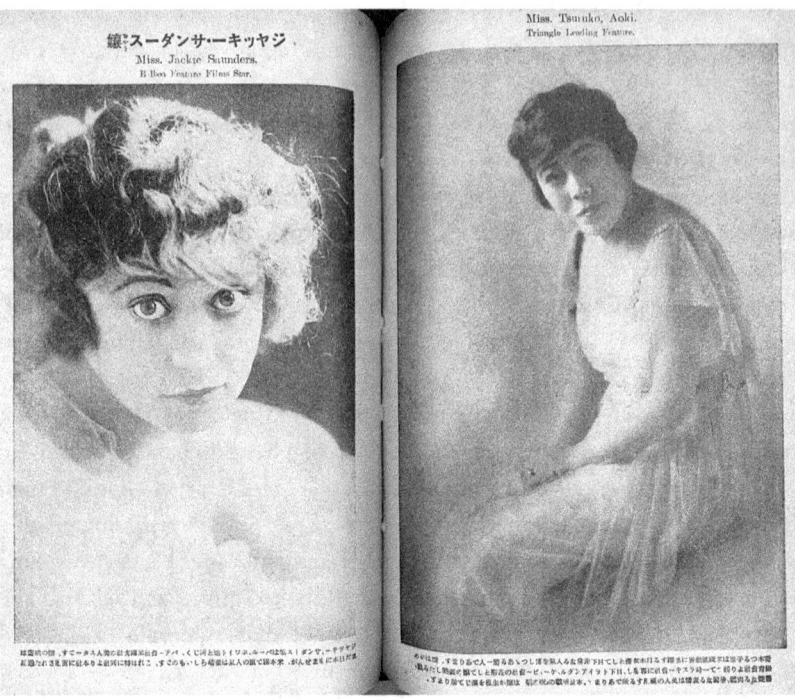

Figure E.4. *Katsudō Shashin Zasshi* 3, no. 12 (December 1917).

section that was usually reserved for Western stars and noted, "Miss Aoki Tsuruko is a Japanese actress in the American film industry and she is one of the most popular stars.... We are fascinated by her sensual body and gorgeous facial expressions."[48] The opposite page displays a close-up of the face of another female star, Jackie Saunders, in typical Hollywood three-point lighting. The unblemished big round eyes and the shining blond hair are striking in the Saunders photo, but relatively strong sidelight emphasizes Aoki's sensual chest loosely covered with a white gown while softer fill light enhances her graceful, motherly facial expression.

Aoki's Japanese body was appreciated in Hollywood because it provided authenticity to the Orientalist fantasy of *Madame Butterfly*. Her female body was appreciated in Japan because it provided authenticity to cinematic representations of sexuality with skillfully incorporated "cinematic" styles such as close-up, three-point lighting, and soft focus. The only thing that the Japanese film reformists had to do was to combine the two and produce their own version of *Madame Butterfly*. What they wanted in their project of nativizing

Orientalism (producing films for export) as well as internalizing Orientalism (identifying with Hollywood's position against the premodern, uncinematic filmmaking in Japan) was a Japanese female actor who could play their own Cio-Cio-San in their cinematic films.

According to Fujiki, Kurishima Sumiko, arguably the first female star in Japanese cinema and one of the most popular female actors of the 1920s, did not only embody the sexuality of her physical body but also represented "a typical traditional Japanese beauty."[49] But the image of the "traditional Japanese beauty" that Kurishima embodied was in fact the one that had been presupposed in Europe and in Hollywood. Aoki's Hollywood stardom had constantly been publicized in Japanese film magazines well before Kurishima appeared. If Aoki's stardom prepared a template for female film actors in Japan, the impact that Fujiki claims American star images had upon the emergence of those actresses turned out to be more complicated. What was imported was not limited to the image of immediacy of physical bodies. The image of archetypal Japanese femininity had already been formulated in Europe and popularized in Hollywood within an Orientalist imagination. Kurishima was the first Japanese female film star who Japanized the image of *Madame Butterfly*, a product of Japonisme, embodied by Aoki.

Shōchiku Company appointed "Henry" Kotani Sōichi to create the visual star image for Kurishima. After appearing in films with Aoki and Hayakawa at Ince's company, Kotani had worked as a cinematographer in Hollywood under renowned filmmaker Cecil B. DeMille. In 1920, eagerly pursued by the representatives of Shochiku and highly recommended by DeMille, Kotani returned to Japan.

First, disliking the Kabuki's makeup, Kotani used Max Factor cosmetics, imported directly from the US, to make up Kurishima in *Gubijinsō* (The Poppy, 1921), in order to create a more natural and authentic appearance of a female face and to enhance the lighting effects.[50] Second, Kotani used backlight for Kurishima to perform "the less self-conscious tasks of defining space and adding a normative degree of aesthetic polish" in order to imitate the photographic techniques of Hollywood.[51] In Hollywood, Kotani had been assigned as a cinematographer for Laila Lee, a Paramount star, in *The Heart of Youth* (Robert G. Vignola, 1919), *Puppy Love* (R. William Neill, 1919), *Rustling a Bride* (Irvin Willat, 1919), and *The Secret Garden* (G. Butler Clonebough, 1919). Thus, Kotani recreated a Hollywood-style sensual physical entity around Kurishima. Like Aoki's, Kurishima's Japanese body was displayed in Hollywood-style cinematography.

At the same time, Shōchiku used Kurishima mostly in films with shinpa-style narratives and obedient and self-sacrificing heroines. Often called *shinpa*

Figure E.5. Kurishima Sumiko in *Gubijinsō* (The Poppy), 1921. © Henry Kotani Production.

daihigeki (a grand tragedy), shinpa tended to be a sentimental drama with a tragic ending.[52] In other words, there is no critical difference between shinpa and *Madame Butterfly* in terms of their characterizations of their heroines. The narrative of *Hototogisu* (*The Cuckoo*, 1922), directed by Ikeda Gishin, a would-be husband of Kurishima, has the theme of a Japanese woman's self-sacrifice and retains a structure very similar to that of *Madame Butterfly*. Lieutenant General Viscount Kataoka's daughter Namiko, played by Kurishima, and Navy Ensign Baron Kawashima Takeo have an arranged yet happy marriage, but she soon turns out to be suffering from tuberculosis. Finding her vomiting blood and fearing infection, her mother-in-law, Okei, forces her to divorce Takeo and return to her parents' hometown while he is away on an official trip. The film closes with scenes in which she is dying in bed and the funeral is held. As with *Madame Butterfly*, "blood" intervenes in an initial marriage, a hero's family member asks the heroine to leave, and the heroine chooses to die alone in the end in order to protect the hero. Stylistically, the film contributes to the construction of Kurishima's character as an obedient heroine like Cio-Cio-San. The film contains close-ups of Namiko's face and emphasizes the fact that Kurishima as an actual woman, not an impersonator, is playing the heroine. Yet compared to the portrait of Myrtle Gonzalez in *Katsudo Gahō*, lighting is not fully used to enhance the sensual attraction or material reality of the actress throughout the film. Instead, as Fujiki points out, in most parts of the film Kurishima looks down and displays her reserved nature.⁵³ In the end, the heroine sacrifices herself for the career of the hero in compositions that emphasize shinpa-style tableaux that occupy the majority of screen time. Critic Īzuka Tōkin claimed in his review of this film that Kurishima "represented Japanese ladies' gracefulness."⁵⁴

In publicity efforts, such a star image of Kurishima was explicitly connected to conventional Japanese womanliness and femininity. As Fujiki suggests, the photogravure and its caption of Kurishima in *Kamata*, a fan magazine for Shōchiku films, are a typical example.⁵⁵ In the portrait photograph the close-up showcases her casting down her eyes, wearing a kimono, and having her hair done up in the traditional Japanese *yuigami* style with an ornament *kanzashi* hairpin. This picture is captioned by the comment "The woman unique to Japan who symbolizes 'obedience' in that she can never complain even if abused and admonished. That is the woman that Miss Sumiko performs."⁵⁶ The critic Tsuda Kōzō described Kurishima as nothing but a "good wife, wise mother," the idealized Japanese woman of the time.⁵⁷

Fujiki connects such a publicity strategy that emphasized the traditional Japanese style in Kurishima's star image to the attributes of the onnagata. As an example, Fujiki points out that Kurishima, who was proficient at *nihon buyō*, Japanese traditional dancing, often displayed her dance in her star vehicles. Fujiki argues that Kurishima's Japanese dance connects her to the onnagata and its idealized Japanese womanliness: "Though such scenes [of Kurishima dance] might have provoked the audience's sexual interest, mostly she as well as [the onnagata actor] Tachibana [Teijirō] was covered by *kimono*" so that "she didn't look that different from an onnagata actor."⁵⁸ But I want to stress that Japanese traditional dancing also existed at the core of the Orientalist fantasy. Many films with Aoki produced in Hollywood, including *The Dragon Painter*, included dance scenes with Aoki in kimono.

With her female Japanese body, Kurishima provided a sense of authenticity to female roles in Japanese cinema, contrary to the onnagata. Her body was sensualized by the Hollywood-style cinematic techniques, as was Aoki's. At the same time, combined with such new and modern technology was an image of obedient womanhood: that of "good wife, wise mother." Kurishima faithfully followed the template that Aoki's stardom had prepared along with the image of *Madame Butterfly*.

Thus, the first female film star in Japan was born as a result of *nativizing* as well as *internalizing* the Orientalist fantasy about Japan. Following the

Hollywood-made stardom of Aoki, Kurishima's star image incorporated the Orientalist image of *Madame Butterfly* for the dream of export of Japanese-made films to international markets. It was a conscious act of self-exoticization of Japanese cinema for the potential foreign gaze. In this sense, Kurishima's stardom occupied a central part in the project of modernization of Japanese cinema with an attitude of nativized Orientalism. At the same time, Kurishima was a "Japanese sweetheart." The formation of her stardom was targeted to a Japanese audience that was about to consume Japanese-made films as an emblem of Japanese modernity. To aid this process, the Orientalist image of Cio-Cio-San, which was embodied by Aoki in Hollywood cinema, was consciously rearticulated as an image of ideal Japanese womanhood in Kurishima's stardom. It was a twisted formation of subjectivity in a modernizing nation that consciously identified its position with the creator of the Orientalist fantasy.

As such, Cio-Cio-San was brought back to Japan. Mission complete.

NOTES

Introduction

1. Some of the Lumière films have official English titles or the ones that are used in Jacques Rittaud-Hutinet, *Auguste et Louis Lumière: Les 1000 Premiers Films* (Paris: Philippe Sers Éditeur, 1990). I list those English titles in italics. Otherwise, the accompanying English titles that are not in italics are my translation. So are the titles of paintings. All translations of non-English texts (mainly from the French and Japanese) in this book are mine unless otherwise noted. The Cinématographe Lumière was a compact device capable of photographing, making copies, and projecting images in 35mm celluloid strips that extend seventeen meters, each about fifty seconds in duration.
2. Arthur Lenning, *The Silent Voice: A Text* (Albany, NY: Lane, 1969), 14.
3. Marshall Deutelbaum, "Structural Patterning in the Lumière Films," in *Film before Griffith*, ed. John L. Fell (Berkeley: University of California Press, 1983), 312.
4. If I may use André Gaudreault's term, this film enters into the "paradigm of monstration," in which the person filming goes beyond "the autonomy of the object being depicted by showing it in its absolute temporal integrity and by attempting to reveal its properly attractional quality" and starts to "fiddle with what is being shown or to act upon its representation." Gaudreault, *Film and Attraction: From Kinematography to Cinema*, trans. Timothy Barnard (Urbana: University of Illinois Press, 2011), 58.
5. Komatsu Hiroshi, *Kigen no eiga* [Cinema of origin] (Tokyo: Seido sha, 1991), 87.
6. Komatsu, *Kigen no eiga*, 89. As another film historian, Tom Gunning, echoes, "The Lumière films create an expansive sense of the world through a series of compositional devices well established in pictorial representation at that time, especially a contrast between foreground and background, as well as visual devices unique to the medium of motion pictures, such as freedom of movement beyond the frame." Tom Gunning, "New Thresholds of Vision: Instantaneous Photography and the Early Cinema of Lumière," in *Impossible Presence: Surface and Screen in the Photogenic Era*, ed. Terry Smith (Chicago: University of Chicago Press, 2001), 78.
7. Auguste Lumière and Louis Lumière, "La photographie oeuvre d'art" [The photography work of art], in *Lumières sur Lumière*, ed. Bernard Chardère (Lyon: Institut Lumière/Presses Universitaires de Lyon, 1987), 100–105.
8. Françoise Heilbrun, "Impressionism and Photography," *History of Photography* 33, no. 1 (February 2009): 19.
9. Lionel Lambourne, *Japonisme: Cultural Crossings between Japan and the West* (London: Phaidon, 2005), 220.

10 Armond Fields, *Henri Rivière* (Salt Lake City: Gibbs M. Smith, 1983), 30; Gabriel P. Weisberg, *Japonisme: Japanese Influence on French Art 1840–1910* (Cleveland: Cleveland Museum of Art, 1975), 58–59.
11 Lenning, *The Silent Voice*, 14.
12 Inaga Shigemi, *Kaiga no tasogare: Eduāru Mane botsugo no tōsō* [The twilight of painting: The posthumous fight of Édouard Manet] (Nagoya: Nagoya daigaku shuppan kai, 1997), 276.
13 Siegfried Wichmann, *Japonisme: The Japanese Influence on Western Art in the 19th and 20th Centuries* (New York: Harmony, 1981), 57.
14 Klaus Berger, *Japonisme in Western Painting from Whistler to Matisse*, trans. David Britt (Cambridge: Cambridge University Press, 1992), 187.
15 All the Lumière films that I discuss in this book are preserved and accessible at the Institut Lumière. I would like to thank Armelle Bourdoulous, Jean-Marc Lamotte, and Nathalie Morena of the Institut Lumière for their valuable help.
16 I have preserved Japanese name order, which places the family name first (e.g., Katsushika Hokusai), except for famous persons and scholars based in the English-speaking countries who are commonly referred to by their given names first (e.g., Sessue Hayakawa).
17 Gaudreault, *Film and Attraction*, 43.
18 Discussing anime, or Japanese animation, in the late twentieth century to the early twenty-first century, the media scholar Thomas LaMarre writes that "an anime series or film might thus be thought of as the nodal point in a *transmedial network* that entails proliferating series of narrative and non-narrative forms across media interfaces and platforms, such as the computer, television, movie theater, and cell phone. So dynamic and diverse are the worlds that unfold around anime that we do better to think always in the plural, in terms of *animations*." Thomas LaMarre, *The Anime Machine: A Media Theory of Animation* (Minneapolis: University of Minnesota Press, 2009), xiv; italics in the original. I prefer the term *transmedia* over *intermedia*, which might have been a little more accepted, because the latter seems to presuppose specificity in each medium and emphasizes interactions between them. As for the terms *intermedia* and *transmedia*, see Kinoshita Chika, *Mizoguchi Kenji ron: Eiga no bigaku to seijigaku* [On Mizoguchi Kenji: Cinema's aesthetics and politics] (Tokyo: Hōsei daigaku shuppan kyoku, 2016), 7–8. I am also inspired by film historian Yuri Tsivian's argument that connects the films of Yevgenii Bauer and Franz Hofer in the 1910s to painting, including turn-of-the-century symbolist art. See Yuri Tsivian, "Two 'Stylists' of the Teens: Franz Hofer and Yevgenii Bauer," in *A Second Life: German Cinema's First Decades*, ed. Thomas Elsaesser and Michael Wedel (Amsterdam: Amsterdam University Press, 1996), 264–76.
19 Thomas Elsaesser, *Film History as Media Archeology: Tracking Digital Cinema* (Amsterdam: Amsterdam University Press, 2016), 25.
20 Elsaesser, *Film History as Media Archeology*, 19, 25.
21 Edward Said, *Orientalism* (New York: Pantheon, 1978), 1–28.

22 Geneviève Lacambre, "Les milieux japonisants à Paris, 1860-1880," in *Japonisme in Art: An International Symposium*, ed. the Society for the Study of Japonisme (Tokyo: Kodansha International, 1980), 49-50. See also Atsuko Ukai, "The History of Japonisme as a Global Study," in *Translation, History and Arts: New Horizons in Asian Interdisciplinary Humanities Research*, ed. Ji Meng and Atsuko Ukai (Newcastle upon Tyne, UK: Cambridge Scholars Publishing, 2013), 70-84.
23 Daisuke Miyao, *The Aesthetics of Shadow: Lighting and Japanese Cinema* (Durham, NC: Duke University Press, 2013), 7.
24 Stuart Hall, "Encoding/Decoding," in *Culture, Media, Language*, ed. Stuart Hall et al. (London: Hutchinson, 1980), 128-38.
25 Daisuke Miyao, *Sessue Hayakawa: Silent Cinema and Transnational Stardom* (Durham, NC: Duke University Press, 2007); Miyao, *The Aesthetics of Shadow*, 84-118.
26 Godard called the Lumière brothers "the last Impressionists" in *La Chinoise* (1967); Steven Z. Levine, "Monet, Lumière, and Cinematic Time," *Journal of Aesthetics and Art Criticism* 36, no. 4 (summer 1978): 441-47.
27 "Lumière Peintres," the Institut Lumière.
28 Lenning, *The Silent Voice*, 14.
29 Jonathan Crary, *Suspensions of Perception: Attention, Spectacle, and Modern Culture* (Cambridge, MA: MIT Press, 1999), 7, 9.
30 Crary, *Suspensions of Perception*, 9.
31 Michelle Aubert and Jean-Claude Seguin, *La Production cinématographique des Frères Lumière* [The cinematographic production of the Lumière brothers] (Paris: Librairie du Premier Siècle du Cinéma, Bibliothèque du film, Editions Mémoires de cinema, Diffusion, CDE, 1996), 72. See also Michael Allan, "Deserted Histories: The Lumière Brothers, the Pyramids and Early Film Form," *Early Popular Visual Culture* 6, no. 2 (July 2008): 160.
32 The term *nativized Orientalism* was coined by the art historian Norman Bryson. Norman Bryson, "Furansu no orientarizumu kaiga ni okeru 'tasha'" ["The Other" in French Orientalist paintings], in *Bijutsu shi to tasha* [Art history and the Other], ed. Shimamoto Kan and Kasuya Makoto (Kyoto: Kōyō shobō, 2000), 83.
33 H. D. Harootunian, *Overcome by Modernity: History, Culture, and Community in Interwar Japan* (Princeton, NJ: Princeton University Press, 2000), xvii, xxi; italics in the original.
34 Stefan Tanaka, *Japan's Orient: Rendering Pasts into History* (Berkeley: University of California Press, 1993), 22. Tanaka argues that Japan eventually became captive to its own discourse of defining itself by the foreign viewpoint.
35 Weihong Bao, "The Trouble with Theater: Cinema and the Geopolitics of Medium Specificity," *Framework* 56, no. 2 (fall 2015): 350.
36 Elsaesser, *Film History as Media Archeology*, 35.

Chapter 1: The À Travers Cinema

1 Noël Burch, *Life to Those Shadows*, trans. Ben Brewster (Berkeley: University of California Press, 1990), 15.
2 Burch, *Life to Those Shadows*, 15.

3   There are four films with the same title, *Sortie d'usine*, in the Lumière catalog. Except for the last one, *Sortie d'usine*, [IV], which shows a more modernized building that looks like a warehouse, they were filmed at the same location. In the second version, probably shot in March 1896, the camera is placed a little farther back from the factory so that the street in front of it is more visible. Another difference is that the small door on the wall is closed at the beginning and opens during the action in the second film. Because of the door opening, the viewers become more aware of the movements between the frontal and the back in the second film. In addition, because of the greater distance between the camera and the factory exit, the second film rather consciously emphasizes horizontal movements, in addition to the movements between the front and the back. Women pass from left to right in front of the camera. A small girl runs from left to right. A dog walks off from left to right and comes back from the right offscreen space. The film ends again when a carriage comes out and is about to turn left. As a result, the effect of the kinzō-gata-kōzu/chūkei-datsuraku/en=kin-hō composition is less, and the sense of depth goes more along with the linear perspective. The third version, probably shot in August 1896, has a clear sense of the beginning and the ending because the film begins when the two doors, the big one on the right and the small one on the left, open and ends when they close. The camera is placed at almost the same distance as in *Sortie d'usine, [I]*. There is no carriage appearing in this film, so there is no action "to be continued." In other words, arguably Louis Lumière once again experiments with the ukiyo-e style composition with movements. This version begins with a two-dimensional composition, turns into three-dimensional with the kinzō-gata-kōzu/chūkei-datsuraku/en=kin-hō composition between the front and the back, and then ends with the initial composition. The fourth version was shot probably in February 1897 in front of a different factory building.

4   The four films titled *Sortie d'usine* were shot at four different times: March 1895, March 1896, August 1896, and February 1897. There is no record of who shot the three later films.

5   Angela Dalle Vacche, "Cezanne and the Lumière Brothers," in *Film, Art, New Media: Museum without Walls?*, ed. Angela Dalle Vacche (London: Palgrave Macmillan, 2012), 46.

6   Thomas Looser, "Superflat and the Layers of Image and History in 1990s Japan," *Mechademia* 1 (2006): 97.

7   Oliver Grau, *Virtual Art: From Illusion to Immersion*, trans. Gloria Custance (Cambridge, MA: MIT Press, 2003), 40.

8   Grau, *Virtual Art*, 40. Similarly, as the film theorist Vivian Sobchack states, "Because perspective is a *theoretical construct*, a *represented* way of seeing and being in the world, it is not the only possibility for signifying the significance of either existence or representation." Vivian Sobchack, *The Address of the Eye: A Phenomenology of Film Experience* (Princeton, NJ: Princeton University Press, 1992), 96; italics in the original. Sobchack's concept of "cinesthetic" in her phenomenological approach to moving images leads us to the totality of bodily experiences and sensory

perceptions of moving images that goes beyond the primacy of vision, which is often theoretically constructed: like Renaissance perspective. She addresses the difficulty of singling out "vision or the particular physiological function" of one's eyes "as discrete and localized organs of perception" dividing itself from one's "entire *perceptive* body in its activity." As she continues, "Indeed, seeing gains its specific meaning as an activity lived through and for that body in a multiplicity of intentional and *cooperative* projects that mark the ongoing act of becoming that is being" (96). My approach to Lumière cinema is not as comprehensive as the phenomenology of intermediality that Sobchack proposes, but it tries to be physiologically astute in order to emphasize the Lumière brothers' project of focusing on the operative function of bodily organs in the age of mechanical reproduction.

9   Jonathan Crary, *Techniques of the Observer: On Vision and Modernity in the Nineteenth Century* (Cambridge, MA: MIT Press, 1990), 48.
10 Kobayashi Yasuo, *Hyōshō bunka ron kōgi: Kaiga no bōken* [Lectures in cultural representations: Adventures of pictures] (Tokyo: Tokyo daigaku shuppan kai, 2016), 174.
11 Ishitani Haruhiro, *Genshi to riarizumu: Kūrube kara Pisaro e Furansu kindai kaiga no saikō* [Illusion and realism: From Courbet to Pissaro, reconsidering French modern painting] (Kyoto: Jinbun shoin, 2011), 44.
12 Kobayashi, *Hyōshō bunka ron kōgi*, 134.
13 Ishitani, *Genshi to riarizumu*, 43.
14 Ishitani, *Genshi to riarizumu*, 47.
15 Mary Ann Doane, "Temporality, Storage, Legibility: Freud, Marey, and the Cinema," in *Endless Night: Cinema and Psychoanalysis, Parallel Histories*, ed. Janet Bergstrom (Berkeley: University of California Press, 1999), 68.
16 Doane, "Temporality, Storage, Legibility," 81.
17 O. Winter, "The Cinematograph," *New Review*, May 1896, 507–13, accessed November 13, 2017, http://picturegoing.com/?p=4166.
18 Jonathan Crary, "Techniques of the Observer," *October* 45 (Summer 1988): 35.
19 Hase Masato, *Eiga to iu tekunorojī taiken* [Cinema and technological experience] (Tokyo: Seikyū sha, 2010), 72.
20 Hase, *Eiga to iu tekunorojī taiken*, 73.
21 Dai Vaughan, *For Documentary* (Berkeley: University of California Press, 1999), 5. See also Lorrain Daston and Peter Galison, "The Image of Objectivity," *Representations* 40 (Fall 1992): 81–128.
22 This notion of the cinematographer-beholder, as well as my focus on the corporeality of the cinematographer, is inspired by the art historian Michael Fried's notion of the "painter-beholder." Fried argues that Courbet's ambition was to overcome the conventional theatrical relationship between artwork and spectator by absorbing "the painter-beholder as if bodily in painting." Michael Fried, *Courbet's Realism* (Chicago: University of Chicago Press, 1990), 132.
23 Hirashima Masao, Sugano Akimasa, and Takashina Shūji, *Tettei tōgi 19seiki no bungaku geijutsu* [Through discussion: Literature and art of the nineteenth century] (Tokyo: Seido sha, 1974), 267.

24 Hirashima, Sugano, and Takashina, *Tettei tōgi 19seiki no bungaku geijutsu*, 401-2.
25 Paul Souriau, *The Aesthetics of Movement*, trans. and ed. Manon Souriau (Amherst: University of Massachusetts Press, 1983), 114-21; Mary Ann Doane, *The Emergence of Cinematic Time: Modernity, Contingency, the Archive* (Cambridge, MA: Harvard University Press, 2002), 83-84.
26 Inaga Shigemi, *Kaiga no tasogare: Eduāru Mane botsugo no tōsō* [The twilight of painting: The posthumous fight of Édouard Manet] (Nagoya: Nagoya daigaku shuppan kai, 1997), 276. The value of *dessin* had been valued highly in Europe as early as in 1550, though Giorgio Vasari, an Italian painter, architect, writer, and historian, claimed that it was Giotto who used dessin to establish painting around the year 1300 to be the representation of nature. See Kobayashi, *Hyōshō bunka ron kōgi*, 10-11.
27 Théodore Duret, *Histoire de Édouard Manet et de son oeuvre* (Paris 1902), quoted and translated into Japanese in Inaga, *Kaiga no tasogare*, 284.
28 Théodore Duret, "L'art japonais" (ca. 1883-85) in *Critique d'avant-garde* (Paris: Charpentier, 1885), quoted and translated into Japanese in Inaga Shigemi, *Kaiga no rinkai: Kindai higashi Ajia bijutsushi no shikoku to meiun* [Images on the edge: A historical survey of East Asian trans-cultural modernities] (Nagoya: Nagoya daigaku shuppan kai, 2014), 103.
29 At the 1878 Exposition in Paris, painters Watanabe Shōtei and Yamamoto Hōsui displayed their dessin skills in front of the European audience. See Mabuchi Akiko, *Japonisumu: Gensō no Nippon* [Japonisme: Imaginary Japan] (Tokyo: Brücke, 1997), 56.
30 Jill DeVonyar and Richard Kendall, *Degas and the Art of Japan* (Reading, PA: Reading Public Museum, 2007), 23; Siegfried Wichmann, *Japonisme: The Japanese Influence on Western Art in the 19th and 20th Centuries* (New York: Harmony, 1981), 36; Kobayashi, *Hyōshō bunka ron kōgi*, 192.
31 Maurice Letouzé, "La Peinture japonaise" [Japanese painting], *L'Exposition et ses attractions*, Tome XVI (Paris, 1900), 49-52, quoted and translated into Japanese in Tano Yasunori, "Pari bankokuhakurankai to Nihon bijutsu" [Paris Exposition Universelle and Japanese art], in *Nippon bijutsuin hyakunenshi*, 2 kan jō (zuhan hen) [One-hundred-year history of Nippon bijutsuin, vol. 2-1 (graphics)], ed. Nippon bijutsuin hyakunenshi henshūshitsu (Tokyo: Nippon bijutsuin, 1990), 445. Amazement at how the ukiyo-e painters capture the movements of living things with mechanical precision by physically using their hands is typically expressed in the following quotation from *Artistic Japan: A Monthly Illustrated Journal of Arts and Industries*, a representative magazine of Japonisme published in 1889: "Movement! It is everywhere in Japanese Art—in architecture, in sculpture, in drawing. Only the Great Buddha is quiescent, and he is so eternally; but at his feet life multiplies itself, and works in immoderate haste. A swarm of pigmies moves round him—one might say the same of a mad flight of insects dancing in a ray of sunlight round a lotus bloom. Japanese artists delight in liveliness. Stiffness, heaviness, straight lines, logical and carefully set rules are their aversion. They throw themselves recklessly into amusement, only to stop when destitute of

breath. Their means of expression, simplified as much as possible, lend themselves admirably to rendering hurried movements and spontaneity of action: as they are minute observers, so they reproduce actions that we take no cognizance of." Ary Renan, "Hokusai's 'Man-gwa' (Concluded)," *Artistic Japan* 2, no. 9 (January 1889): 99–100. Impressionists were not the first who paid attention to the mechanism of movements and pursued how to express them, though. Leonardo da Vinci had already studied them from various fields, including optics, anatomy, zoology, and architecture.

32 Richard Shiff, *Cézanne and the End of Impressionism: A Study of the Theory, Technique, and Critical Evaluation of Modern Art* (Chicago: University of Chicago Press, 1984), 108; italics in the original.
33 Shiff, *Cézanne and the End of Impressionism*, 108.
34 Klaus Berger, *Japonisme in Western Painting from Whistler to Matisse*, trans. David Britt (Cambridge: Cambridge University Press, 1992), 74. The high-angle composition that was adopted by such a painting of the street as *Boulevard des Capucines* provided a compositional model for the street films of the Lumière brothers. *Place Bellecour*, an 1896 film by Louis Lumière, is a typical example. The camera was placed at a certain height of a building that was located at the northeast corner of Place Bellecour to capture the movements of people and coaches on the street under the strong sunlight.
35 Aaron Scharf, *Art and Photography* (London: Allen Lane, 1968), 170–72.
36 Inaga, *Kaiga no tasogare*, 304.
37 Mutobe Akinori, "Mone 'Tsumiwara' rensaku no saikō: Mochīfu, shunkansei, koten" (Rethinking Monet's series painting *Haystacks*: Motifs, instantaneity, private exhibition), in *Furansu kindai bijutsu shi no genzai: Nyū āto hisutorī igo no shiza kara* [French modern art history now: From the post-new art history viewpoint], ed. Nagai Takanori (Tokyo: Sangen sha, 2007), 188. Mutobe argues that physicality was lost in the postimpressionist paintings by painters such as George Seurat and Paul Signac when they started to approach colors more scientifically and formulate the theory of colors (177).
38 See Françoise Albera and Maria Tortajada, "The 1900 Episteme," in *Cinema beyond Film: Media Epistemology in the Modern Era*, ed. Françoise Albera and Maria Tortajada (Amsterdam: Amsterdam University Press, 2010), 28.
39 Naruse Fujio, "Edo kara Pari e" [From Edo to Paris], *Kikan Geijutsu* 40 (winter 1979): 86–105.
40 Naruse, "Edo kara Pari e," 86–105.
41 Kishi Fumikazu, *Edo no enkinhō: Uki-e no shikaku* [Perspective in Edo: *Uki-e*'s vision] (Tokyo: Keisō shobō, 1994), 4–5.
42 Kishi (*Edo no enkinhō*, 38) argues that there were two different purposes behind such a coexistence of two styles. Linear perspective was used to increase the amount of information in the frontal plane and to create an illusion of depth, whereas bird's-eye perspective was used to provide the geographical information of the space.
43 Imahashi Riko, *The Akita Ranga School and the Cultural Context in Edo Japan*, trans. Ruth S. McCreery (Tokyo: International House of Japan, 2016), x–xi.

44 Inaga Shigemi, *Kaiga no tōhō: Orientarizumu kara Japonizumu e* [The Orient of the painting: From Orientalism to Japonisme] (Nagoya: Nagoya daigaku shuppan kai, 1999), 99.
45 Inaga, *Kaiga no tōhō*, 120.
46 Inaga, *Kaiga no tōhō*, 97.
47 Inaga, *Kaiga no tōhō*, 73. As art historian Uchibayashi Shun similarly argues, "Kinzō-gata-kōzu was considered to be a unique technique in Japan to create a sense of depth, where the scientific idea of linear perspective was not correctly understood." Uchibayashi Shun, *Kaiga ni kogareta shashin: Nihon shashin shi ni okeru pikutoriarizumu no seiritsu* [The photography that longs for the painting: The emergence of pictorialism in the history of Japanese photography] (Tokyo: Shinwa sha, 2015), 182.
48 Inaga, *Kaiga no rinkai*, 102.
49 "Western-Style 'Hokusai' Artworks Found," *Yomiuri Shimbun*, October 23, 2016, accessed October 24, 2016, https://article.wn.com/view/2016/10/23/Westernstyle_Hokusai_artworks_found.
50 In this sense, as art historian Laurinda S. Dixon argues, the public perception of Japanese prints that entered Europe in the nineteenth century as distinctly "Japanese" was actually preconditioned by their discernibly Western characteristics, intended originally to appease Dutch sensibilities. Laurinda S. Dixon, "Trade and Tradition: Japan and the Dutch Golden Age," in *The Orient Expressed: Japan's Influence on Western Art 1854–1918*, ed. Gabriel P. Weisberg (Jackson: Mississippi Museum of Art, 2011), 91.
51 Looser, "Superflat," 101.
52 Thomas LaMarre, *The Anime Machine: A Media Theory of Animation* (Minneapolis: University of Minnesota Press, 2009), 119. Art historian Henry D. Smith II makes a connection between cinema and ukiyo-e by Hokusai and Hiroshige by way of Sergei Eisenstein's 1929 essay, "The Cinematographic Principle and the Ideogram," in which Eisenstein reproduced a diagram from a Japanese elementary-school art manual of 1910 demonstrating ways of composing a painting of a branch. Smith's argument is basically limited to the kinzō-gata-kōzu/chūkei-datsuraku/en=kin-hō, or "near-far," composition and does not say much about the mobile vision that such a composition would initiate. Henry D. Smith II, "'He Frames a Shot!': Cinematic Vision in Hiroshige's One Hundred Famous Views of Edo," *Orientations* 31, no. 3 (2000): 90–96.
53 Mabuchi, *Japonisumu*, 91. The literary critics Edmond and Jules de Goncourt wrote in their journal dated February 17, 1892, "As we were leafing through the big plates of *Fujiyama* by Hokusai, Manzi said to me: 'Look, here are Monet's great yellow areas.' And he was right. People are not sufficiently aware of how much our contemporary landscape artists have borrowed from those pictures, especially Monet, whom I often encounter at Bing's in the little attic where Lévy is in charge of the Japanese prints." Edmond de Goncourt and Jules de Goncourt, *Paris and the Arts, 1851–1896: From the Goncourt Journal*, ed. and trans. by George J. Becker and Edith Philips (Ithaca, NY: Cornell University Press, 1971), 292–93.
54 Mabuchi, *Japonisumu*, 98.

55 Virginia Spate and David Bromfield, "A New and Strange Beauty: Monet and Japanese Art," in *Monet & Japan*, ed. Pauline Green (Canberra: National Gallery of Australia, 2001), 14.
56 Mabuchi, *Japonisumu*, 99.
57 Mabuchi, *Japonisumu*, 99.
58 The art historian Miyazaki Katsumi claims that Corot's work "had the major influence" on Monet's composition. Miyazaki Katsumi, "'Sukashi' to 'tōshi zuhō': Kūkan no Japonisumu shō" ["Openwork" and "linear perspective": Japonisme of the space, abstract], in *Tankyū to hōhō: Furansu kin gendai bijutsu shi o kaibō suru: Bunken gaku, bijutsukan gyōsei kara seishin bunseki, jendā ron ikō e* [Search and method: Anatomy of modern and contemporary French art history from philology, museum politics, psychoanalysis, gender criticism, and beyond], ed. Nagai Takanori (Kyoto: Kōyō shobō, 2014), 122–23.
59 Miyazaki, "'Sukashi' to 'tōshi zuhō,'" 123.
60 Spate and Bromfield, "A New and Strange Beauty," 16.
61 Mabuchi, *Japonisumu*, 91.
62 Spate and Bromfield, "A New and Strange Beauty," 14. Monet was not the first who was conscious of multiple layers within a pictorial space. Whether or not he was acutely aware of the sense of vision from a physiological standpoint, as art historian Kobayashi Yasuo points out, "in the spaces of Tintoretto's paintings, different things are happening simultaneously." Kobayashi, *Hyōshō bunka ron kōgi*, 66. Examining Tintoretto's *The Annunciation* (1582–87), Kobayashi argues that "the annunciation here is an attack of the elliptic movements from the Heaven toward the space of this world depicted in the perspective." Kobayashi, 68.
63 Spate and Bromfield, "A New and Strange Beauty," 20.
64 Charles F. Stucky, "Monet's Art and the Act of Vision," in *Aspects of Monet: A Symposium on the Artist's Life and Times*, ed. John Rewald and Frances Weitzenhoffer (New York: Abrams, 1984), 113.
65 Jonathan Crary, *Suspensions of Perception: Attention, Spectacle, and Modern Culture* (Cambridge, MA: MIT Press, 1999), 30.
66 B. Joy Jeffries, *The Eye in Health and Disease. Being a Series of Articles on the Anatomy and Physiology of the Human Eye, and Its Surgical and Medical Treatment* (Boston: Alexandre Moore, 1871), 77, quoted in Lynda Neade, *The Haunted Gallery: Painting, Photography, Film c. 1900* (New Haven, CT: Yale University Press, 2007), 30.
67 Crary, *Suspensions of Perception*, 291.
68 Hal Foster, ed., *Vision and Visuality* (Seattle: Bay Press, 1988), 25.
69 Berger, *Japonisme in Western Painting*, 112.
70 Crary, *Suspensions of Perception*, 46, 295. Mikhail Iampolski considers Crary's view on the transition in the nineteenth century from the objective and rational epistemology embodied by camera obscura to subjective vision and illusion suggested by such psychologists as Johannes Müller and Hermann von Helmholtz to be too simplistic. Iampolski argues that the arbitrary relation between sensations and their causes does not liberate vision from referentiality, thus rendering it subjective, as Crary claims. See Mikhail Iampolski, "The Logic of an Illusion: Notes on

the Genealogy of Intellectual Cinema," in *Camera Obscura, Camera Lucida: Essays in Honor of Annette Michelson*, ed. Richard Allen and Malcolm Turvey (Amsterdam: Amsterdam University Press, 2003), 35–50. Examining the validity of each claim is beyond the scope of this chapter. Instead, what I want to stress is that the Lumière brothers appeared to be engaged in the late nineteenth-century trend of scientific experiments of human eyes, using their films.

71 Crary, *Suspensions of Perception*, 288. Klaus Berger similarly claims that Cézanne was moving "towards the enduring painterly structure behind which illusionistic space dwindles and disintegrates" and that the "beholder is not immobile." Berger, *Japonisme in Western Painting*, 114–15.

72 Crary, *Suspensions of Perception*, 289.

73 Crary, *Suspensions of Perception*, 289. The art historian Richard Shiff similarly regards Cézanne as one of the forerunners of modernist image-makers who emphasized touch over vision. In Shiff's view, modernist paintings are characterized by the "metonymic exchange between an artist's or a viewer's human physicality and the material, constructed physicality of artwork." While Shiff argues about modernism's emphasis on touch over vision, what I want to stress in Lumière cinema is its consciousness about the physicality, mobility, and transient nature of vision rather than the sense of touch. Richard Shiff, "Constructing Physicality," *Art Journal* 50 (Spring 1991): 43.

74 Crary, *Suspensions of Perception*, 344.

75 *Joachim Gasquet's Cézanne*, trans. Christopher Pemberton (London: Thames and Hudson, 1991), 152.

76 Hayashi Michio and Matsuura Hisao, "Efude no hitofuri: Sezannu to tomoni kangaeru tameni" [One stroke of a pen: To think with Cézanne], *Yuriika* 44, no. 4 (April 2012): 51.

77 Crary, *Suspensions of Perception*, 342; italics in the original.

78 Crary, *Suspensions of Perception*, 344.

79 Norman Bryson, *Vision and Painting: The Logic of the Gaze* (New Haven, CT: Yale University Press, 1983), 94.

80 Jacques Aumont, *L'Oeil interminable: peinture et cinema* (Paris: Editions Seguier, 1989), 37–72. See also Jacques Aumont, "The Variable Eye, or the Mobilization of the Gaze," trans. Charles O'Brien and Sally Shafto, in *The Image in Dispute: Art and Cinema in the Age of Photography*, ed. Dudley Andrew (Austin: University of Texas Press, 1997), 231–58. Similarly, the art historian Erwin Panofsky focused on the mobility of the spectator of motion pictures and wrote in 1934 that "the spectator occupies a fixed seat, but only physically, not as the subject of an aesthetics experience. Aesthetically, he is in permanent motion as his eye identifies itself with the lens of the camera, which permanently shifts in distance and direction." Erwin Panofsky, "Style and Medium in the Motion Pictures," in *The Visual Turn: Classical Film Theory and Art History*, ed. Angela Dalle Vacche (New Brunswick, NJ: Rutgers University Press, 2003), 72.

81 Auguste Lumière and Louis Lumière, "La photographie oeuvre d'art" [The photography work of art], in *Lumières sur Lumière*, ed. Bernard Chardère (Lyon: Institut Lumière/Presses Universitaires de Lyon, 1987), 101.

82 Lumière and Lumière, "La photographie oeuvre d'art," 102.
83 Virgilio Tosi, *Cinema before Cinema: The Origins of Scientific Cinematography*, trans. Sergio Angelini (London: British Universities Film & Video Council, 2005), 127.
84 Richard Abel, *The Ciné Goes to Town: French Cinema 1896–1914* (Berkeley: University of California Press, 1994), 11.
85 Burch, *Life to Those Shadows*, 18. Tom Gunning also stresses that while sharing the curiosity about the new photographic process with the contemporary amateur photography culture, the Lumière brothers were also pursuing the "visual investigations [that] combined a strong faith in the accuracy and scientific value of photography." As evidence, Gunning examines a Lumière instantaneous photograph of Auguste Lumière leaping over a kitchen chair that was published in the February 1, 1887, issue of *L'Amateur photographe* and was accompanied by "precise indications on the lens, shutter, exposure time, the developing process that combined to make this image of suspended motion possible." Tom Gunning, "New Thresholds of Vision: Instantaneous Photography and the Early Cinema of Lumière," in *Impossible Presence: Surface and Screen in the Photogenic Era*, ed. Terry Smith (Chicago: University of Chicago Press, 2001), 86.
86 Alan Williams, "The Lumière Organization and 'Documentary Realism,'" in *Film before Griffith*, ed. John L. Fell (Berkeley: University of California Press, 1983), 157. The apparatus was not yet called the Cinématographe, which means "writing in movement." Georges Sadoul, "Louis Lumière: The Last Interview," in *Film Makers on Film Making: Statements on Their Art by Thirty Directors*, ed. Harry M. Geduld (Bloomington: Indiana University Press, 1967), 22.
87 Gunning, "New Thresholds of Vision," 94.
88 Abel, *The Ciné Goes to Town*, 11.
89 Williams, "The Lumière Organization and 'Documentary Realism,'" 158.
90 Quoted in Williams, "The Lumière Organization and 'Documentary Realism,'" 158. Auguste devoted most of his life to medical research.
91 Autochrome Lumière was the principal color photography process based on the anatomical study of the human eye by the English physiologist Thomas Young as well as the German physician and physicist Hermann von Helmholtz. In 1802 Young discerned the trichrome mechanism of color vision, or three separate color receptors in the eye. Photoreceptor cells that line the back of the retina have differential chromatic sensitivities, being optimally receptive to light in the red, green, or violet portion of the visible light spectrum. In his 1867 volume *Handbook of Physiological Optics*, Helmholtz extended Young's work, defining more precisely the nature of the physiological primary colors. It was on the basis of these physiological discoveries that the three-color processes, including Lumière Autochrome, were developed. They were all based on the fundamental nature of color vision of the human eye. See Bertrand Lavédrine and Jean-Paul Gandolfo, *The Lumière Autochrome: History, Technology, and Preservation*, trans. John McElhone (Los Angeles: Getty Conservation Institute, 2013), 60. In his 1908 book *The Colorist*, J. Arthur Hatt identified the "juxtaposit" technique of combining colors, in which the colors were blended by being placed side by side. This juxtaposing

method was used in Lumière Autochrome and was essentially the method of painting referred to as chromatic divisionism among the impressionists. According to art historian Anne Hammond, artists and critics were excited to discover this apparent demonstration of impressionist theory: another link between impressionism and Lumière. Anne Hammond, "Impressionist Theory and the Autochrome," *History of Photography* 15, no. 2 (1991): 98. In addition, the Lumière Company produced films in color as early as 1897. *Ballet: "Le carnaval de Venise," II* (Ballet: "Venice carnival," II), shot by an anonymous cinematographer, displays women's skirts in either red or blue and the walls at the background in green.

92 Tom Gunning, "Loïe Fuller and the Art of Motion: Body, Light, Electricity, and the Origins of Cinema," in *Camera Obscura, Camera Lucida: Essays in Honor of Annette Michelson*, ed. Richard Allen and Malcolm Turvey (Amsterdam: Amsterdam University Press, 2003), 77–78.

93 Burch, *Life to Those Shadows*, 12.

94 *Bulletin de la Société francaise de photographie*, 1895, 423, quoted in Tosi, *Cinema before Cinema*, 40.

95 *Catalogue du 'Musée centennal' de la classe 12 (photographie) à l'exposition universelle internationale de 1900 à Paris: métrophotographie et chronophotographie, deuxième partie*, 23–35, quoted in Tosi, *Cinema before Cinema*, 123.

96 Burch, *Life to Those Shadows*, 12.

97 Étienne-Jules Marey, *Animal Mechanism: A Treatise on Terrestrial and Aerial Locomotion* (London: Henry S. King, 1874), 1, quoted in Burch, *Life to Those Shadows*, 12.

98 Burch, *Life to Those Shadows*, 12.

99 Burch, *Life to Those Shadows*, 12.

100 Doane, *The Emergence of Cinematic Time*, 10–11.

101 Doane, *The Emergence of Cinematic Time*, 11.

102 Crary, *Suspensions of Perception*, 318, 12.

103 In addition, the Lumière brothers' cinema combined commercialism and the avant-garde. The popularity of ukiyo-e prints was based on the development of the mass market in Japan in the eighteenth century. Ukiyo-e prints were the products of capitalist industry: producers, painters, and printmakers formed the production group. Initially separating themselves from the capitalist economy, impressionist painters individually pursued artistic experiments inspired by the styles of ukiyo-e prints. The Lumière brothers' cinema brought back this avant-gardism of impressionism to the mass art form. See Ōshima Seiji, *Japonisumu: Inshō-ha to ukiyo-e no shūhen* [Japonisme: On impressionism and ukiyo-e] (Tokyo: Bijutsu kōron sha, 1980), 11.

104 Doane, *The Emergence of Cinematic Time*, 84.

105 Crary, *Suspensions of Perception*, 51.

106 Takashina Shūji, *Zōho Nihon bijutsu o miru me: Higashi to nishi no deai* [The eyes that look at Japanese art: The encounter between East and West, expanded edition] (Tokyo: Iwanami shoten, 2009), 80. Siegfried Wichmann calls this the "grille motif" and argues that Manet, Gauguin, and Vuillard also employed the same method of spatial blocking and dividing. "On the one hand," argues Wichmann,

"it was intended to cut the foreground off from the landscape behind, and on the other to create a spatial unity with often startling visual progressions." Wichmann, *Japonisme*, 235.
107 Quoted in Takashina, *Zōho Nihon bijutsu o miru me*, 77.
108 Takashina, *Zōho Nihon bijutsu o miru me*, 86.
109 I emphasize "physiologically" here in order to distinguish my argument from Hugo Münsterberg's argument on the motion picture spectator. Münsterberg also discusses the spectatorial perception of depth and movement, but the focus of his argument is on psychology and not on the à travers effect: *"Depth and movement alike come to us in the moving picture world, not as hard facts but as a mixture of fact and symbol. They are present yet they are not in the things. We invest the impressions with them."* Allan Langdale, ed., *Hugo Münsterberg on Film: A Psychological Study and Other Writings* (New York: Routledge, 2002), 78; italics in the original.
110 André Bazin, "The Ontology of the Photographic Image," trans. Huge Gray, *Film Quarterly* 13, no. 4 (summer 1960): 7.
111 Angela Dalle Vacche, "The Difference of Cinema in the System of the Arts," in *Opening Bazin: Postwar Film Theory and Its Afterlife*, ed. Dudley Andrew with Hervé Joubert-Laurencin (New York: Oxford University Press, 2011), 148; Dudley Andrew, *The Major Film Theories: An Introduction* (New York: Oxford University Press, 1976), 135.
112 See Joel Snyder, "Visualization and Visibility," in *Picturing Science, Producing Art*, ed. Caroline A. Jones and Peter Galison (New York: Routledge, 1998), 379–97.
113 Bazin, "The Ontology of the Photographic Image," 7.
114 Andrew, *The Major Film Theories*, 145.
115 Andrew, *The Major Film Theories*, 163.
116 Jacques Rancière, "L'historicité du cinéma," in *De l'histoire au cinéma*, ed. Antoine de Baecque and Christian Delage (Bruxelles: Éditions Complexe, 1998), 49. See also Joseph J. Tanke, *Jacques Rancière: An Introduction* (London: Continuum, 2011), 113.
117 Andrew, *The Major Film Theories*, 169; italics in the original.
118 Andrew, *The Major Film Theories*, 169.
119 Andrew, *The Major Film Theories*, 169.
120 André Bazin, *What Is Cinema?* (Berkeley: University of California Press, 1967), 1:22.
121 Tom Gunning, "The World in Its Own Image: The Myth of Total Cinema," in *Opening Bazin: Postwar Film Theory and Its Afterlife*, eds. Dudley Andrew with Hervé Joubert-Laurencin (New York: Oxford University Press, 2011), 123.
122 Gunning, "The World in Its Own Image," 124.
123 Jean-Louis Comolli, *Cinema against Spectacle: Techniques and Ideology Revisited*, trans. and ed. Daniel Fairfax (Amsterdam: Amsterdam University Press, 2015), 198.
124 Comolli, *Cinema against Spectacle*, 198; italics in the original.
125 As Comolli stated, "We know what perspective brought with it, and thus what depth of field enabled to enter into cinematic image as its *constitutive codes*: namely, the pictorial and theatrical codes of classical Western representation. . . . Not only is depth of field the mark, in the primitive cinematic image, of its

submission to these representative codes, and to the histories and ideologies that perforce determine these codes and make them function ..., but, more generally speaking, it signals that the ideological apparatus of the cinema is itself produced within these codes and by these systems of representation, as their complement, their refinement and their supersession." Comolli, *Cinema against Spectacle*, 214; italics in the original.

126 *Sortie d'usine* was remade at least three more times, so this motif of launching and the resulting abrupt forming of the kinzō-gata-kōzu/chūkei-datsuraku/en=kin-hō composition was repeated several times in different locations. *Kiel: lancement du "Fürst-Bismarck"* (Kiel: Launch of the *Fürst-Bismarck*) and *Naples: lancement du cuirasse* (Naples: Launch of a cuirass), which were shot in September 1897 by unknown cinematographers, as well as *Départ d'un bateau sur la Tamise* (Departure of a boat on the Thames, 1897) by Alexandre Promio, are such examples. *Expérience du ballon dirigeable de M. Santos-Dumont: I. Sortie du ballon* (Mr. Santos-Dumont's airship experience: Balloon exit, 1900) is a version with a gigantic airship.

127 Georges Sadoul, *Histoire du cinéma mondial: des origines à nos jours* [History of world cinema: From origins to the present day] (1949; Paris: Flammarion, 1972), 21.

128 Sadoul, *Histoire du cinéma mondial*, 21.

129 Michael Allan, "Deserted Histories: The Lumière Brothers, the Pyramids and Early Film Form," *Early Popular Visual Culture* 6, no. 2 (July 2008): 160.

130 Jean-Claude Seguin, *Alexandre Promio ou les énigmes de la Lumière* [Alexandre Promio or the enigmas of the Lumière] (Paris: Éditions L'Harmattan, 1999), 87.

131 *The Lumière Brothers First Films*. DVD. (New York: Kino, 1996). *Milan: les canotiers* (Milan: The Boaters), a film shot by an anonymous cinematographer most likely in 1896, has similar three-layered actions. In the frontal plane, an accident happens: one boat tips over, and two swimmers pull the boat out. In the middle plane, a boat and a canoe move across. At the background, a man comically slips and falls over and over again on the ground in front of a big house. Similarly, Gabriel Veyre used three separate planes to depict the laborers at a mine in Vietnam in *Les mines de charbon de Hon Gay* (Hon Gay coal mines), photographed in December 1899. A line of laborers pushes mining carts in the frontal plane, a person works in front of a hut in the second plane, and a number of laborers dig the ground at the slope of a mountain in the background. The Lumière Company also started editing, or cuts, as early as in 1897, in order to punctuate actions that happen in different planes and/or in different moments. The first film in the Lumière catalog that explicitly used cuts and editing was *Espagne: courses de taureaux, II* (Spain: Bull races, II), a film that records a bullfight in Barcelona shot by Francis Doublier on March 7, 1897. This film consists of three extreme long shots of a bullfight: (1) a bull jumps out of the frame to the left, (2) the bull pushes over a horse and moves toward the far end, and (3) the bull is back at the middle ground. By 1899, such editing became used more strategically to draw the viewer's attention. In an 1899 bullfight film, *Estocade, I*, following the initial extreme long shot of two bullfighters, the closer shot displays the final sword thrust by one of them. Then, in another film shot in 1899, *M. Loubet aux courses* (Mr. Loubet

at the races), the match-on-action technique is used over two connected shots. A man with a beard walks to the center of the frame. Cut. The following shot shows him standing in the same position from a different angle.

132 Seguin, *Alexandre Promio ou les énigmes de la Lumière*, 91.
133 There are other films by Promio with the same effect. In *Lanciers de la reine, charge* (Queen's lancers, charge), a June 1896 film shot in Madrid, he combined horizontal movements and depth movements in a dramatic manner. When the film begins, a coach and two men on horses slowly move from the left to the offscreen right. A dog runs after them. At that point, we see the cavalry run from the far left toward the middle ground. In other words, the initial horizontal composition is taken over by the composition of depth in accordance with the approaching movement of the cavalry. Moreover, in *Grande roue (Ferris Wheel)*, a September 1896 film shot in Chicago, Promio combined the slow circular movement of the Ferris wheel at the background with the high-speed horizontal movement of a tram that crosses the frame from left to right in the middle ground and with the medium-speed diagonal movement of a coach from the frontal left to the center of the frame, curving to the offscreen left. But these two films should be categorized in Type III, instead of Type II. In addition to the composition, Promio was also experimenting with temporal suspense. In *Artillerie (exercice du tin)* (Artillery [tin exercise]), another film that he photographed in Madrid in 1896, two cannons are carried into the frame (the frontal plane and the background). Soldiers place the cannons onto the ground and prepare for firing. The film ends when the two cannons fire one after the other. Moreover, Promio was the first Lumière cinematographer who used two separate films to tell one story. In September 1897 he photographed *Faust: apparition de Méphistophélès* (*Faust*: Appearance of Mephistopheles), and *Faust: metamorphose de Faust* (*Faust*: Metamorphosis of Faust) in Paris. Both are trick films that use two shots to depict the appearance of Méphistophélès (the first film) and the transformation of Faust (the second film). Then, in 1898, Promio photographed a thirteen-film series of the life of Jesus Christ. In the sixth film, *La vie et la passion de Jésus-Christ VI. La cène* (*Life and Passion of Jesus Christ: Last Supper*), Promio uses two shots to show Jesus suddenly appearing at the table from nowhere. In the tenth film, *X. La mise en croix* (The cross), Promio uses strong spotlight from the left to bring a dramatic effect to the set of Calvary.
134 Jacques Rittaud-Hutinet, ed., *Letters: Auguste and Louis Lumière*, trans. Pierre Hodgson (London: Faber and Faber, 1995), 142.
135 Alexandre Promio, "Notes sur la photographie" [Notes on the photograph], *Le Progrès illustré*, October 30, 1898, quoted in Seguin, *Alexandre Promio ou les énigmes de la Lumière*, 135–36.
136 Promio, "Notes sur la photographie" [Notes on the photograph], *Le Progrès illustré*, January 8, 1899, quoted in Seguin, *Alexandre Promio ou les énigmes de la Lumière*, 138.
137 Similarly, in *Cherbourg: débarqument des souverains russes* (Cherbourg: Landing of Russian sovereigns) and *Cherbourg: entrée des souverains russes et du président de la Republique sous le hall* (Cherbourg: Entry of Russian sovereigns and the president

of the Republic under the hall), Girel recorded the visit by Russian Tsar Nicolas II and Empress Alexandra Feodorovna to the Cherbourg site on October 5, 1896, in extreme long shots when unexpected objects blocked the frame in both cases: people passed from right to left in an extreme close-up in the former, and a spectator's elbow is visible in an extreme close-up up to the middle of the film in the latter. Another Lumière cinematographer, Francisco Felicetti, also encountered such an accidental appearance of the *kinzō-gata-kōzu* composition when he photographed a launching event of a boat in Livourne, Italy. The film *Après le lancement: sortie des invités et du public* (After the launch: The guests and the audience leave, 1899) displays the exit of the crowd in an extreme long shot when a man appears all of a sudden in close-up and shows a funny face.

138 Constant Girel, "Cologne, 22 septembre 1896," trans. Victor LeGrand. Girel's letters are preserved at the Institut Lumière.

139 In *Roi et reine d'Italie* (King and queen of Italy, 1896), Girel placed the Cinématographe Lumière at a compositionally crafty place to photograph the Italian king Humbert II and queen Marguerite de Savoie leaving the royal palace to get on a coach. The black coach waiting in the frontal plane occupies about one-third of the frame while the royal couple first moves away and then approaches the camera by stepping down the zigzagging stairs. This is a Type I film with complex movements at the back to create the à travers effect.

140 For instance, *Cuirassiers: en fourrageurs (charge)* (Cuirassiers: As foragers [load]), an 1896 film shot by an unknown cinematographer at the military camp of La Valbonne in Beligneux, has a deep-space composition in which the cavalry rides quite a distance from the back to the middle ground and goes offscreen to both right and left. Similarly, in *Pigeons sur la place Saint-Marc* (Pigeons in St. Mark's Square), an 1896 film shot in Venice by Charles Moisson, chief mechanic in the Lumière factories and working with Louis Lumière on the design of the prototype of the Cinématographe Lumière, a woman (Marie Moisson) walks toward the camera as she feeds a huge number of pigeons. In *Berlin: Hallesches Thor*, photographed by an unknown cinematographer in 1896, two electric lines for trams that appear from the top of the frame and extend to the center emphasize the composition of the linear perspective. *Descente de la grande pyramide* (Descent from the Great Pyramid), shot by Promio in Egypt in 1897, incorporated height in the linear perspective composition. A group of people descends the rocks of the pyramid from the far right end and walks to the frontal left. In *Le charpentier maladroit* (The clumsy carpenter), an 1897 staged comedy shot by Promio, two actions occur in separate planes. Two hand-drawn carts collide at the background while, in the frontal plane, a man with a long board on his shoulder hits the head of another man with his board every time he turns to a different direction. It looks as if the initial collision of the carts occurred because the man was heading toward them, but the supposed chain reaction is not clearly explained.

141 Even though it does not explicitly use the kinzō-gata-kōzu/chūkei-datsuraku/en=kin-hō composition and the à travers effect, *Passage d'un tunnel en chemin de fer* (Passage of a railway tunnel), an 1898 film shot by an anonymous cinematog-

rapher in Lyon, uses lighting effectively to achieve a spectacular kaleidoscopic vision. *Panorama pris d'un ballon captif* (Panorama taken from a captive balloon), another 1898 film shot by an anonymous cinematographer, displays an unusual view as well because the camera is directed vertically toward the ground from an unstably ascending balloon.

142 Girel was arguably the first Lumière cinematographer who used the traveling camera technique to achieve a panoramic view. In *Panorama pris d'un bateau* (Panorama taken from a boat), the film that he photographed in Cologne, Germany, in September 1896, he placed the Cinématographe Lumière on a boat and captured the panoramic movement of the riverbank from left to right.

143 Another example of a panoramic film with a constantly transforming kinzō-gata-kōzu/chūkei-datsuraku/en=kin-hō composition, or more specifically the blocking effect in this case, is *Nice: panorama sur la ligne de Beaulieu à Monaco, I* (Nice: Panorama on the line from Beaulieu to Monaco I), a film consisting of two shots photographed by Felix Mesguich, an Algerian-born cinematographer at the Lumière Company, in February 1900. The camera is most likely placed on a window of a steam locomotive facing toward the moving front. The frontal left space within the frame is occupied by the first train of the locomotive. The view of rocky mountains on the far left and the Mediterranean Sea on the far right is not only contrasted with the moving train in the frontal plane but is also constantly blocked by the white steam that the locomotive produces. When that occurs, the screen first becomes rather two-dimensional without background, then almost completely a whiteout.

144 In contrast, although *Vue prise d'une baleiniere en marche* (View of a whaling boat on the move), photographed by an anonymous cinematographer probably in 1897, also displays a panoramic traveling shot from the camera placed on a boat with shaky up-and-down movements because of the unstable setting of the camera, the focus is on the faces of the sailors who row the boat captured in medium close-ups, instead of a contrast between the frontal plane (sailors) and the background (the ocean blocked by their faces and bodies).

Chapter 2: Japonisme and Nativized Orientalism

1 Takanashi Kōji, *Inabata Katsutarō kun den* [Biography of Mr. Inabata Katsutarō] (Osaka: Inabata Katsutarō ō kiju kinen denki hensan kai, 1938), appendix 4–5.

2 Inabata Katsutarō, "Shinematogurafu o yunyū shita zengo" [The time when I imported the Cinématographe], *Kinema Junpō*, November 11, 1935, 71.

3 According to Girel's letter to his family, Girel departed Marseille on the *Polynesian* on December 6, 1896. He changed onto the *Natal* at the port of Colombo. Girel, "Marseille, 6 décembre 1896."

4 Mitsuda Yuri, "Jireru to Vēru: Seikimatsu Nihon o otozureta futari no eiga gishi" [Girel and Veyre: Two cinematographers who visited Japan at the end of the century], in *Eiga denrai: Cinematogurafu to "Meiji no Nippon"* [The arrival of cinema: The Cinématographe and "Meiji Japan"], ed. Yoshida Yoshishige, Yamaguchi Masao, and Kinoshita Naoyuki (Tokyo: Iwanami shoten, 1995), 47; Tsukada

Yoshinobu, *Nihon eiga shi no kenkyū: Katsudō shashin torai zengo no jijō* [A study of Japanese film history: Facts around the time when motion pictures arrived] (Tokyo: Gendai shokan, 1980), 92–93. Based on the records of exhibition, Tsukada assumes that at least four Cinématographe Lumière entered Japan with Inabata and Girel.

5   Denise Bohem-Girel, "Un Lumière Operature: Constant Girel (1873–1952)" [A Lumière Operator: Constant Girel (1873–1952)], in *L'aventure du Cinématographe: Actes du Congrès mondial Lumière* [The adventure of the Cinématographe: Proceedings of the World Lumière Conference] (Lyon: Aléas, 1999), 71. According to the official request of a motion picture exhibition (with a hired foreigner) that Miki Fukusuke submitted to the mayor of Osaka on February 3, 1897, Girel's address was a French mission (Tenshudō) at Kawaguchi Furukawabashi in Tomijimachō of the Kita district of Osaka. This document is preserved at Institute Lumière in Lyon.

6   Three Cinématographe Lumière in Japan at that time looked to be fully employed. According to newspaper advertisements, Cinématographe was exhibited at three different locations: the Tōkōza Theater in Kyoto Shinkyōgoku from March 1 to June 1, at the Kawakamiza Theater in Tokyo Kanda Misaki-chō on March 8–28, and at the Kadoza Theater in Osaka starting on March 9. Mitsuda, "Jireru to Vēru," 47–48. According to Inabata's biography, the first screening was at Shinkyōgoku Tōkōza Theater in Kyoto. Takanashi, *Inabata Katsutarō kun den*, 300.

7   Girel, "16 août 97, Hakodate, Japon Borál."

8   Veyre was officially invited by the Japanese empress to attend a party of appreciating chrysanthemums on November 16, 1898. Mitsuda, "Jireru to Vēru," 65.

9   Girel, "Kyoto, 28 avril 97."

10 Quoted in Maekawa Kumio, *Meiji ki Hokkaidō eiga shi* [The movie history of Hokkaido in the Meiji era] (Sapporo: Alice sha, 2012), 21.

11 Mitsuda, "Jireru to Vēru," 77.

12 Koga Futoshi, "Kamera ga toraeta Nippon: 'Meiji no Nippon' kara 'Ryumiēru eiga Nippon hen' e" [Japan that a camera captured: From "Meiji Japan" to "Lumière Japan films"], in *Eiga denrai: Cinematogurafu to "Meiji no Nippon"* [The arrival of cinema: The Cinématographe and "Meiji Japan"], ed. Yoshida Yoshishige, Yamaguchi Masao, and Kinoshita Naoyuki (Tokyo: Iwanami shoten, 1995), 28.

13 Koga, "Kamera ga toraeta Nippon," 40.

14 As André Bazin famously noted, the novelty of cinematic realism lies in its capacity to stage duration: "Now, for the first time, the image of things is likewise the image of their duration, change mummified as it were." André Bazin, "The Ontology of the Photographic Image," trans. Hugh Gray, *Film Quarterly* 13, no. 4 (summer 1960): 8. See also Michael Allan, "Deserted Histories," 167.

15 Bryson, "Furansu no orientarizumu kaiga ni okeru 'tasha,'" 84.

16 Elizabeth Grosz, "Criticism, Feminism, and the Institution: An Interview with Gayatri Chakravorty Spivak," *Thesis Eleven* 10/11 (1984/85): 183–84.

17 Gayatri Chakravorty Spivak, "Subaltern Studies: Deconstructing Historiography," in *Selected Subaltern Studies*, ed. Ranajit Guha and Gayatri Chakravorty Spivak (Oxford: Oxford University Press, 1988), 3–32.

18　Gayatri Chakravorty Spivak, *Outside in the Teaching Machine* (New York: Routledge, 1993), 4.
19　Girel's album is also preserved by the Institut Lumière in Lyon and was exhibited at the "Lumière! Le cinéma inventé" exposition at Grand Palais in Paris (March 27–June 14, 2015) and at Musée des Confluences in Lyon (June 13, 2017–February 25, 2018).
20　Saitō Takio, *Bakumatsu Meiji Yokohama shashinkan monogatari* [A story of Yokohama photographs at the end of the Tokugawa era and the Meiji period] (Tokyo: Yoshikawa kōbunkan, 2004), 170–71.
21　Satō Morihiro, "'Ōrudo Japan' no hyōshō: Yokohama shashin to 19 seiki kōhan no shikaku bunka" [Representations of "Old Japan": Yokohama photographs and the visual culture of the late nineteenth century], *Eizōgaku/Iconics* 71 (2003): 70.
22　Satō, "'Ōrudo Japan' no hyōshō," 76.
23　Satō, "'Ōrudo Japan' no hyōshō," 78.
24　Satō, "'Ōrudo Japan' no hyōshō," 79.
25　W. J. T. Mitchell, "Imperial Landscape," in *Landscape and Power*, ed. W. J. T. Mitchell (Chicago: University of Chicago Press, 1994), 5.
26　Satō, "'Ōrudo Japan' no hyōshō," 79.
27　Giorgio Bertellini, *Italy in Early American Cinema: Race, Landscape, and the Picturesque* (Bloomington: Indiana University Press, 2010), 4, 276.
28　Linda Nochlin, *The Politics of Vision: Essays on Nineteenth-Century Art and Society* (New York: Harper and Row, 1989), 33–59.
29　It is noteworthy that three photographs taken in Saigon are inserted in the middle of this album out of the blue. For Girel, Japan and Vietnam were not essentially very different as premodern spaces. French Indochina did not have as much of an ambivalent image as Japan.
30　The order of the photographs is based on the exhibit at the "Lumière! Le cinéma inventé" exposition at Musée des Confluences in Lyon (June 13, 2017–February 25, 2018).
31　Yokohama kaikō shiryōkan, ed., *Saishoku arubamu Meiji no Nippon: "Yokohama shashin" no sekai* [Colored album Japan in the Meiji era: The world of "Yokohama photographs"] (Yokohama: Yūrindō, 1990), 23. In addition to this photo, "Group de geishas prenant le thé" (in color) in Girel's album was most likely photographed at the River Kamo in Kyoto and appears to be very similar to a Yokohama photograph, "Kamogawa Shijō fukin" (The River Kamo near Shijō). "Rivière avec barque à voile devant le Mont Fuji" (in color) in Girel's album is very similar to "Numagawa ryūiki, Ukishimagahara yori nozomu" (Mt. Fuji seen from Ukishimagahara of the River Numa) (128, 109).
32　Usui accompanied British naturalist Francis Henry Hill Guillemard when he visited Japan in 1882 as a part of his exploration cruise from Kamchatka to New Guinea. Guillemard collected Usui's photos of Japan to use them in his travelogue, which was published in 1888. Guillemard's photos, including those taken by Usui, and his travel diaries are preserved at the University of Cambridge. Koyama Noboru, *Kenburijji daigaku hizō Meiji koshashin: Mākēza gō no Nihon ryokō* [Early

photographs of the Meiji era at the University of Cambridge: The journey of the marchesa in Japan] (Tokyo: Heibon sha, 2005), 1–3.
33 Koyama, *Kenburijji daigaku hizō Meiji koshashin*, 38–39.
34 Girel, "Kyoto, 28 avril 97."
35 There are at least two other photos of cherry blossoms in Girel's album, "Allée de cerisiers en fleurs" (Alley of cherry blossoms) and "Route bordée de cerisiers en fleurs" (Road lined with cherry blossoms), even though the shooting locations are not listed.
36 Tsukada Yoshinobu, "Jurēru to 'Meiji no Nippon' o megutte" [On Girel and "Meiji Japan"], *Eiga Shiryō Hakkutsu* 10 (June 15, 1973): 262. As Girel wrote in his September 18 letter from Kyoto to his parents, "Yesterday, the weather was beautiful so I took the opportunity to make six films." Girel, "Kyoto, 18 septembre 97." His letter from Kyoto on September 21 stated that the good weather came back and that the departure time on the following day—most likely for filming—would be at six in the morning. Girel, "Kyoto, 21 Sept." There is no record of which six films were made on September 17 and of whether the filming was actually done on September 22.
37 These three films were photographed at Nanchi-Kayūen in Osaka on May 27, 1897.
38 Tsukada Yoshinobu, "Jurēru to 'Meiji no Nippon' o megutte sono 2" [On Girel and "Meiji Japan" part 2], *Eiga Shiryō Hakkutsu* 13 (December 1973): 288.
39 Nihon eiga terebi gijutsu kyōkai, "Nihon eiga gijutsu shi nenpu No. 14" [Chronology of Japanese film technology], *Eiga Terebi Gijutsu* 236 (April 1972): 75. The film historian Tsukada Yoshinobu conducted profound research on exactly when this film with Sadanji I was filmed. See Tsukada, *Nihon eiga shi no kenkyū*, 150–63.
40 The realism of the cinema differentiated this act of Sadanji I from other acts that he normally performed on the Kabuki stage. Right before striking the decisive pose, as the film critic Hasumi Shigehiko also points out, Sadanji I pours real water over himself. On the stage, this would never happen: his act was exclusively for the film. Hasumi Shigehiko, "Hikari no shito: Ryumiēru kyōdai to Gaburieru Vēru" [The apostles of light: Lumière brothers and Gabriel Veyre], in *Ryumiēru gannen: Gaburieru Vēru to eiga no rekishi* [The first year of Lumière: Gabriel Veyre and the history of cinema], ed. Hasumi Shigehiko (Tokyo: Chikuma shobō, 1995), 31.
41 The maiden name of Girel's mother was d'Anna Berlioz. Christianity went under suppression in Japan from around 1620 through nearly two centuries after that. After Japan abandoned its locked-door policy in the 1850s, Japan was formed into a vicarte apostolic, administrated by the Paris Foreign Missions Society. Stephen R. Tumbull, *Japan's Hidden Christians, 1549–1999*, vol. 1, *Open Christianity in Japan, 1549–1639* (Surrey: Curzon, 2000), 155. Even before the efforts by Bishop Berlioz, the missionary John Batchelor had played a significant role in proselytizing for the "salvation of the Ainu" after he arrived in Hakodate in 1877 on a mission for the Anglican Church. As the number of converts increased, Batchelor established schools and a hospital in Hakodate, Sapporo, and Horobetsu. Yōichi Komori, Helen J. S. Lee, and Michele Mason, "Rule in the Name of Protection: The Japanese State, the Ainu and the Vocabulary of Colonialism," *Asia-Pacific Journal* 11, no. 8-2 (2013): 15.

42 Girel, "Kyoto, 28 avril 97"; "Samedi soir, 12 juin 97"; "Kyoto, 21 Sept."
43 Sophie O'Brien, "The Lessons of the Colonial Exhibition in Paris. I. The Missionaries," *Irish Monthly* 59 (October 1931): 634-35.
44 Girel, "16 aout 97, Hakodate, Japon Boréal." According to this letter, Girel needed to return from his first Hokkaido trip to Kyoto to receive new rolls of film sent from the Lumière brothers.
45 Girel, "Hakodate, 18 octobre 97," trans. Victor LeGrand.
46 Girel, "Hakodate, 18 octobre 97."
47 Muroran kyōkai, "Muroran kyōkai no rekishi" [The history of Muroran church], accessed September 14, 2017, http://catholic-m.goodplace.jp/gaiyo/index.html. According to the January–April 1895 issue of the *Dublin Review*, "Diocese of Hakodate.—Contains 24 catechists, 12 nuns, and 5 schools, with 536 pupils. The speciality [sic] of this mission is that it embraces that curious aboriginal race, the Ainus, of Yezo, the evangelisation of whom was seriously taken in hand by Bishop Berlioz in 1893." "The Catholic Church in Japan," *Dublin Review* 116 (January–April 1895): 281.
48 "Muroran kyōkai no rekishi."
49 "Muroran kyōkai no rekishi."
50 Girel, "Hakodate, 18 octobre 97."
51 Girel, "Hakodate, 18 octobre 97."
52 Luke Gartlan, *A Career of Japan: Baron Raimund von Stillfried and Early Yokohama Photography* (Leiden: Brill, 2016), 127.
53 Girel, "Hakodate, 18 octobre 97."
54 Girel, "Hakodate, 18 octobre 97."
55 Girel, "Hakodate, 18 octobre 97."
56 Bohem-Girel, "Un Lumière Operature: Constant Girel," 71.
57 Gartlan, *A Career of Japan*, 105.
58 Komori, Lee, and Mason, "Rule in the Name of Protection," 10.
59 Komori, Lee, and Mason, 10.
60 Komori, Lee, and Mason, 11.
61 Gartlan, *A Career of Japan*, 105-6.
62 Komori, Lee, and Mason, "Rule in the Name of Protection," 14.
63 Komori, Lee, and Mason, 12-13.
64 Gartlan, *A Career of Japan*, 220, 233.
65 Gartlan, 202. The historian Saitō Takio similarly argues that Stillfried used actors to create his Yokohama photographs not because "feudal Japan" had disappeared but because the customs of "feudal Japan" went under the strong controls of the modernizing state. For instance, nudity in public spaces became unlawful in 1873 even though laborers were working naked after that in reality. Still, it was easier for Stillfried to photograph naked actors in his studio under such sociopolitical conditions. Saitō, *Bakumatsu Meiji Yokohama shashinkan monogatari*, 161-62.
66 Komori, Lee, and Mason, "Rule in the Name of Protection," 15-16.
67 An official document was submitted to the mayor of Osaka, Utsumi Tadakatsu, by an exhibitor, Miki Fukusuke, to hire Girel as a "shashin gishi" (photo

technician) for the film exhibition at Nanchi Enbujō in Osaka. The document is preserved at the Ministry of Foreign Affairs in Japan.

68 Gartlan, *A Career of Japan*, 141.
69 Girel, "Hakodate, 18 octobre 97."
70 According to the *Shin Aichi* newspaper (June 30, 1899), ten Japanese-made Lumière films (supposedly the ones photographed by Girel) were scheduled to be screened at Shinmoriza Theater on July 1, 1899: *Nagoya teishajō chakusha no zattō* (most likely *Arrivée d'un train*); *Kyoto Toyokuni sai kinen odori* (Kyoto Toyokuni festival dance: unknown film); *Osaka haiyū Udanji, Ganjirō, Kasen, Enzaburō, Shijyaku goyū no danmari* (most likely *Une scène au theater japonais*; the name of Udanji is incorrect, but Sadanji was in the film); *Gion Shinchi geiko sanbu* (most likely *Danseuses japonaises*); *Kyoto Rokujō sōko gaisha shukka no kōkei* (A fire at Kyoto Rokujō warehouse: not extant); *Butokukai no kakkoku kenshi shiai* (most likely *Lutteurs japonais*); *Hokkaidō dojin Aino no kuma odori* (most likely *Les Aïnos à Yeso, I*); *Yasaka Jinja mikoshi togyo no nigiwai* (most likely *Procession shintoïste*); *Tokyo haiyū Sadanji Maruhashi Chyūya meshitorizuka ido no mizuzukai* (most likely *Acteurs japonais: Bataille au sabre*); and *Dai Nippon kyūshu no batai Shirakawa kihei no mizuoyogi* (Swimming of Shirakawa cavalry team: not extant). "'Meiji no Nippon' jōei kiroku" [Record of the Exhibition of "Meiji Japan"], in *Eiga denrai: Cinématogurafu to "Meiji no Nippon"* [The arrival of cinema: The Cinématographe and "Meiji Japan"], ed. Yoshida Yoshishige, Yamaguchi Masao, and Kinoshita Naoyuki (Tokyo: Iwanami shoten, 1995), 189–90. The identification of the Japanese titles and the actual Lumière films in the parentheses is hypothetical. I assume that the train film was included most likely because it was shot at Nagoya Station. *Une scène au theater japonais* and *Acteurs japonais: Bataille au sabre* were screened because famous Kabuki actors appeared in them. *Danseuses japonaises* was because of the geishas. I discuss this issue of Kabuki and geisha in films in chapter 3. *Lutteurs japonais* and *Procession shintoïste* were most likely considered to be authentic, as was *Les Aïnos à Yeso, I*. Other films photographed in Japan, both by Girel and Veyre, were kept in France until 1960, when André Malraux, minister of culture, handed them to the director of the National Museum of Modern Art in Tokyo. After that, twenty-nine films out of the thirty-three Japanese-made films were collectively titled "Meiji no Nippon" and screened in Japan on several occasions. See Koga, "Kamera ga toraeta Nippon," 25.
71 Gabriel Veyre, *Opérateur Lumière: autour du monde avec le Cinématographe correspondance (1896–1900)* (Lyon: Institut Lumière/Actes Sud, 1996), 272.
72 G. W. Harris, "Japanese Pictures," *Outlook* 81, no. 9 (October 28, 1905): 496.
73 Kinoshita Naoyuki, "Egakareta 'Meiji no Nippon': Nippon e no/Nippon kara no manazashi" [Represented "Meiji Japan": Gazes to and from Japan], in *Eiga denrai: Cinématogurafu to "Meiji no Nippon"* [The arrival of cinema: The Cinématographe and "Meiji Japan"], ed. Yoshida Yoshishige, Yamaguchi Masao, and Kinoshita Naoyuki (Tokyo: Iwanami shoten, 1995), 157.
74 Kinoshita claims that it is easy to find the motifs of rice mowing and a waterwheel for rice fields in Yokohama photographs. He provides an exemplary photograph, "Hataraku nōmin" (A working farmer), from the collection of Yokohama

photographs that looks similar to Veyre's film with the waterwheel. Kinoshita, "Egakareta 'Meiji no Nippon,'" 156. The 1909 French *Almanach des postes et des télégraphes* used three Japanese images drawn by Georges Bigot: two women riding a rickshaw, a geisha dance accompanied by a shamisen player, and a farmer stepping on a waterwheel. Despite Bigot's firsthand experiences in Japan, it is clear that these images had reached the status of Japanese stereotypes in popular visual culture in France by 1909. See Shimizu Isao, *Bigō no 150 nen: Ishoku Furansu jin gaka to Nippon* [Bigot's 150 years: Unique French artist and Japan] (Tokyo: Rinsen shoten, 2011), 188. Veyre was aware of the artificial relationship between the photographer and the photographed. He made a self-referential film about filmmaking as early as 1899. *La sortie de l'arsenal* (The exit of the arsenal), which he filmed in Saigon on April 28, 1899, was a kind of remake of *Sortie d'usine* with a man cranking a Cinématographe Lumière at the left edge of the screen.

75 Michelle Aubert and Jean-Claude Seguin, *La Production cinématographique des Frères Lumière* [The cinematographic production of the Lumière Brothers] (Paris: Librairie du Premier Siècle du Cinéma, Bibliothèque du film, Editions Mémoires de cinema, Diffusion, CDE, 1996), 357.

76 Wirgman and Beato together established a photo studio in Yokohama in 1863 and started a magazine, *Japan Punch* (later *The Far East*), for foreign tourists in Japan. Beato began selling photo albums around 1868. Baron Raimund von Stillfried took over Beato's studio in 1877. Saitō, *Bakumatsu Meiji Yokohama shashinkan monogatari*, 157.

77 With its capacity of mechanical reproduction and photographic realism, cinema functioned to provide authenticity to the image of the geisha. Japan and the Japanese people became popular subjects for films, including newsreels and travelogues. *The American Film Institute Catalog 1893-1910* lists ninety-four films that were released in the US under the category of "Japan and Japanese," and the same catalog of *1911-1920* lists forty-three films under the categories of "Japan" and "Japanese" combined. Elias Savada, comp., *The American Film Institute Catalog of Motion Pictures Produced in the United States: Film Beginnings, 1893-1910* (Metuchen, NJ: Scarecrow, 1995), 350. Patricia King Hanson and Alan Gevinson, ed., *The American Film Institute Catalog of Motion Pictures Produced in the United States: Feature Films, 1911-1920* (Berkeley: University of California Press, 1989), 338. In particular, fully half of the films that were released in the US from 1909 to 1915 portraying cross-cultural relations took the form of ill-fated romance, which were the reworkings of *Madame Butterfly*'s narrative of doomed romance between a Japanese woman and an American man. Gregory Waller, "Historicizing, a Test Case: Japan on American Screens, 1909-1915," unpublished manuscript obtained from Sumiko Higashi.

78 Yoko Kawaguchi, *Butterfly's Sisters: The Geisha in Western Culture* (New Haven, CT: Yale University Press, 2010), 5.

79 Veyre, *Opérateur Lumière*, 274.

80 Veyre, *Opérateur Lumière*, 275-76.

81 Kinoshita, "Egakareta 'Meiji no Nippon,'" 127.

82 Gartlan, *A Career of Japan*, 201.

83 *British Journal of Photography*, October 26, 1877, 515; *Photographic News*, November 9, 1877, 532, quoted in Gartlan, *A Career of Japan*, 201.
84 Kinoshita, "Egakareta 'Meiji no Nippon,'" 126.
85 Kinoshita, "Egakareta 'Meiji no Nippon,'" 127.
86 Kinoshita, "Egakareta 'Meiji no Nippon,'" 135-37.
87 Kinoshita, "Egakareta 'Meiji no Nippon,'" 144-45.
88 Aimé Humbert, *Le Japon illustré* [The illustrated Japan] (Paris: Librairie de L. Hachette et CLE, 1870), 108.
89 Kinoshita, "Egakareta 'Meiji no Nippon,'" 143.
90 Shimizu Isao, *Bigō o yomu: Meiji rearisumu hanga 200 ten no sekai* [Reading Bigot: The world of 200 realist prints of the Meiji era] (Tokyo: Rinsen shoten, 2014), 96-102.
91 Shimizu, *Bigō no 150 nen*, 119.
92 Kinoshita, "Egakareta 'Meiji no Nippon,'" 141.
93 Girel, "Kyoto, 21 Sept."
94 Takanashi, *Inabata Katsutarō kun den*, 302.
95 Edward McDonald, *Learning Chinese, Turning Chinese: Challenges to Becoming Sinophone in a Globalised World* (New York: Routledge, 2011), 150.
96 Morishige Kazuo, "The Life and Times of Shimooka Renjō," in *Shimooka Renjō: A Pioneer of Japanese Photography*, ed. Mitsui Keishi and Toriumi Saki (Tokyo: Kokusho kankō kai, 2014), 13-14.
97 Ozawa Takeshi, *Bakumatsu Meiji no shashin* [Photography in the final years of the Edo period and the Meiji period] (Tokyo: Chikuma shobō, 1997), 117, 124.
98 Amano Keigo, "Yamaguchi Saiichirō 'Shashin jireki' gendaigo yaku" [Yamaguchi Saiichirō, "Case history of photography" modern translation], in *Shimooka Renjō: A Pioneer of Japanese Photography*, ed. Mitsui Keishi and Toriumi Saki (Tokyo: Kokusho kankō kai, 2014), 195.
99 Kinoshita, "Egakareta 'Meiji no Nippon,'" 150. Art historian Martin Jay points out "a *frisson* of reciprocity," or "crossing of gazes," in Manet's painting, in which the spectator's gaze meets an intersubjective return look from the figure in the painting. *Vision and Visuality*, ed. Hal Foster (Seattle: Bay Press, 1988), 27.
100 Kinoshita, "Egakareta 'Meiji no Nippon,'" 149-50.
101 Gartlan, *A Career of Japan*, 176. In contrast, in Felice Beato's photos, which were taken mainly in the 1860s, before the period of Westernization of Japan, Japanese people were often looking in the direction of the camera. As a result of the returning gaze, Saitō argues, we could detect "tensions" and "relations between human beings" regarding the photographer and the photographed in Beato's work. Saitō, *Bakumatsu Meiji Yokohama shashinkan monogatari*, 104.
102 Livio Belloï, "Lumière and His View: The Cameraman's Eye in Early Cinema," *Historical Journal of Film, Radio and Television* 154, no. 4 (1995): 464.
103 Belloï, "Lumière and His View," 463.
104 Belloï, "Lumière and His View," 469.
105 Belloï, "Lumière and His View," 469-70.
106 Belloï, "Lumière and His View," 470.
107 Belloï, "Lumière and His View," 470.

108 Belloï, "Lumière and His View," 472.
109 Belloï, "Lumière and His View," 472.
110 Edison Manufacturing Company, which started production of Kinetoscope in April 1894, photographed a Kinetoscope film about Japanese dancing women, *Imperial Japanese Dance/Japanese Dance/Jap Dance*, at Black Maria in West Orange, New Jersey, in October-November 1894. Charles Musser, *Edison Motion Pictures 1890-1900: An Annotated Filmography* (Washington, DC: Smithsonian, 1997), 153. A single long shot depicts three Japanese women in kimono dancing with a long white cloth and a fan. The film historian Iwamoto Kenji speculates that these three women were the ones who danced at the Imperial Theater in Chicago in 1893 right after the Universal Exposition of that year, as geishas from Osaka and Kobe under the direction of Uenishi Keizō. These women also appeared in *The Mikado* at the Fifth Avenue Theater in New York in June 1894 and were called the "Sarashe Sisters." That was probably when the Edison Company brought them to Black Maria and photographed them. Iwamoto Kenji, "Eiga no torai: Ejison eiga to Nihon" [The arrival of cinema: Edison films and Japan], in *Nihon eiga no tanjō* [The birth of Japanese cinema], ed. Iwamoto Kenji (Tokyo: Shinwa sha, 2011), 19-20. See also Kurata Yoshihiro, *Kaigai kōen kotohajime* [The beginning of overseas performance] (Tokyo: Tokyo shoseki, 1994), 203. If we consider Edison's Kinetoscope to be cinema, these three Japanese women appeared in cinema four years before Veyre photographed geisha using Cinématographe Lumière. The Edison Company also sent a crew (producer James H. White and cinematographer Frederick Blechynden) to Japan in April 1898, which preceded Veyre's visit. Iwamoto, "Eiga no torai," 23.

Chapter 3: Japonisme and Internalized Orientalism

1 The two actors played *Momijigari* together at the Kabukiza Theater for twenty-five days, until November 1. Tanaka Junichirō, "Satsuei gishu, Shibata Tsunekichi" [Cinematographer Shibata Tsunekichi], *Eiga Gijutsu* 4, no. 6 (December 1942): 56.
2 Tanaka Junichirō, "'Yunyū kamera dai 1 gō' kō" [Thought on the "first imported camera"], *Eiga Terebi Gijutsu* 220 (December 1970): 85.
3 Tanaka, "Satsuei gishu, Shibata Tsunekichi," 57.
4 The Meiji Period on Film, accessed October 10, 2019, https://meiji.filmarchives.jp/works/01.html.
5 Hisashi Okajima, the chief curator of the National Film Center, National Museum of Modern Art, Tokyo (National Film Archive of Japan since 2018), estimates the survival rate for Japanese films of the prewar period to be only about 4 percent. Hisahi Okajima, "Japan's Case: Hopeful or Hopeless?" *Bulletin FIAF* 45 (1992): 2.
6 Irie Yoshirō, "Saiko no Nihon eiga ni tsuite: Konishi Honten seisaku no katsudō shashin" [The earliest Japanese movie: Motion pictures produced by Konishi Honten], *Bulletin of the National Museum of Modern Art, Tokyo* 13 (2009): 65-91.
7 Irie, "Saiko no Nihon eiga ni tsuite," 65.

8   Tanaka, "Satsuei gishu, Shibata Tsunekichi," 56.
9   Irie, "Saiko no Nihon eiga ni tsuite," 89. Unfortunately, none of those Konishi films are extant, except a few frames of two of them photographed by Asano or Shibata: *Okanesarashi* (aka *Nunosarashi*, Exposing clothes to the sun, 1898) and *Nagauta Ikioijishi* (Long song: Vigorous lion, 1898), which are preserved at the Tsubouchi Memorial Theater Library of Waseda University. Usui Michiko, "Engeki Hakubutsukan korekushon ni miru, Nihon eizō shi no genryū" [The origin of the history of moving images in Japan seen in the Tsubouchi Memorial Theater Library collection], *Yomiuri Online*, accessed December 29, 2016, http://www.yomiuri.co.jp/adv/wol/culture/080711.html. It is not clear whether it was Asano or Shibata who photographed these two films. In a 1940 interview Asano said that he photographed them. Ōtsuka Shirō et al., "Yonjūnen mae no satsueiki to satsuei o kiku zadankai" [A round-table talk about the camera and cinematography of forty years ago], *Kinema Junpō*, January 1, 1940, 152. Yet the film historian Tanaka Junichirō claimed that these films of geisha's dances were photographed by Shibata, "who was a famous photographer working for Mitsukoshi kimono fabric store at that time and was well known in the entertainment world." Tanaka Junichirō, *Nihon eiga shi hakkutsu* [Excavating Japanese film history] (Tokyo: Tōju sha, 1980), 63. Citing Asano's words, in 1948 Tanaka wrote that these two films were photographed by Asano. Tanaka Junichirō, *Nihon eigashi I* [Japanese film history I] (Tokyo: Saitō shoten, 1948), 85–86. Tanaka admitted that all the early films with geishas were not solely photographed by Asano but also by Shibata as well as another photographer, Shirai Kanzō. As for these two films, in 1985 Tanaka changed his claim and wrote that they had been photographed by Shibata. Tanaka Junichirō, *Katsudō shashin ga yattekita* [Moving photography has arrived] (Tokyo: Chūō kōron sha, 1985), 68–69. Still photographs of films that were presumably screened at the Meijiza Theater on July 14–31, 1899, one of the first exhibitions of Japanese-made films by Konishi honten and Hiromeya, were published in the April 7, 1900, issue of *Shashin Geppō*. According to Irie, the titles of these films were presumably *Nagauta Tsurukame* (Long song: Crane and turtle), probably photographed by Asano, *Hauta Matsuzukushi* (Song: Pine trees) by Asano, and *Kappore* by Asano. One other still photograph of a film presumably screened at the Meijiza Theater at the same time was published in the November 1942 issue of *Eiga Gijutsu*. According to Irie, the film was presumably *Genroku hanami odori* (Genroku period's flower dance) by Asano. All of these films depict singing, playing the shamisen, and geisha dancing at Japanese restaurants. Irie Yoshirō, "Nihon eiga no hatsu kōkai: Meiji sanjūninen no kōgyō to jōei bangumi" [The first showing of Japanese cinema: The exhibition in 1899 and its titles], in *Nihon eiga no tanjō* [The birth of Japanese cinema], ed. Iwamoto Kenji (Tokyo: Shinwa sha, 2011), 146–47. These two films were presumably screened at the Hongō Harukiza Theater from August 11 to 25, 1899. Irie, "Nihon eiga no hatsu kōkai," 154–56.
10 Tanaka, "Satsuei gishu, Shibata Tsunekichi," 57.
11 Matsumoto Kōshirō, *Geidan issei ichidai* [Talk on arts: Once in a lifetime] (Tokyo: Ubun sha, 1948), 67.

12 Ueda Manabu, *Nihon eiga sōsō ki no kōgyō to kankyaku: Tokyo to Kyoto o chūshin ni* [The exhibition and audience during the early period of Japanese cinema: In Tokyo and Kyoto] (Tokyo: Waseda daigaku shuppan bu, 2012), 174.

13 "Nihon eiga shi sokō 22" [Draft of the History of Japanese Cinema], *Kinema Junpō*, May 11, 1936, 82; "Nihon eiga shi sokō 23," *Kinema Junpō*, May 21, 1936, 75–76.

14 Kamiyama Akira, "Eiga 'Momijigari' zengo to Dangiku igo: 'Edosodachi' to 'kosei' no aida" [Before and after the film *Maple Viewing* and after Dangiku: Between "Growing up in Edo" and "Personality"], *Kabuki Kenkyū to Hihyō* 32 (2004): 7.

15 Kamiyama, "Eiga 'Momijigari' zengo to Dangiku igo," 7.

16 Nihon eiga terebi gijutsu kyōkai, "Nihon eiga gijutsu shi nenpu No. 16," *Eiga Terebi Gijutsu* 238 (June 1972): 77; Nihon eiga terebi gijutsu kyōkai, "Nihon eiga gijutsu shi nenpu No. 20," *Eiga Terebi Gijutsu* 242 (October 1972): 75.

17 "1900 nen Pari bankoku hakurankai jimu hōkoku 3" [Report of the Head Office for the 1900 Paris Exposition Universelle, vol. 3], in *Meiji zenki sangyō hattatsu shi shiryō kangyō hakurankai shiryō 203* [Data of the industrial development history in the early Meiji period and data of industrial exposition, vol. 203], ed. Fujiwara Masato (Tokyo: Meiji bunken shiryō kankō kai, 1976), 634.

18 I borrow the term *dream of export* from Aaron Gerow when he discusses the goal of the pure film movement of the late 1910s to early 1920s. Aaron Gerow, *Visions of Japanese Modernity: Articulations of Cinema, Nation, and Spectatorship, 1895–1925* (Berkeley: University of California Press, 2010), 114.

19 "1900 nen Pari bankoku hakurankai jimu hōkoku 3," 634–35.

20 Yokoyama Akio, "Mone to Nihonshumi sono ichi sokumen: Ra Japonēzu no ishō kara mieru mono" [A thought on Monet and Japonisme: What we can see in the costume of *La Japonaise*], *Bijutsushi Ronshū* 12 (2012): 132–34.

21 Helena Gaudekova, "The Kimono of Monet's 'La Japonaise,'" *Fuuryuu: Researching Traditional Japanese Arts and Crafts*, January 11, 2015, accessed December 29, 2016, http://www.fuuryuu.eu/news/the-kimono-of-monets-la-parisienne.

22 Geneviève Lacambre, "Pari no bijutsushō to Hayashi Tadamasa" [Art merchants in Paris and Hayashi Tadamasa], trans. Oki Yukio, in *Hayashi Tadamasa: Japonisumu to bunka kōryū* [Hayashi Tadamasa: Japonisme and cultural communication], ed. Hayashi Tadamasa shimpojiumu jikkō iinkai (Tokyo: Brücke, 2007), 169.

23 Mabuchi Akiko, *Japonisumu: Gensō no Nippon* [Japonisme: Imaginary Japan] (Tokyo: Brücke, 1997), 62.

24 "1900 nen Pari bankoku hakurankai jimu hōkoku 3," 635.

25 Koga Futoshi, "Kamera ga toraeta Nippon: 'Meiji no Nippon' kara 'Ryumiēru eiga Nippon hen' e" [Japan that a camera captured: From "Meiji Japan" to "Lumière Japan films"], in *Eiga denrai: Cinematogurafu to "Meiji no Nippon"* [The arrival of cinema: The Cinématographe and "Meiji Japan"], ed. Yoshida Yoshishige, Yamaguchi Masao, and Kinoshita Naoyuki (Tokyo: Iwanami shoten, 1995), 33.

26 Koga, "Kamera ga toraeta Nippon," 34.

27 There is a possibility that Asano photographed films for the Lumière Company. Because Asano and Shibata had various interests in common, I think many of my arguments would still be valid if Asano was the cinematographer.

28 Kume Keiichirō, "Shin-Inshōha no eikyō" [The influence of postimpressionism], *Taiyō*, June 1, 1911, 111.
29 According to Tanaka Junichirō, this film was first screened at the Kabukiza Theater in June 1899. Tanaka Junichirō, *Nihon eiga hattatsu shi I: Katsudō shashin jidai* [The history of the development of Japanese cinema I: The period of moving photography] (Tokyo: Chūō kōron sha, 1975), 74.
30 As noted earlier in this chapter, a few frames of two other 1898 films by Asano and/or Shibata are also preserved at the Tsubouchi Memorial Library. The films are *Okanesarashi* and *Nagauta Ikioijishi*. The two preserved frames of *Okanesarashi* display two (or possibly three) geisha in front of a black curtain in a long shot. One of them waves a white cloth. The two white objects at the top right corner are possibly other cloths being waved by a third geisha, whose body is barely seen in the frame. There is a white backdrop pinned on the black curtain, which reads "Hiromeya" and "Kaikarō." Hiromeya is obviously the exhibitor of the film. Kaikarō is the name of a Japanese restaurant in Kanda, Tokyo. According to Irie Yoshirō, it was a regular practice to show the name of the restaurant in films in order to inform the audience of the location of the filming. Irie presumes that Asano or Shibata invited some geisha to the restaurant to photograph this film. Irie, "Nihon eiga no hatsu kōkai," 141, 155.
31 Quoted in Tanaka, *Nihon eiga hattatsu shi I*, 73–74.
32 Saeki Junko, "'Geisha' no hakken: 'Tasha' ka sareru Nippon" [Discovering geisha: Japan that is turned into the Other], in *Bijutsu shi to tasha* [Art history and the Other], ed. Shimamoto Kan and Kasuya Makoto (Kyoto: Kōyō shobō, 2000), 148.
33 Two books that were written during the modernization period of Japan by renowned authors represented nativized Orientalism and internalized Orientalism. *Bushido: The Soul of Japan* (1900) by the diplomat Nitobe Inazō embodied the former, and *In Praise of Shadows* (1933–34) by the novelist Tanizaki Juni'chirō did the latter. Referring to a notion that was popularized during the period of Japonisme, Nitobe strategically presented a cultural image to non-Japanese readers. The notion was *bushido*, or the code of samurai, handed down through generations. Nitobe explained Japanese nationalism by emphasizing the codes of loyalty and filial piety in bushido: "The samurai grew to be the beau ideal of the whole race. . . . Bushido was and still is the animating spirit, the motor force of our country." Inazo Nitobe, *Bushido: The Soul of Japan* (Tokyo: Kodansha International, 2002), 135, 141. The first edition of *Bushido* appeared in the US in 1900 and had modest sales. The revised version, released by Putnam in July 1905, received much favorable publicity "at the high tide of interest" in the Russo-Japanese War of 1904 and 1905. *Bushido* was translated into Polish, German, Hungarian, Norwegian, French, Spanish, Russian, Italian, and Chinese. When the book was translated into Japanese in 1908, Japanese readers identified with the non-Japanese readership of the book. Here a transition from nativized Orientalism to internalized Orientalism was observable. The cultural image of Japan was first formulated in order to cater to foreign readers and then accepted back in Japan to be naturalized

as the essence of the Japanese spirit. No matter how imaginary it was, the Western recognition of the exoticism of Japanese culture had an impact on the formation of Japanese national identity. In contrast, Tanizaki did not anticipate foreign readers when he published *In Praise of Shadows* in a series of essays in the 1930s. Since then, *In Praise of Shadows* has been considered by many Japanese people to be one of the most influential writings that explain Japanese aesthetics. In his discussion of Japanese architecture, Tanizaki wrote, "Ultimately, it is the magic of shadows. Were the shadows to be banished from the corners, the alcove [in a Japanese room] would in that instant revert to mere void. This was the genius of our [Japanese] ancestors—that by cutting off the light from this empty space they imparted to the world of shadows that formed there a quality of mystery and depth superior to that of any wall painting or ornament." Tanizaki Jun'ichirō, *In Praise of Shadows*, trans. Thomas J. Harper and Edward G. Seidensticker (London: Vintage, 2001), 32–33. "The magic of shadows" was Tanizaki's expression of internalized Orientalism. In fact, Tanizaki's essay was not exactly based on the actuality of the Japanese landscape and architecture of the time. When Tanizaki wrote *In Praise of Shadows*, Japan was leading the world in the vogue of neon signs. See Miya Elise Mizuta, "Luminous Environment: Light, Architecture and Decoration in Modern Japan," *Japan Forum* 18, no. 3 (2006): 339–60. As the historian Harry Harootunian claims, "In Japan and elsewhere, modernity was seen as a spectacle of ceaseless change (the narrative of historical progress and the law of capitalist expansion) and the specter of unrelieved uncertainty introduced by a dominant historical culture no longer anchored in fixed values but in fantasy and desire." What emerged was "an immense effort to recall older cultural practices (religious, aesthetic, literary, linguistic) that derived from a remote past before the establishment of modern, capitalist society, and that were believed to be still capable of communicating an authentic experience of the people[,] . . . race[,] or folk that historical change could not disturb." According to Harootunian, people like Tanizaki "looked longingly to some moment in the past, or simply the past itself as an indefinite moment, as the place of community or culture, that would serve as the primordial and originary condition of the Japanese folk. . . . This image of culture and community was as timeless and frozen as the commodity form itself." H. D. Harootunian, *Overcome by Modernity: History, Culture, and Community in Interwar Japan* (Princeton, NJ: Princeton University Press, 2000), xix, xxvi. That is, Tanizaki identified with the Orientalist fantasy about "timeless and frozen" Japanese culture when he strategically presented it to Japanese readers during the period of Japanese modernity. It was his way of formulating Japan's cultural identity for the Japanese domestic audience by identifying with the Orientalist standpoint. Thomas LaMarre similarly points out the "form of colonial ambivalence, a structure of disavowal and displacement, which entails a repeating, reprising, or redirecting of Western hierarchies based on whiteness, sex appeal, and industriousness" in Tanizaki's writings from the early 1930s. Thomas LaMarre, *Shadows on the Screen: Tanizaki Jun'ichirō on Cinema and "Oriental" Aesthetics* (Ann Arbor: Center for Japanese Studies, University of Michigan, 2005), 14.

34 Specialized areas included religion (*Nihon no Kyōgaku* by Hakubunkan, 1887–90), commerce (*Nihon Shyōgyō Zasshi* by Hakubunkan, 1890–95), agriculture (*Nihon Nōgyō Zasshi* by Hakubunkan, 1892–95), law (*Nihon no Hōritsu* by Hakubunkan, 1888–95), and children (*Nihon no Shōnen* by Hakubunkan, 1889–95). More ideologically goal-oriented publications included *Kokumin no Tomo* (*The Nation's Friend*, 1887–89), published by Tokutomi Sohō's Minyū sha, which supported Western-style populism (*heimin shugi*); *Meiroku Zasshi* (1874–75), the journal for Meiroku sha, an intellectual society that attempted to enlighten Japanese people by introducing Western thoughts and ethics; *Rikugō Zasshi* (1880–1921), the YMCA magazine in Tokyo that introduced Christian thought as well as Marxism later; and *Fujo Zasshi* (1891–95), the women's journal published by Hakubunkan. Suzuki Sadami, "Meiji ki *Taiyō* no enkaku, oyobi ichi" [The history and the position of *Taiyō* in the Meiji era], in *Zasshi* Taiyō *to kokumin bunka no keisei* [*Taiyō* Magazine and the formation of the national culture], ed. Suzuki Sadami (Tokyo: Shibunkaku shuppan, 2001), 14; Hibi Yoshitaka, "Sōkanki *Taiyō* no sōga shashin: Fūkei shashin to manazashi no seijigaku" [Photographs in early periods of *Taiyō*: The politics of landscape photography and the gaze], in *Shokuminchi shugi to Ajia no hyōshō* [Colonialism and the representation of Asia], ed. Tsukuba daigaku bunka hihyō kenkyūkai (Tsukuba: Tsukuba daigaku bunka hihyō kenkyūkai, 1999), 61–87. The only exception might have been *Nihon Taika Ronshū* [*The collection of essays by eminent writers in Japan*] (1887–94), published by Hakubunkan. *Nihon Taika Ronshū* was an anthology of academic essays that had been published elsewhere. Because the magazine was a compilation of unauthorized reproductions of published articles in various areas, including law, medicine, and religion, other publishers frowned on it. Yet because of its inexpensive price, *Nihon Taika Ronshū* sold very well. It formed the basis of the publication of *Taiyō*.

35 Suzuki, "Meiji ki *Taiyō* no enkaku, oyobi ichi," 14. The state nationalism that *Taiyō* presented was distinguished from *kokusui shugi* or *kokusui hozon shugi* (ultranationalism), which criticized the Meiji government's Westernization policy and explored the values (truth, goodness, and beauty) in Japanese tradition. *Taiyō* did publish ultranationalist essays, including the literary critic Takayama Chogyū's "Nihon shugi o sansu" (Praising Japanese nationalism) in June 1897. But the magazine also published essays with opinions opposing Takayama, including those by the novelist/critic/playwright/translator Tsubouchi Shōyō. Suzuki, "Meiji ki *Taiyō* no enkaku, oyobi ichi," 22. Such inclusiveness made the magazine accessible to any kind of reader: merchants read the economy section, students read the literary section, and housewives read the home section. By 1909, however, when Ukita Kazutami, doctor of law, became the editor in chief, *Taiyō* had grown more openly supportive of constitutionalism and imperialism. Owada Shigeru, "Henshū shukan Ukita Kazutami no ichi" [Ukita Kazutami's position as the editor in chief], in *Zasshi* Taiyō *to kokumin bunka no keisei* [*Taiyō* Magazine and the formation of the national culture], ed. Suzuki Sadami (Tokyo: Shibunkaku shuppan, 2001), 201.

36 Ōhashi Shintarō, "*Taiyō* no hakkan" [Publication of *Taiyō*], *Taiyō*, January 5, 1895, 2.

37 Suzuki, "Meiji ki *Taiyō* no enkaku, oyobi ichi," 7–8.
38 Suzuki, "Meiji ki *Taiyō* no enkaku, oyobi ichi," 38–39.
39 Tsubotani Zenshirō, *Hakubunkan gojūnen shi* [The fifty-year history of Hakubunkan] (Tokyo: Hakubunkan, 1937), 88–89, 93.
40 "Shashin jutsu ōyō no hattatsu" [The development of how to apply the technology of photography], *Taiyō*, January 5, 1895, 186.
41 The magazine *Shashin Geppō* [Photography Monthly], which publicized photo technology, was founded by Konishi honten in February 1894, eleven months before the publication of the first issue of *Taiyō*.
42 Kaneko Tsutomu, "Shoki *Taiyō* ni miru Meiji shashin jutsu no tenkai" [The development of the photographic techniques in the Meiji period seen in the early period of *Taiyō*], in *Zasshi* Taiyō *to kokumin bunka no keisei* [*Taiyō* Magazine and the formation of the national culture], ed. Suzuki Sadami (Tokyo: Shibunkaku shuppan, 2001), 104. In 1906 Hakubunkan organized a nationwide photographers' group, Teikoku shashin kai (the Imperial Group of Photography), to stabilize the supply for its photojournalism. Kaneko, "Shoki *Taiyō* ni miru Meiji shashin jutsu no tenkai," 105.
43 Shibata Tsunekichi, "Kenshō shashin no shinsa" [Evaluation of the contest photos], *Taiyō*, March 1, 1905, 160. The "hazy style" (*mōrō tai*) was Shibata's reference to a movement in Japanese art led by Yokoyama Taikan that challenged conventions. By doing so, according to Kaneko, Shibata distinguished photography from painting, which could be less realistic and more personal. Kaneko, "Shoki *Taiyō* ni miru Meiji shashin jutsu no tenkai," 104. Later in 1911, however, Shibata changed his opinion and claimed in an interview for *Taiyō*, "In the past photography was regarded as a simple form of entertainment. It has been recently considered to be an artistic product. It is the effect of recent school education and social education that has enriched general thoughts on art. I am delighted with this contemporary phenomenon." See "Mistukoshi shashin bu gishichō Shibata Tsunekichi kun dan" [Interview with Shibata Tsunekichi, the chief technician of Mitsukoshi's Department of Photography], *Taiyō*, February 15, 1911, 145. Shibata's change of mind might have been an indication of *Taiyō*'s attitude toward the role of photography after the end of the Russo-Japanese War—possibly the move from its emphasis on transparency to its more specific political and/or artistic inclination.
44 Shibata, "Kenshō shashin no shinsa," 160.
45 As the critic Tsubouchi Yūzō claims, the inclusion of a number of portraits of the royal family members as well as photos of battleships indicated *Taiyō*'s conservative political position. Tsubouchi Yūzō, "Henshusha Ōhashi Otowa" [Editor Ōhashi Otowa], in *Zasshi* Taiyō *to kokumin bunka no keisei* [*Taiyō* Magazine and the formation of the national culture], ed. Suzuki Sadami (Tokyo: Shibunkaku shuppan, 2001), 161.
46 Hibi, "Sōkanki *Taiyō* no sōga shashin."
47 Hibi, "Sōkanki *Taiyō* no sōga shashin."
48 "Kyoto Shijōgawara nōryō" [Summer evening on the Shijō River, Kyoto], *Taiyō*, January 5, 1895, 73.

49 Satō Morihiro, *Topogurafi no Nihon kindai: Edo doroe, Yokohama shashin, geijutsu shasin* [Topography and Japanese modernity: Edo mud paintings, Yokohama photographs, art photography] (Tokyo: Seikyū sha, 2011), 136.
50 Kōjin Karatani, *Origins of Modern Japanese Literature*, ed. and trans. Brett de Bary (Durham, NC: Duke University Press, 1993), 11–44.
51 Gerow, *Visions of Japanese Modernity*, 20.
52 Eric Hobsbawm and Terence Ranger, eds., *The Invention of Tradition* (Cambridge: Cambridge University Press, 1983).
53 Endō Miyuki, "Tokyo Shashin Kenkyū kai 'Kenten' to 'geijutsu shashin' no keisei" [The exhibition of the Tokyo Photographic Research Society and emergence of "art photography": Rethinking Japanese pictorialism], *Waseda Daigaku Daigakuin Bungaku Kenkyūka Kiyō*, Dai 3 bunsatsu 60 (2014): 138.
54 In addition, Shibata contributed two photographic views of Mt. Fuji, "Fujikawabashi no fuji" [Fuji viewed from Fujikawa] and "Suzukawa no sakasa fuji" [Inverted Fuji viewed from Suzukawa], to another magazine, *Bijutsu Gahō* [Illustrated News on Arts], January 31, 1899, n.p.
55 The themes of the three other works by Shibata can be also found in Yokohama photographs: "Ōzutsu oyobi Hitachiyama no torikumi" [Wrestling of Hitachiyama and Ōzutsu]), *Taiyō*, February 5, 1902, n.p.; "Amida Minegashira Hōkō Funbo" [The tomb of Taikō and the ceremonies], with three small photographs, *Taiyō*, May 20, 1898, n.p.; and "Hōtaikō mokuzō" [The wooden sculpture of Hōtaikō, and his tomb in Kōtaiji], with three small photographs, *Taiyō*, May 20, 1898, n.p.
56 Shibata Tsunekichi, "Suishōsekai (Honnen ichigatsu yōka no asageshiki)" [The crystal world: The morning view on January 8 of this year], *Taiyō*, February 5, 1902, n.p.
57 Shibata Tsunekichi, "Hachigatsu nijūsan nichi yoru no denkō" [The lightning in the stormy night of August 23], *Taiyō*, September 5, 1898, n.p.
58 Ueda, *Nihon eiga sōsō ki no kōgyō to kankyaku*, 175. The cancellation was caused by Kikugorō V's death earlier that year, leading Danjurō IX to approve the substitute screening of *Momijigari*. Alternately, according to Tanaka Junichirō, the Nakaza Theater needed a program before Nakamura Ganjirō I's Kabuki troop could return from its tour of Kyoto and approached Inoue Takejirō, the executive of the Kabukiza Theater in Tokyo, who owned the print of *Momijigari*. Tanaka, "Satsuei gishu, Shibata Tsunekichi," 58. Whatever the case, the screening of *Momijigari* was a last-minute substitute for a Kabuki performance. For further discussions on the ambiguous status of *Momijigari* as a "film," see Daisuke Miyao, "Reviewing *Maple Viewing (Momijigari*, 1899)," in *The Oxford Handbook of Silent Cinema*, ed. Charlie Keil and Rob King (Oxford: Oxford University Press, forthcoming).
59 In 1908 Yokota shōkai started producing narrative films and joined industrial efforts in the mass production of cinema by other companies, including Yoshizawa shōten, which constructed its first film studio in Meguro, Tokyo, in January of the same year. Irie, "Saiko no Nihon eiga ni tsuite," 88.
60 Ueda, *Nihon eiga sōsō ki no kōgyō to kankyaku*, 185.
61 It is difficult to identify exactly which Pathé films corresponded to these titles.

62 "Nihon eiga shi sokō 43," *Kinema Junpō*, June 11, 1937, 83.
63 Tsukada Yoshinobu, *Eiga Shiryō Hakkutsu*, July 15, 1975, 1. Tsukada included a photocopy of the newspaper report but could not identify which newspaper it was.
64 Ueda, *Nihon eiga sōsō ki no kōgyō to kankyaku*, 183–84.
65 Ueda, *Nihon eiga sōsō ki no kōgyō to kankyaku*, 184.

Epilogue

1 Emmanuelle Toulet, "Cinema at the Universal Exposition, Paris, 1900," trans. Tom Gunning, *Persistence of Vision* 9 (1991): 10.
2 Toulet, "Cinema at the Universal Exposition, Paris, 1900," 11, 13.
3 *Rapport general administrative et technique*, vol. IV, 121, quoted in Toulet, "Cinema at the Universal Exposition, Paris, 1900," 15.
4 Toulet, "Cinema at the Universal Exposition, Paris, 1900," 15.
5 Toulet, "Cinema at the Universal Exposition, Paris, 1900," 16.
6 Ayako Kano, *Acting Like a Woman in Modern Japan: Theater, Gender and Nationalism* (New York: Palgrave, 2001), 57–84.
7 In 1897 the Privy Council of Japan ordered the acting ambassador Katō Tsunetada to inform the French Head Office that the following five types of exhibitions would need prior approval from the Japanese Head Office in order to avoid any possible damage to the image of Japan: "(1) Exhibiting any kinds of Japanese products; (2) Setting up stores, cafés, restaurants, and tea houses that sell Japanese products; (3) Exhibiting and selling Japanese products outside of the Japanese pavilion; (4) Exhibiting Japanese entertainment, such as music, dance, and theatrical performances; (5) Wearing of Japanese costumes by Japanese people hired by French or any other foreign exhibitors." "1900 nen Pari bankoku hakurankai jimu hōkoku 4" [Report of the Head Office for the 1900 Paris Exposition Universelle, vol. 4], in *Meiji zenki sangyō hattatsu shi shiryō kangyō hakurankai shiryō 204* [Data of the industrial development history in the early Meiji period and data of industrial exposition, vol. 204], ed. Fujiwara Masato (Tokyo: Meiji bunken shiryō kankō kai, 1976), 901.
8 Kaneo Tanejirō, ed., *Kawakami Otojirō Sadayakko manyūki* [The travelogue of Kawakami Otojirō and Sadayakko] (Tokyo: Kaneo bunen dō, 1901), 16. In addition to exoticizing the content, Kawakami was aware that he would need to incorporate Western theatrical techniques in their performance to be received by the non-Japanese audience. During their stay in New York before arriving in Paris, the Kawakami troupe visited the American Academy of Dramatic Arts and observed lectures on makeup, acting, etc. In particular, Kawakami was impressed by the "Delsarte System," the acting method created by François Delsarte, which actors could refer to when they connected their body movements to their emotional expressions. Joseph L. Anderson, *Enter a Samurai: Kawakami Otojirō and Japanese Theatre in the West* (Tucson, AZ: Wheatmark, 2011), 402.
9 Yukio Hayakawa, "Tsuru Aoki: A Flower of Japan," *Rafu Shinpo Magazine* (June 19, 1998): 3–5, 16–18.
10 "Miss Tsura Aoki, Japanese Actress," *Moving Picture World*, February 14, 1914, 825.
11 *Variety*, December 12, 1913, 12.

12 *Reel Life*, November 1, 1913; February 7, 1914; June 20, 1914.
13 Mari Yoshihara, *Embracing the East: White Women and American Orientalism* (New York: Oxford University Press, 2003), 10. Japanese art and culture was nostalgically and Orientalistically regarded as a premodern and primitive existence and dichotomized as an alternative or a reaction to modernity that was threatening to the Victorian morality of the Progressive era. Jane Converse Brown, "'Fine Arts and Fine People': The Japanese Taste in the American Home, 1876-1916," in *Making the American Home: Middle-Class Women & Domestic Material Culture 1840-1940*, ed. Marilyn Ferris Motz and Pat Browne (Bowling Green, OH: Bowling Green State University Popular Press, 1988), 123; Yoshihara, *Embracing the East*, 28. Also, during the Progressive era art became viewed not as an end unto itself but as a tool that would teach a lesson in morality. Aestheticism was considered to be the sign of a "refined mind." Edward Dewson, "Estheticism," *Decorator and Furnisher* 3 (1883): 89. In such middle-class discourses, Brown argues, the "Japanese Taste" reflected "an exemplum of middle-class women's desire to carry out moral reforms in their own households and to present their families and themselves favorably to the public," and Japanese art was considered to incorporate "a number of moral and spiritual qualities." Brown, "'Fine Arts and Fine People,'" 1, 155. It is noteworthy that Japanese art was perversely used in Christian homes to enhance morality, purity, and good taste, only because it was justified by its evocative relationship between nature and religion in the imagination of the American middle class.
14 Gregory Waller, "Historicizing, a Test Case: Japan on American Screens, 1909-1915," unpublished manuscript obtained from Sumiko Higashi. Japan and the Japanese people became popular subjects for early American films, including newsreels and travelogues. *The American Film Institute Catalog 1893-1910* lists ninety-four films that were released in the US under the category of "Japan and Japanese," and the same catalog of 1911-20 lists forty-three films under the categories of "Japan" and "Japanese" combined. Elias Savada, comp., *The American Film Institute Catalog of Motion Pictures Produced in the United States: Film Beginnings, 1893-1910* (Metuchen, NJ: Scarecrow, 1995), 350. Patricia King Hanson and Alan Gevinson, ed., *The American Film Institute Catalog of Motion Pictures Produced in the United States: Feature Films, 1911-1920* (Berkeley: University of California Press, 1989), 338.
15 *Moving Picture World*, January 31, 1914, 554.
16 "Japanese Film Actress Marries," *New York Clipper*, May 9, 1914, 16.
17 Hayakawa, "Tsuru Aoki," 3-5, 16-18.
18 Nick Browne, "The Undoing of the Other Woman: Madame Butterfly in the Discourse American Orientalism," in *The Birth of Whiteness: Race and the Emergence of U.S. Cinema*, ed. Daniel Bernardi (New Brunswick, NJ: Rutgers University Press, 1996), 234.
19 For a more detailed analysis of *The Wrath of the Gods* in relation to the stardom of Sessue Hayakawa, see Daisuke Miyao, *Sessue Hayakawa: Silent Cinema and Transnational Stardom* (Durham, NC: Duke University Press, 2007), 57-65.
20 For more information about the fan magazine discourse on the formation of Hayakawa's stardom, see Miyao, *Sessue Hayakawa*, 136-50.

21 Sara Ross, "The Americanization of Tsuru Aoki: Orientalism, Melodrama, Star Image, and the New Woman," *Camera Obscura* 20, no. 3 (2005): 144.
22 Warren Reed, "The Tradition Wreckers: Two People Who Became Famous, though Few People without Almond Eyes Can Pronounce Their Names," *Picture-Play*, March 1917, 64.
23 Miyao, *Sessue Hayakawa*, 140–41.
24 Margaret I. MacDonald, *Moving Picture World*, October 4, 1919, 161.
25 *Kinema Junpo*, April 1, 1922, 12.
26 Miyao, *Sessue Hayakawa*, 179–80.
27 Grace Kingsley, "That Splash of Saffron: Sessue Hayakawa, a Cosmopolitan Actor, Who for Reasons of Nativity, Happens to Peer from Our White Screens with Tilted Eyes," *Photoplay* 9.4 (March 1916): 139.
28 Sessue Hayakawa, *Zen Showed Me the Way . . . to Peace, Happiness and Tranquility* (Indianapolis, IN: Bobbs-Merrill, 1960), 138–39, 143.
29 Miyao, *Sessue Hayakawa*, 153–67. In addition, there was another context behind the emphasis on the Orientalist fantasy in Hayakawa films after 1919. Throughout the year 1919, Robertson-Cole, the distribution company, restructured its system and began to have a stronger influence on Haworth films, so Hayakawa started to lose control over his company. Robertson-Cole continued to distribute Haworth films through 1920, when Haworth was integrated into Robertson-Cole, which by then had also begun producing films. As Robertson-Cole rapidly expanded its position in the film distribution and production businesses, it became necessary for Hayakawa to negotiate more seriously with it regarding the production of his star vehicles. See Miyao, *Sessue Hayakawa*, 168–76. Aoki and Hayakawa's balancing act failed as anti-Japanese sentiment grew in California. Hayakawa moved to France and tried to maintain his stardom there. French intellectuals formulated a theoretical film concept of *photogénie* based on Hayakawa's facial expressions captured in close-ups. The theorist and filmmaker Jean Epstein called the close-ups of Hayakawa's face on the screen "*photogénie*, cadenced movement." Jean Epstein, "The Senses I (b)," in *French Film Theory and Criticism: A History/Anthology 1907–1939*, vol. I, *1907–1929*, ed. Richard Abel (Princeton, NJ: Princeton University Press, 1988), 243. The critic and filmmaker Louis Delluc argued that "photogénie" changes "real" into something else without eliminating the "realness" using the camera/screen, and makes people "see ordinary things as they had never been before." See Richard Abel, ed., *French Film Theory and Criticism: A History/Anthology 1907–1939*, vol. I, *1907–1929* (Princeton, NJ: Princeton University Press, 1988), 110. Five decades later, the film critic André Bazin revived the notion of photogénie by repeating the same words as the ones that Delluc used: "Photography affects us like a phenomenon in nature, like a flower or a snowflake whose vegetable or earthly origins are an inseparable part of their beauty." André Bazin, *What Is Cinema?* trans. Hugh Gray (Berkeley: University of California Press, 1967), 1:13. Via viewing Hayakawa's body, according to the film scholar Steven Shaviro, French film theorists developed the "utopian vision of an originary, phenomenological plentitude of perception, preserved and extended by the cinematic apparatus."

Steven Shaviro, *The Cinematic Body* (Minneapolis: University of Minnesota Press, 1993), 18. The act of those French intellectuals paralleled the practice of impressionist and postimpressionist painters who were impressed by Japanese paintings and incorporated their styles in their work. In that regard the French reception of Hayakawa initiated another wave of Japonisme.

30 Terada Shirō, "Teisō no kuni no onna Ochō fujin" [Cio-Cio-San, the Woman from a Faithful Country], *Fujin Kōron*, April 1921, 70.

31 Suzuki Yō, "Shinsetsu na Hayakawa Sesshū to Tsuruko fujin" [Kind Sessue Hayakawa and Mrs. Tsuruko], in *Sesshū*, ed. Kōda Honami (Tokyo: Shin jidai sha, 1922), 16–20.

32 Shigeno Yukiyoshi, "Beikoku dewa Nihongeki ga donnna kankyō de torareruka" [Why films about Japan were made in the US], *Katsudō Kurabu*, February 1920, 28.

33 Kano, *Acting Like a Woman in Modern Japan*, 39.

34 Mari Yoshihara, "The Flight of the Japanese Butterfly: Orientalism, Nationalism, and Performance of Japanese Womanhood," *American Quarterly* 56, no. 4 (December 2004): 982.

35 Shibata Tamaki, "Joyū ni tsukite" [To be an actress], trans. Mari Yoshihara, *Chūō Kōron*, December 1911, 100.

36 Aokusa-sei, "Kamome tobu Koreamaru no kanpan de: Aoki Tsuruko san no omoide" [On the deck of Korea-maru: Memoir of Miss Aoki Tsuruko], *Katsudō Gahō*, June 1920, 51.

37 Joanne Bernardi, *Writing in Light: The Silent Scenario and the Japanese Pure Film Movement* (Detroit, MI: Wayne State University Press, 2001), 13.

38 Tamura Chiho, "Eiga joyū no tanjō: Aruiwa Nana no monogatari" [The emergence of female motion picture actors, or a story of Nana], in *Nihon eiga wa ikiteiru dai 5 kan: Kantoku to haiyū no bigaku* [Japanese cinema is alive, vol. 5, The aesthetics of directors and actors], ed. Kurosawa Kiyoshi et al. (Tokyo: Iwanami shoten, 2010), 174–81.

39 Sasō Tsutomu, *1923 Mizoguchi Kenji Chi to rei* [1923 Mizoguchi Kenji *Blood and Soul*] (Tokyo: Chikuma shobō, 1991), 19.

40 Aaron Gerow, *Visions of Japanese Modernity*, 114.

41 Kaeriyama Norimasa, "Jiko o shireriya?" [Do we know ourselves?], *Kinema Record*, January 10, 1915, 2.

42 Gerow, "'Nihonjin' Kitano Takeshi: *Hana-Bi* to nashonaru shinema no keisei" [The "Japanese" Kitano Takeshi: *Fireworks* and the formation of a national cinema], *Yuriika* rinji zōkan 30, no. 3 (February 1998): 42–51.

43 Hideaki Fujiki, *Making Personas: Transnational Film Stardom in Modern Japan* (Cambridge, MA: Harvard University Asia Center, 2013), 213.

44 *Katsudō Gahō*, March 1917, n.p. See also Fujiki, *Making Personas*, 192–95.

45 Fujiki, *Making Personas*, 192.

46 Fujiki, *Making Personas*, 203.

47 *Kinema Record*, November/December 1917, 14.

48 *Katsudō Shashin Zasshi*, December 1917, n.p.

49 Fujiki, *Making Personas*, 235, 240.

50 Kurishima Sumiko, "'Gubijinsō' no koro" [Days of "The Poppy"], *Eiga Terebi Gijutsu* 238 (June 1972): 21–22; Okabe Ryū, "Amerika jidai no Henrī Kotani" [Henry Kotani, American period], *Eigashi Kenkyū* 2 (1973): 25; Tamaki Junichirō, *Nihon eiga seisui ki* [Record of the adolescence of Japanese cinema] (1938; Tokyo: Yumani shobō, 2006), 109.
51 Patrick Keating, "The Birth of Backlighting in the Classical Cinema," *Aura* 6 (2000): 49.
52 Mitsuhiro Yoshimoto, *Kurosawa: Film Studies and Japanese Cinema* (Durham, NC: Duke University Press, 2000), 208–9.
53 Fujiki, *Making Personas*, 232.
54 Īzuka Tōkin, "*Hototogisu* to *Chikyōdai* o mite, nihon eiga no zento ni kitaisu" [Watching *The Cuckoo* and *Foster Sisters*: Expecting the bright future of Japanese cinema], *Katsudō Kurabu*, June 1922, 52.
55 Fujiki, *Making Personas*, 186–87.
56 Fujiki, *Making Personas*, 186–87. Translation of the first sentence is by Fujiki, and translation of the second sentence is by Miyao.
57 Tsuda Kōzō, "Kurishima-gata to Satsuki-gata" [Kurishima-type and Satsuki-type], *Kamata*, November 1924, 20–22.
58 Fujiki, *Making Personas*, 240.

BIBLIOGRAPHY

Abel, Richard. *The Ciné Goes to Town: French Cinema 1896–1914*. Berkeley: University of California Press, 1994.
Abel, Richard, ed. *French Film Theory and Criticism: A History/Anthology 1907–1939*. Vol. I, *1907–1929*. Princeton, NJ: Princeton University Press, 1988.
Albera, Françoise, and Maria Tortajada. "The 1900 Episteme." In *Cinema beyond Film: Media Epistemology in the Modern Era*, edited by Françoise Albera and Maria Tortajada, 25–44. Amsterdam: Amsterdam University Press, 2010.
Allan, Michael. "Deserted Histories: The Lumière Brothers, the Pyramids and Early Film Form." *Early Popular Visual Culture* 6, no. 2 (July 2008): 159–70.
Amano, Keigo. "Yamaguchi Saiichirō 'Shashin jireki' gendaigo yaku" [Yamaguchi Saiichirō, "Case history of photography" modern translation]. In *Shimooka Renjō: A Pioneer of Japanese Photography*, edited by Mitsui Keishi and Toriumi Saki, 186–98. Tokyo: Kokusho kankō kai, 2014.
Anderson, Joseph L. *Enter a Samurai: Kawakami Otojirō and Japanese Theatre in the West*. Tucson, AZ: Wheatmark, 2011.
Andrew, Dudley. *The Major Film Theories: An Introduction*. New York: Oxford University Press, 1976.
Aokusa-sei. "Kamome tobu Koreamaru no kanpan de: Aoki Tsuruko san no omoide" [On the deck of Korea-maru: Memoir of Miss Aoki Tsuruko]. *Katsudō Gahō*, June 1920, 50–51.
Aubert, Michelle, and Jean-Claude Seguin. *La Production cinématographique des Frères Lumière* [The cinematographic production by the Lumière brothers]. Paris: Librairie du Premier Siècle du Cinéma, Bibliothèque du film, Editions Mémoires de cinema, Diffusion, CDE, 1996.
Aumont, Jacques. *L'Oeil interminable: peinture et cinema*. Paris: Editions Seguier, 1989.
Aumont, Jacques. "The Variable Eye, or the Mobilization of the Gaze." Translated by Charles O'Brien and Sally Shafto. In *The Image in Dispute: Art and Cinema in the Age of Photography*, edited by Dudley Andrew, 231–58. Austin: University of Texas Press, 1997.
Bao, Weihong. "The Trouble with Theater: Cinema and the Geopolitics of Medium Specificity." *Framework* 56, no. 2 (fall 2015): 350–67.
Bazin, André. "The Ontology of the Photographic Image." Translated by Hugh Gray. *Film Quarterly* 13, no. 4 (summer 1960): 4–9.
Bazin, André. *What Is Cinema?* Berkeley: University of California Press, 1967.
Belloï, Livio. "Lumière and His View: The Cameraman's Eye in Early Cinema." *Historical Journal of Film, Radio and Television* 154, no. 4 (1995): 461–74.
Berger, Klaus. *Japonisme in Western Painting from Whistler to Matisse*. Translated by David Britt. Cambridge: Cambridge University Press, 1992.

Bernardi, Joanne. *Writing in Light: The Silent Scenario and the Japanese Pure Film Movement*. Detroit, MI: Wayne State University Press, 2001.

Bertellini, Giorgio. *Italy in Early American Cinema: Race, Landscape, and the Picturesque*. Bloomington: Indiana University Press, 2010.

Bohem-Girel, Denise. "Un Lumière Operature: Constant Girel (1873-1952)" [A Lumière operator: Constant Girel (1873-1952)]. In *L'aventure du Cinématographe: Actes du Congrès mondial Lumière* [The adventure of the Cinématographe: Proceedings of the World Lumière Conference], 69-72. Lyon: Aléas, 1999.

Brown, Jane Converse. "'Fine Arts and Fine People': The Japanese Taste in the American Home, 1876-1916." In *Making the American Home: Middle-Class Women and Domestic Material Culture 1840-1940*, edited by Marilyn Ferris Motz and Pat Browne, 121-39. Bowling Green, OH: Bowling Green State University Popular Press, 1988.

Browne, Nick. "The Undoing of the Other Woman: Madame Butterfly in the Discourse of American Orientalism." In *The Birth of Whiteness: Race and the Emergence of U.S. Cinema*, edited by Daniel Bernardi, 227-56. New Brunswick, NJ: Rutgers University Press, 1996.

Bryson, Norman. "Furansu no orientarizumu kaiga ni okeru 'tasha'" ["The Other" in French Orientalist paintings]. In *Bijutsu shi to tasha* [Art history and the Other], edited by Shimamoto Kan and Kasuya Makoto, 69-86. Kyoto: Kōyō shobō, 2000.

Bryson, Norman. *Vision and Painting: The Logic of the Gaze*. New Haven, CT: Yale University Press, 1983.

Burch, Noël. *Life to Those Shadows*. Translated by Ben Brewster. Berkeley: University of California Press, 1990.

"The Catholic Church in Japan." *Dublin Review* 116 (January-April 1895): 257-89.

Comolli, Jean-Louis. *Cinema against Spectacle: Techniques and Ideology Revisited*. Translated and edited by Daniel Fairfax. Amsterdam: Amsterdam University Press, 2015.

Crary, Jonathan. *Suspensions of Perception: Attention, Spectacle, and Modern Culture*. Cambridge, MA: MIT Press, 1999.

Crary, Jonathan. "Techniques of the Observer." *October* 45 (summer 1988): 3-35.

Crary, Jonathan. *Techniques of the Observer: On Vision and Modernity in the Nineteenth Century*. Cambridge, MA: MIT Press, 1990.

Daston, Lorrain, and Peter Galison. "The Image of Objectivity." *Representations* 40 (fall 1992): 81-128.

de Goncourt, Edmond, and Jules de Goncourt. *Paris and the Arts, 1851-1896: From the Goncourt Journal*. Edited and translated by George J. Becker and Edith Philips. Ithaca, NY: Cornell University Press, 1971.

Deutelbaum, Marshall. "Structural Patterning in the Lumière Films." In *Film before Griffith*, edited by John L. Fell, 299-310. Berkeley: University of California Press, 1983.

DeVonyar, Jill, and Richard Kendall. *Degas and the Art of Japan*. Reading, PA: Reading Public Museum, 2007.

Dewson, Edward. "Estheticism." *Decorator and Furnisher* 3 (1883): 89.

Dixon, Laurinda S. "Trade and Tradition: Japan and the Dutch Golden Age." In *The Orient Expressed: Japan's Influence on Western Art 1854-1918*, edited by Gabriel P. Weisberg, 77-93. Jackson: Mississippi Museum of Art, 2011.

Doane, Mary Ann. *The Emergence of Cinematic Time: Modernity, Contingency, the Archive*. Cambridge, MA: Harvard University Press, 2002.

Doane, Mary Ann. "Temporality, Storage, Legibility: Freud, Marey, and the Cinema." In *Endless Night: Cinema and Psychoanalysis, Parallel Histories*, edited by Janet Bergstrom, 57–87. Berkeley: University of California Press, 1999.

Elsaesser, Thomas. *Film History as Media Archeology: Tracking Digital Cinema*. Amsterdam: Amsterdam University Press, 2016.

Endō, Miyuki. "Tokyo Shashin Kenkyū kai 'Kenten' to 'geijutsu shashin' no keisei" [The exhibition of the Tokyo Photographic Research Society and emergence of "art photography": Rethinking Japanese pictorialism]. *Waseda Daigaku Daigakuin Bungaku Kenkyūka Kiyō*, Dai 3 bunsatsu 60 (2014): 133–50.

Epstein, Jean. "The Senses I (b)." In *French Film Theory and Criticism: A History/Anthology 1907–1939*, edited by Richard Abel. Princeton, NJ: Princeton University Press, 1988.

Fields, Armond. *Henri Rivière*. Salt Lake City: Gibbs M. Smith, 1983.

Foster, Hal, ed. *Vision and Visuality*. Seattle: Bay Press, 1988.

Fried, Michael. *Courbet's Realism*. Chicago: University of Chicago Press, 1990.

Fujiki, Hideaki. *Making Personas: Transnational Film Stardom in Modern Japan*. Cambridge, MA: Harvard University Asia Center, 2013.

Gartlan, Luke. *A Career of Japan: Baron Raimund von Stillfried and Early Yokohama Photography*. Leiden: Brill, 2016.

Gaudekova, Helena. "The Kimono of Monet's 'La Japonaise.'" *Fuuryuu: Researching Traditional Japanese Arts and Crafts*, January 11, 2015. Accessed December 29, 2016. http://www.fuuryuu.eu/news/the-kimono-of-monets-la-parisienne.

Gaudreault, André. *Film and Attraction: From Kinematography to Cinema*. Translated by Timothy Barnard. Urbana: University of Illinois Press, 2011.

Gerow, Aaron. "'Nihonjin' Kitano Takeshi: *Hana-Bi* to nashonaru shinema no keisei" [The "Japanese" Kitano Takeshi: *Fireworks* and the formation of a national cinema]. *Yuriika* rinji zōkan 30, no. 3 (February 1998): 42–51.

Gerow, Aaron. *Visions of Japanese Modernity: Articulations of Cinema, Nation, and Spectatorship, 1895–1925*. Berkeley: University of California Press, 2010.

Grau, Oliver. *Virtual Art: From Illusion to Immersion*. Translated by Gloria Custance. Cambridge, MA: MIT Press, 2003.

Grosz, Elizabeth. "Criticism, Feminism, and the Institution: An Interview with Gayatri Chakravorty Spivak." *Thesis Eleven* 10/11 (1984/85): 175–87.

Gunning, Tom. "Loïe Fuller and the Art of Motion: Body, Light, Electricity, and the Origins of Cinema." In *Camera Obscura, Camera Lucida: Essays in Honor of Annette Michelson*, edited by Richard Allen and Malcolm Turvey, 75–89. Amsterdam: Amsterdam University Press, 2003.

Gunning, Tom. "New Thresholds of Vision: Instantaneous Photography and the Early Cinema of Lumière." In *Impossible Presence: Surface and Screen in the Photogenic Era*, edited by Terry Smith, 71–99. Chicago: University of Chicago Press, 2001.

Gunning, Tom. "The World in Its Own Image: The Myth of Total Cinema." In *Opening Bazin: Postwar Film Theory and Its Afterlife*, edited by Dudley Andrew with Hervé Joubert-Laurencin, 119–26. New York: Oxford University Press, 2011.

Hall, Stuart. "Encoding/Decoding." In *Culture, Media, Language*, edited by Stuart Hall, Dorothy Hobson, Andrew Lowe, and Paul Willis, 128-38. London: Hutchinson, 1980.

Hammond, Anne. "Impressionist Theory and the Autochrome." *History of Photography* 15, no. 2 (1991): 96-100.

Hanson, Patricia King, and Alan Gevinson, eds. *The American Film Institute Catalog of Motion Pictures Produced in the United States: Feature Films, 1911-1920*. Berkeley: University of California Press, 1989.

Harootunian, H. D. *Overcome by Modernity: History, Culture, and Community in Interwar Japan*. Princeton, NJ: Princeton University Press, 2000.

Harris, G. W. "Japanese Pictures." *Outlook* 81, no. 9 (October 28, 1905): 496-504.

Hase, Masato. *Eiga to iu tekunorojī taiken* [Cinema and technological experience]. Tokyo: Seikyū sha, 2010.

Hasumi, Shigehiko. "Hikari no shito: Ryumiēru kyōdai to Gaburieru Vēru" [The apostles of light: Lumière brothers and Gabiriel Veyre]. In *Ryumiēru gannen: Gaburieru Vēru to eiga no rekishi* [The first year of Lumière: Gabriel Veyre and the history of cinema], edited by Hasumi Shigehiko, 5-44. Tokyo: Chikuma shobō, 1995.

Hayakawa, Sessue. *Zen Showed Me the Way . . . to Peace, Happiness and Tranquility*. Indianapolis: Bobbs-Merrill, 1960.

Hayakawa, Yukio. "Tsuru Aoki: A Flower of Japan." *Rafu*, June 19, 1998, 3-5, 16-18.

Hayashi, Michio, and Matsuura Hisao. "Efude no hitofuri: Sezannu to tomoni kangaeru tameni" [One stroke of a pen: To think with Cézanne]. *Yuriika* 44, no. 4 (April 2012): 48-65.

Heilbrun, Françoise. "Impressionism and Photography." *History of Photography* 33, no. 1 (February 2009): 18-25.

Hibi, Yoshitaka. "Sōkanki *Taiyō* no sōga shashin: Fūkei shashin to manazashi no seijigaku" [Photographs in early periods of *Taiyō*: The politics of landscape photography and the gaze]. In *Shokuminchi shugi to Ajia no hyōshō* [Colonialism and the representation of Asia], edited by Tsukuba daigaku bunka hihyō kenkyūkai, 61-87. Tsukuba: Tsukuba daigaku bunka hihyō kenkyūkai, 1999.

Hirashima, Masao, Sugano Akimasa, and Takashina Shūji. *Tettei tōgi 19seiki no bungaku geijutsu* [Through discussion: Literature and art of the nineteenth century]. Tokyo: Seido sha, 1974.

Hobsbawm, Eric, and Terence Ranger, eds. *The Invention of Tradition*. Cambridge: Cambridge University Press, 1983.

Humbert, Aimé. *Le Japon illustré* [The illustrated Japan]. Paris: Librairie de L. Hachette et CLE, 1870.

Iampolski, Mikhail. "The Logic of an Illusion: Notes on the Genealogy of Intellectual Cinema." In *Camera Obscura, Camera Lucida: Essays in Honor of Annette Michelson*, edited by Richard Allen and Malcolm Turvey, 35-50. Amsterdam: Amsterdam University Press, 2003.

Imahashi, Riko. *The Akita Ranga School and the Cultural Context in Edo Japan*. Translated by Ruth S. McCreery. Tokyo: International House of Japan, 2016.

Inabata, Katsutarō. "Shinematogurafu o yunyū shita zengo" [The time when I imported the Cinématographe]. *Kinema Junpō*, November 11, 1935, 71-72.

Inaga, Shigemi. *Kaiga no rinkai: Kindai higashi Ajia bijutsushi no shikkoku to meiun* [Images on the edge: A historical survey of East Asian trans-cultural modernities]. Nagoya: Nagoya daigaku shuppan kai, 2014.

Inaga, Shigemi. *Kaiga no tasogare: Eduāru Mane botsugo no tōsō* [The twilight of painting: The posthumous fight of Édouard Manet]. Nagoya: Nagoya daigaku shuppan kai, 1997.

Inaga, Shigemi. *Kaiga no tōhō: Orientarizumu kara Japonizumu e* [The Orient of the painting: From Orientalism to Japonisme]. Nagoya: Nagoya daigaku shuppan kai, 1999.

Irie, Yoshirō. "Nihon eiga no hatsu kōkai: Meiji sanjūninen no kōgyō to jōei bangumi" [The first showing of Japanese cinema: The exhibition in 1899 and its titles]. In *Nihon eiga no tanjō* [The birth of Japanese cinema], edited by Iwamoto Kenji, 127–62. Tokyo: Shinwa sha, 2011.

Irie, Yoshirō. "Saiko no Nihon eiga ni tsuite: Konishi Honten seisaku no katsudō shashin" [The earliest Japanese movie: Motion pictures produced by Konishi Honten]. *Bulletin of the National Museum of Modern Art, Tokyo* 13 (2009): 65–91.

Ishitani, Haruhiro. *Genshi to riarizumu: Kūrube kara Pisaro e Furansu kindai kaiga no saikō* [Illusion and realism: From Courbet to Pissarro, reconsidering French modern painting]. Kyoto: Jinbun shoin, 2011.

Iwamoto, Kenji. "Eiga no torai: Ejison eiga to Nihon" [The arrival of cinema: Edison films and Japan]. In *Nihon eiga no tanjō* [The birth of Japanese cinema], edited by Iwamoto Kenji, 7–41. Tokyo: Shinwa sha, 2011.

Izuka, Tōkin. "*Hototogisu* to *Chikyōdai* o mite, nihon eiga no zento ni kitaisu" [Watching *The Cuckoo* and *Foster Sisters*: Expecting the bright future of Japanese cinema]. *Katsudō Kurabu*, June 1922, 52.

"Japanese Film Actress Marries." *New York Clipper*, May 9, 1914, 16.

Jay, Martin. "Scopic Reigns of Modernity." In *Vision and Visuality*, edited by Hal Foster, 3–28. Seattle: Bay Press, 1988.

Jeffries, B. Joy. *The Eye in Health and Disease. Being a Series of Articles on the Anatomy and Physiology of the Human Eye, and Its Surgical and Medical Treatment*. Boston: Alexandre Moore, 1871.

Joachim Gasquet's Cézanne. Translated by Christopher Pemberton. London: Thames and Hudson, 1991.

Kaeriyama, Norimasa. "Jiko o shireriya?" [Do we know ourselves?]. *Kinema Record*, January 10, 1915, 2–3.

Kamiyama, Akira. "Eiga 'Momijigari' zengo to Dangiku igo: 'Edosodachi' to 'kosei' no aida" [Before and after the film *Maple Viewing* and after Dangiku: Between "growing up in Edo" and "personality"]. *Kabuki Kenkyū to Hihyō* 32 (2004): 5–15.

Kaneko, Tsutomu. "Shoki *Taiyō* ni miru Meiji shashin jutsu no tenkai" [The development of the photographic techniques in the Meiji period seen in the early period of *Taiyō*]. In *Zasshi Taiyō to kokumin bunka no keisei* [*Taiyō* Magazine and the formation of the national culture], edited by Suzuki Sadami, 87–112. Tokyo: Shibunkaku shuppan, 2001.

Kaneo, Tanejirō, ed. *Kawakami Otojirō Sadayakko manyūki* [The travelogue of Kawakami Otojirō and Sadayakko]. Tokyo: Kaneo bunen dō, 1901.

Kano, Ayako. *Acting Like a Woman in Modern Japan: Theater, Gender and Nationalism.* New York: Palgrave, 2001.

Karatani, Kōjin. *Origins of Modern Japanese Literature.* Edited and translated by Brett de Bary. Durham, NC: Duke University Press, 1993.

Kawaguchi, Yoko. *Butterfly's Sisters: The Geisha in Western Culture.* New Haven, CT: Yale University Press, 2010.

Keating, Patrick. "The Birth of Backlighting in the Classical Cinema." *Aura* 6 (2000): 45-56.

Kingsley, Grace. "That Splash of Saffron: Sessue Hayakawa, a Cosmopolitan Actor, Who for Reasons of Nativity, Happens to Peer from Our White Screens with Tilted Eyes." *Photoplay* 9.4 (March 1916): 139-41.

Kinoshita, Chika. *Mizoguchi Kenji ron: Eiga no bigaku to seijigaku* [On Mizoguchi Kenji: Cinema's aesthetics and politics]. Tokyo: Hōsei daigaku shuppan kyoku, 2016.

Kinoshita, Naoyuki. "Egakareta 'Meiji no Nippon': Nippon e no/Nippon kara no manazashi" [Represented 'Meiji Japan': Gazes to and from Japan], in *Eiga denrai: Cinematogurafu to "Meiji no Nippon"* [The arrival of Cinema: The Cinématographe and "Meiji Japan"], edited by Yoshida Yoshishige, Yamaguchi Masao, and Kinoshita Naoyuki, 124-88. Tokyo: Iwanami shoten, 1995.

Kishi, Fumikazu. *Edo no enkinhō: Uki-e no shikaku* [Perspective in Edo: *Uki-e*'s vision]. Tokyo: Keisō shobō, 1994.

Kobayashi, Yasuo. *Hyōshō bunka ron kōgi: Kaiga no bōken* [Lectures in cultural representations: Adventures of pictures]. Tokyo: Tokyo daigaku shuppan kai, 2016.

Koga, Futoshi. "Kamera ga toraeta Nippon: 'Meiji no Nippon' kara 'Ryumiēru eiga Nippon hen' e" [Japan that a camera captured: From "Meiji Japan" to "Lumière Japan films"]. In *Eiga denrai: Cinematogurafu to "Meiji no Nippon"* [The arrival of cinema: The Cinématographe and "Meiji Japan"], edited by Yoshida Yoshishige, Yamaguchi Masao, and Kinoshita Naoyuki, 25-43. Tokyo: Iwanami shoten, 1995.

Komatsu, Hiroshi. *Kigen no eiga* [Cinema of origin]. Tokyo: Seido sha, 1991.

Komori, Yōichi, Helen J. S. Lee, and Michele Mason. "Rule in the Name of Protection: The Japanese State, the Ainu and the Vocabulary of Colonialism." *Asia-Pacific Journal* 11, no. 8-2 (2013): 1-19.

Koyama, Noboru. *Kenburijji daigaku hizō Meiji koshashin: Mākēza gō no Nihon ryokō* [Early photographs of the Meiji era at the University of Cambridge: The journey of the marchesa in Japan]. Tokyo: Heibon sha, 2005.

Kume, Keiichirō. "Shin-Inshōha no eikyō" [The influence of postimpressionism]. *Taiyō*, June 1, 1911, 109-11.

Kurata, Yoshihiro. *Kaigai kōen kotohajime* [The beginning of overseas performance]. Tokyo: Tokyo shoseki, 1994.

Kurishima, Sumiko. "'Gubijinsō' no koro" [Days of "The Poppy"]. *Eiga Terebi Gijutsu* 238 (June 1972): 21-22.

"Kyoto Shijōgawara nōryō" [Summer evening on the Shijō River, Kyoto]. *Taiyō*, January 5, 1895, 73.

Lacambre, Geneviève. "Les milieux japonisants à Paris, 1860–1880." In *Japonisme in Art: An International Symposium*, edited by the Society for the Study of Japonisme, 43–55. Tokyo: Kodansha International, 1980.

Lacambre, Geneviève. "Pari no bijutsushō to Hayashi Tadamasa" [Art merchants in Paris and Hayashi Tadamasa]. Translated by Oki Yukiko. In *Hayashi Tadamasa: Japonisumu to bunka kōryū* [Hayashi Tadamasa: Japonisme and cultural communication], edited by Hayashi Tadamasa shimpojiumu jikkō iinkai, 163–79. Tokyo: Brücke, 2007.

LaMarre, Thomas. *The Anime Machine: A Media Theory of Animation*. Minneapolis: University of Minnesota Press, 2009.

LaMarre, Thomas. *Shadows on the Screen: Tanizaki Jun'ichirō on Cinema and "Oriental" Aesthetics*. Ann Arbor: Center for Japanese Studies, University of Michigan, 2005.

Lambourne, Lionel. *Japonisme: Cultural Crossings between Japan and the West*. London: Phaidon, 2005.

Langdale, Allan, ed. *Hugo Münsterberg on Film: A Psychological Study and Other Writings*. New York: Routledge, 2002.

Lavédrine, Bertrand, and Jean-Paul Gandolfo. *The Lumière Autochrome: History, Technology, and Preservation*. Translated by John McElhone. Los Angeles: Getty Conservation Institute, 2013.

Lenning, Arthur. *The Silent Voice: A Text*. Albany, NY: Lane, 1969.

Levine, Steven Z. "Monet, Lumière, and Cinematic Time." *Journal of Aesthetics and Art Criticism* 36. no. 4 (summer 1978): 441–47.

Looser, Thomas. "Superflat and the Layers of Image and History in 1990s Japan." *Mechademia* 1 (2006): 92–109.

The Lumière Brothers First Films. DVD. New York: Kino, 1996.

Lumière, Auguste, and Louis Lumière. "La photographie oeuvre d'art" [The photography work of art]. In *Lumières sur Lumière*, edited by Bernard Chardère, 100–105. Lyon: Institut Lumière/Presses Universitaires de Lyon, 1987.

Mabuchi, Akiko. *Japonisumu: Gensō no Nippon* [Japonisme: Imaginary Japan]. Tokyo: Brücke, 1997.

MacDonald, Margaret I. *Moving Picture World*, October 4, 1919.

Maekawa, Kumio. *Meiji ki Hokkaidō eiga shi* [The movie history of Hokkaido in the Meiji era]. Sapporo: Alice sha, 2012.

Matsumoto, Kōshirō. *Geidan issei ichidai* [Talk on arts: Once in a lifetime]. Tokyo: Ubun sha, 1948.

McDonald, Edward. *Learning Chinese, Turning Chinese: Challenges to Becoming Sinophone in a Globalised World*. New York: Routledge, 2011.

"'Meiji no Nippon' jōei kiroku" [Record of the exhibition of "Meiji Japan"]. In *Eiga denrai: Cinematogurafu to "Meiji no Nippon"* [The arrival of cinema: The Cinématographe and "Meiji Japan"], edited by Yoshida Yoshishige, Yamaguchi Masao, and Kinoshita Naoyuki, 189–90. Tokyo: Iwanami shoten, 1995.

"Miss Tsura Aoki, Japanese Actress." *Moving Picture World*, February 14, 1914, 825.

"Mistukoshi shashin bu gishichō Shibata Tsunekichi kun dan" (Interview with Shibata Tsunekichi, the chief technician of Mitsukoshi's Department of Photography). *Taiyō*, February 15, 1911, 144–45.

Mitchell, W. J. T. "Imperial Landscape." In *Landscape and Power*, edited by W. J. T. Mitchell, 5–34. Chicago: University of Chicago Press, 1994.

Mitsuda, Yuri. "Jireru to Vēru: Seikimatsu Nihon o otozureta futari no eiga gishi" [Girel and Veyre: Two cinematographers who visited Japan at the end of the century]. In *Eiga denrai: Cinematogurafu to "Meiji no Nippon"* [The arrival of cinema: The Cinématographe and "Meiji Japan"], edited by Yoshida Yoshishige, Yamaguchi Masao, and Kinoshita Naoyuki, 44–82. Tokyo: Iwanami shoten, 1995.

Miyao, Daisuke. *The Aesthetics of Shadow: Lighting and Japanese Cinema*. Durham, NC: Duke University Press, 2013.

Miyao, Daisuke. "Japonisme and the Birth of Cinema: A Transmedial and Transnational Analysis of the Lumière Brothers' Films." *Journal of Japonisme* 1, no. 1 (February 2016): 66–92.

Miyao, Daisuke. "Reviewing *Maple Viewing* (*Momijigari*, 1899)." In *The Oxford Handbook of Silent Cinema*, edited by Charlie Keil and Rob King. Oxford: Oxford University Press, forthcoming.

Miyao, Daisuke. *Sessue Hayakawa: Silent Cinema and Transnational Stardom*. Durham, NC: Duke University Press, 2007.

Miyazaki, Katsumi. "'Sukashi' to 'tōshi zuhō': Kūkan no Japonisumu shō" ["Openwork" and "linear perspective": Japonisme of the space, abstract]. In *Tankyū to hōhō: Furansu kin gendai bijutsu shi o kaibō suru: Bunken gaku, bijutsukan gyōsei kara seishin bunseki, jendā ron ikō e* [Search and method: Anatomy of modern and contemporary French art history from philology, museum politics, psychoanalysis, gender criticism, and beyond], edited by Nagai Takanori, 115–37. Kyoto: Kōyō shobō, 2014.

Mizuta, Miya Elise. "Luminous Environment: Light, Architecture and Decoration in Modern Japan." *Japan Forum* 18, no. 3 (2006): 339–60.

Morishige, Kazuo. "The Life and Times of Shimooka Renjō." In *Shimooka Renjō: A Pioneer of Japanese Photography*, edited by Mitsui Keishi and Toriumi Saki, 6–38. Tokyo: Kokusho kankō kai, 2014.

Muroran kyōkai. "Muroran kyōkai no rekishi" [The history of Muroran church]. Accessed September 14, 2017. http://catholic-m.goodplace.jp/gaiyo/index.html.

Musser, Charles. *Edison Motion Pictures 1890–1900: An Annotated Filmography*. Washington, DC: Smithsonian, 1997.

Mutobe, Akinori. "Mone 'Tsumiwara' rensaku no saikō: Mochīfu, shunkansei, koten" (Rethinking Monet's series painting *Haystacks*: Motifs, instantaneity, private exhibition). In *Furansu kindai bijutsu shi no genzai: Nyū āto hisutorī igo no shiza kara* [French modern art history now: From the post-new art history viewpoint], edited by Nagai Takanori, 163–92. Tokyo: Sangen sha, 2007.

Naruse, Fujio. "Edo kara Pari e" [From Edo to Paris]. *Kikan Geijutsu* 40 (winter 1979): 86–105.

Neade, Lynda. *The Haunted Gallery: Painting, Photography, Film c. 1900*. New Haven, CT: Yale University Press, 2007.

"Nihon eiga shi sokō 22" [Draft of the history of Japanese cinema]. *Kinema Junpō*, May 11, 1936, 81–82.

"Nihon eiga shi sokō 23." *Kinema Junpō*, May 21, 1936, 75–76.
"Nihon eiga shi sokō 43," *Kinema Junpō*, June 11, 1937, 81–84.
Nihon eiga terebi gijutsu kyōkai. "Nihon eiga gijutsu shi nenpu No. 14" [Chronology of Japanese film technology]. *Eiga Terebi Gijutsu* 236 (April 1972): 75–78.
Nihon eiga terebi gijutsu kyōkai. "Nihon eiga gijutsu shi nenpu No. 16." *Eiga Terebi Gijutsu* 238 (June 1972): 75–78.
Nihon eiga terebi gijutsu kyōkai. "Nihon eiga gijutsu shi nenpu No. 20." *Eiga Terebi Gijutsu* 242 (October 1972): 75–78.
"1900 nen Pari bankoku hakurankai jimu hōkoku 3" [Report of the Head Office for the 1900 Paris Exposition Universelle, vol. 3]. In *Meiji zenki sangyō hattatsu shi shiryō kangyō hakurankai shiryō 203* [Data of the industrial development history in the early Meiji period and data of industrial exposition, vol. 203], edited by Fujiwara Masato, 475–728. Tokyo: Meiji bunken shiryō kankō kai, 1976.
"1900 nen Pari bankoku hakurankai jimu hōkoku 4" [Report of the Head Office for the 1900 Paris Exposition Universelle, vol. 4]. In *Meiji zenki sangyō hattatsu shi shiryō kangyō hakurankai shiryō 204* [Data of the industrial development history in the early Meiji period and data of industrial exposition, vol. 204], edited by Fujiwara Masato, 728–953. Tokyo: Meiji bunken shiryō kankō kai, 1976.
Nitobe, Inazo. *Bushido: The Soul of Japan*. Tokyo: Kodansha International, 2002.
Nochlin, Linda. *The Politics of Vision: Essays on Nineteenth-Century Art and Society*. New York: Harper and Row, 1989.
O'Brien, Sophie. "The Lessons of the Colonial Exhibition in Paris. I. The Missionaries." *Irish Monthly* 59 (October 1931): 634–38.
Ōhashi, Shintarō. "*Taiyō* no hakkan" [Publication of *Taiyō*]. *Taiyō*, January 5, 1895, 1–2.
Okabe, Ryū. "Amerika jidai no Henrī Kotani" [Henry Kotani, American period]. *Eigashi Kenkyū* 2 (1973): 15–29.
Okajima, Hisashi. "Japan's Case: Hopeful or Hopeless?" *Bulletin FIAF* 45 (1992): 2–4.
Ōshima, Seiji. *Japonisumu: Inshō-ha to ukiyo-e no shūhen* [Japonisme: On impressionism and ukiyo-e]. Tokyo: Bijutsu kōron sha, 1980.
Ōtsuka, Shirō, Sugiura Rokuemon, Sugiura Sennosuke, Sugiura Sōjirō, Aoji Chūzō, Nakamura Masatoshi, Tamura Yukihiko, and Seiji Mizumachi. "Yonjūnen mae no satsueiki to satsuei o kiku zadankai" [A round-table talk about the camera and cinematography of forty years ago]. *Kinema Junpō*, January 1, 1940, 148–52.
Owada, Shigeru. "Henshū shukan Ukita Kazutami no ichi" [Ukita Kazutami's position as the editor in chief]. In *Zasshi* Taiyō *to kokumin bunka no keisei* [*Taiyō* Magazine and the formation of the national culture], edited by Suzuki Sadami, 193–221. Tokyo: Shibunkaku shuppan, 2001.
Ozawa, Takeshi. *Bakumatsu Meiji no shashin* [Photography in the final years of the Edo period and the Meiji period]. Tokyo: Chikuma shobō, 1997.
Panofsky, Erwin. "Style and Medium in the Motion Pictures." In *The Visual Turn: Classical Film Theory and Art History*, edited by Angela Dalle Vacche, 69–84. New Brunswick, NJ: Rutgers University Press, 2003.
Rancière, Jacques. "L'historicité du cinéma." In *De l'histoire au cinéma*, edited by Antoine de Baecque and Christian Delage, 45–60. Bruxelles: Éditions Complexe, 1998.

Reed, Warren. "The Tradition Wreckers: Two People Who Became Famous, though Few People without Almond Eyes Can Pronounce Their Names." *Picture-Play*, March 1917.

Renan, Ary. "Hokusai's 'Man-gwa' (Concluded)." *Artistic Japan* 2, no. 9 (January 1889): 99–100.

Rittaud-Hutinet, Jacques. *Auguste et Louis Lumière: Les 1000 Premiers Films*. Paris: Philippe Sers Éditeur, 1990.

Rittaud-Hutinet, Jacques, ed. *Letters: Auguste and Louis Lumière*. Translated by Pierre Hodgson. London: Faber and Faber, 1995.

Ross, Sara. "The Americanization of Tsuru Aoki: Orientalism, Melodrama, Star Image, and the New Woman." *Camera Obscura* 20, no. 3 (2005): 129–58.

Sadoul, Georges. *Histoire du cinéma mondial: des origines à nos jours*. 1949. Reprint. Paris: Flammarion, 1972.

Sadoul, Georges. "Louis Lumière: The Last Interview." In *Film Makers on Film Making: Statements on Their Art by Thirty Directors*, edited by Harry M. Geduld, 19–25. Bloomington: Indiana University Press, 1967.

Saeki, Junko. "'Geisha' no hakken: 'Tasha' ka sareru Nippon" [Discovering geisha: Japan that is turned into the Other]. In *Bijutsu shi to tasha* [Art history and the Other], edited by Shimamoto Kan and Kasuya Makoto, 117–52. Kyoto: Kōyō shobō, 2000.

Said, Edward. *Orientalism*. New York: Pantheon, 1978.

Saitō, Takio. *Bakumatsu Meiji Yokohama shashinkan monogatari* [A story of Yokohama photographs at the end of the Tokugawa era and the Meiji period]. Tokyo: Yoshikawa kōbunkan, 2004.

Sasō, Tsutomu. *1923 Mizoguchi Kenji Chi to rei* [1923 Mizoguchi Kenji Blood and Soul]. Tokyo: Chikuma shobō, 1991.

Satō, Morihiro. "'Ōrudo Japan' no hyōshō: Yokohama shashin to 19 seiki kōhan no shikaku bunka" [Representations of "old Japan": Yokohama photographs and the visual culture of the late nineteenth century]. *Eizōgaku/Iconics* 71 (2003): 69–86.

Satō, Morihiro. *Topografi no Nihon kindai: Edo doroe, Yokohama shashin, geijutsu shasin* [Topography and Japanese modernity: Edo mud paintings, Yokohama photographs, art photography]. Tokyo: Seikyū sha, 2011.

Savada, Elias, comp. *The American Film Institute Catalog of Motion Pictures Produced in the United States: Film Beginnings, 1893–1910*. Metuchen, NJ: Scarecrow, 1995.

Scharf, Aaron. *Art and Photography*. London: Allen Lane, 1968.

Seguin, Jean-Claude. *Alexandre Promio ou les énigmes de la Lumière*. Paris: Éditions L'Harmattan, 1999.

"Shashin jutsu ōyō no hattatsu" [The development of how to apply the technology of photography]. *Taiyō*, January 5, 1895, 185–86.

Shaviro, Steven. *The Cinematic Body*. Minneapolis: University of Minnesota Press, 1993.

Shibata, Tamaki. "Joyū ni tsukite" [To be an actress]. Translated by Mari Yoshihara. *Chūō Kōron*, December 1911, 100.

Shibata, Tsunekichi. "Amida Minegashira Hōkō Funbo" [The tomb of Taikō and the Ceremonies]. *Taiyō*, May 20, 1898.

Shibata, Tsunekichi. "Bōen renzu nite satsuei seshi yuki no Fuji" [The snow-clad Fuji sketched by a telephoto]. *Taiyō*, May 1, 1905, n.p.

Shibata, Tsunekichi. "Fujisan chōbō" [View of Mt. Fuji]. *Taiyō*, April 5, 1898, n.p.
Shibata, Tsunekichi. "Gotenba yori nozomu yuki no Fujisan [Snow-clad Fuji from Gotenba]. *Taiyō*, August 20, 1898, n.p.
Shibata, Tsunekichi. "Hachigatsu nijūsan nichi yoru no denkō" [The lightning in the stormy night of August 23]. *Taiyō*, September 5, 1898, n.p.
Shibata, Tsunekichi. "Hōtaikō mokuzō" [The wooden sculpture of Hōtaikō, and his tomb in Kōtaiji]. *Taiyō*, May 20, 1898, n.p.
Shibata, Tsunekichi. "Kenshō shashin no shinsa" [Evaluation of the contest photos]. *Taiyō*, March 1, 1905, 160.
Shibata, Tsunekichi. "Ōzutsu oyobi Hitachiyama no torikumi" [Wrestling of Hitachiyama and Ōzutsu]. *Taiyō*, February 5, 1902, n.p.
Shibata, Tsunekichi. "Suishōsekai (Honnen ichigatsu yōka no asageshiki)" [The crystal world: The morning view on January 8 of this year]. *Taiyō*, February 5, 1902, n.p.
Shibata, Tsunekichi. "Suruga Gotenba no yuki no Fujisan" [Winter view of Mt. Fuji from Gotemba, Suruga]. *Taiyō*, September 5, 1898, n.p.
Shibata, Tsunekichi. "Yuki no Fuji" [Snowy Fuji]. *Taiyō*, April 1, 1905, n.p.
Shiff, Richard. *Cézanne and the End of Impressionism: A Study of the Theory, Technique, and Critical Evaluation of Modern Art*. Chicago: University of Chicago Press, 1984.
Shiff, Richard. "Constructing Physicality." *Art Journal* 50 (spring 1991): 42–47.
Shigeno, Yukiyoshi. "Beikoku dewa Nihongeki ga donnna kankyō de torareruka" [Why films about Japan were made in the US]. *Katsudō Kurabu*, February 1920, 26–29.
Shimizu, Isao. *Bigō no 150 nen: Ishoku Furansu jin gaka to Nippon* [Bigot's 150 years: Unique French artist and Japan]. Tokyo: Rinsen shoten, 2011.
Shimizu, Isao. *Bigō o yomu: Meiji rearisumu hanga 200 ten no sekai* [Reading Bigot: The world of 200 realist prints of the Meiji era]. Tokyo: Rinsen shoten, 2014.
Smith II, Henry D. "'He Frames a Shot!': Cinematic Vision in Hiroshige's One Hundred Famous Views of Edo." *Orientations* 31, no. 3 (March 2000): 90–96.
Snyder, Joel. "Visualization and Visibility." In *Picturing Science, Producing Art*, edited by Caroline A. Jones and Peter Galison, 379–97. New York: Routledge, 1998.
Sobchack, Vivian. *The Address of the Eye: A Phenomenology of Film Experience*. Princeton, NJ: Princeton University Press, 1992.
Souriau, Paul. *The Aesthetics of Movement*. Translated and edited by Manon Souriau. Amherst: University of Massachusetts Press, 1983.
Spate, Virginia, and David Bromfield. "A New and Strange Beauty: Monet and Japanese Art." In *Monet & Japan*, edited by Pauline Green, 1–63. Canberra: National Gallery of Australia, 2001.
Spivak, Gayatri Chakravorty. *Outside in the Teaching Machine*. New York: Routledge, 1993.
Spivak, Gayatri Chakravorty. "Subaltern Studies: Deconstructing Historiography." In *Selected Subaltern Studies*, edited by Ranajit Guha and Gayatri Chakravorty Spivak, 3–32. Oxford: Oxford University Press, 1988.
Stucky, Charles F. "Monet's Art and the Act of Vision." In *Aspects of Monet: A Symposium on the Artist's Life and Times*, edited by John Rewald and Frances Weitzenhoffer, 107–21. New York: Abrams, 1984.

Suzuki, Sadami. "Meiji ki *Taiyō* no enkaku, oyobi ichi" [The history and the position of *Taiyō* in the Meiji era]. In *Zasshi* Taiyō *to kokumin bunka no keisei* [*Taiyō* Magazine and the formation of the national culture], edited by Suzuki Sadami, 3–39. Tokyo: Shibunkaku shuppan, 2001.

Suzuki, Yō. "Shinsetsu na Hayakawa Sesshū to Tsuruko fujin" [Kind Sessue Hayakawa and Mrs. Tsuruko]. In *Sesshū*, edited by Kōda Honami, 16–20. Tokyo: Shin jidai sha, 1922.

Takanashi, Kōji. *Inabata Katsutarō kun den* [Biography of Mr. Inabata Katsutarō]. Osaka: Inabata Katsutarō ō kiju kinen denki hensan kai, 1938.

Takashina, Shūji. *Zōho Nihon bijutsu o miru me: Higashi to nishi no deai* [The eyes that look at Japanese art: The encounter between East and West, expanded edition]. Tokyo: Iwanami shoten, 2009.

Tamaki, Junichirō. *Nihon eiga seisui ki* [Record of the adolescence of Japanese cinema]. 1938. Reprint, Tokyo: Yumani shobō, 2006.

Tamura, Chiho. "Eiga joyū no tanjō: Aruiwa Nana no monogatari" [The emergence of female motion picture actors, or a story of Nana]. In *Nihon eiga wa ikiteiru dai 5 kan: Kantoku to haiyū no bigaku* [Japanese cinema is alive, vol. 5: The aesthetics of directors and actors], edited by Kurosawa Kiyoshi, Yomota Inuhiko, Yoshimi Shunya, and Ri Bonu, 174–81. Tokyo: Iwanami shoten, 2010.

Tanaka, Junichirō. *Katsudō shashin ga yattekita* [Moving photography has arrived]. Tokyo: Chūō kōron sha, 1985.

Tanaka, Junichirō. *Nihon eiga hattatsu shi I: Katsudō shashin jidai* [The history of the development of Japanese cinema I: The period of moving photography]. Tokyo: Chūō kōron sha, 1975.

Tanaka, Junichirō. *Nihon eiga shi hakkutsu* [Excavating Japanese film history]. Tokyo: Tōju sha, 1980.

Tanaka, Junichirō. *Nihon eigashi I* [Japanese film history I]. Tokyo: Saitō shoten, 1948.

Tanaka, Junichirō. "Satsuei gishu, Shibata Tsunekichi" [Cinematographer Shibata Tsunekichi]. *Eiga Gijutsu* 4, no. 6 (December 1942): 56–60.

Tanaka, Junichirō. "'Yunyū kamera dai 1 gō' kō" [Thought on the "first imported camera"]. *Eiga Terebi Gijutsu* 220 (December 1970): 83–85.

Tanaka, Stefan. *Japan's Orient: Rendering Pasts into History*. Berkeley: University of California Press, 1993.

Tanizaki, Jun'ichirō. *In Praise of Shadows*. Translated by Thomas J. Harper and Edward G. Seidensticker. London: Vintage, 2001.

Tanke, Joseph J. *Jacques Rancière: An Introduction*. London: Continuum, 2011.

Tano, Yasunori. "Pari bankokuhakurankai to Nihon bijutsu" [Paris Exposition Universelle and Japanese art]. In *Nippon bijutsuin hyakunenshi*, 2 kan jō (zuhan hen) [One-hundred-year history of Nippon bijutsuin, vol. 2-1 (graphics)], edited by Nippon bijutsuin hyakunenshi henshūshitsu, 435–59. Tokyo: Nippon bijutsuin, 1990.

Terada, Shirō. "Teisō no kuni no onna Ochō fujin" [Cio-Cio-San, the woman from a faithful country]. *Fujin Kōron*, April 1921, 66–70.

Tosi, Virgilio. *Cinema before Cinema: The Origins of Scientific Cinematography*. Translated by Sergio Angelini. London: British Universities Film and Video Council, 2005.

Toulet, Emmanuelle. "Cinema at the Universal Exposition, Paris, 1900." Translated by Tom Gunning. *Persistence of Vision* 9 (1991): 10-36.
Tsivian, Yuri. "Two 'Stylists' of the Teens: Franz Hofer and Yevgenii Bauer." In *A Second Life: German Cinema's First Decades*, edited by Thomas Elsaesser and Michael Wedel, 264-76. Amsterdam: Amsterdam University Press, 1996.
Tsubotani, Zenshirō. *Hakubunkan gojūnen shi* [The fifty-year history of Hakubunkan]. Tokyo: Hakubunkan, 1937.
Tsubouchi, Yūzō. "Henshusha Ōhashi Otowa" [Editor Ōhashi Otowa]. In *Zasshi Taiyō to kokumin bunka no keisei* [*Taiyō* Magazine and the formation of the national culture], edited by Suzuki Sadami, 153-67. Tokyo: Shibunkaku shuppan, 2001.
Tsuda, Kōzō. "Kurishima-gata to Satsuki-gata" [Kurishima-type and Satsuki-type]. *Kamata*, November 1924, 20-22.
Tsukada, Yoshinobu. *Eiga Shiryō Hakkutsu* 18 (July 15, 1975): 1.
Tsukada, Yoshinobu. "Jurēru to 'Meiji no Nippon' o megutte" [On Girel and "Meiji Japan"]. *Eiga Shiryō Hakkutsu* 10 (June 15, 1973): 245-63.
Tsukada, Yoshinobu. "Jurēru to 'Meiji no Nippon' o megutte sono 2" [On Girel and "Meiji Japan," part 2]. *Eiga Shiryō Hakkutsu* 13 (December 1973): 285-92.
Tsukada, Yoshinobu. *Nihon eiga shi no kenkyū: Katsudō shashin torai zengo no jijō* [A study of Japanese film history: Facts around the time when motion pictures arrived]. Tokyo: Gendai shokan, 1980.
Tumbull, Stephen R. *Japan's Hidden Christians, 1549-1999*. Vol. 1, *Open Christianity in Japan, 1549-1639*. Surrey, UK: Curzon, 2000.
Uchibayashi, Shun. *Kaiga ni kogareta shashin: Nihon shashin shi ni okeru pikutoriarizumu no seiritsu* [The photography that longs for the painting: The emergence of pictorialism in the history of Japanese photography]. Tokyo: Shinwa sha, 2015.
Ueda, Manabu. *Nihon eiga sōsō ki no kōgyō to kankyaku: Tokyo to Kyoto o chūshin ni* [The exhibition and audience during the early period of Japanese cinema: In Tokyo and Kyoto]. Tokyo: Waseda daigaku shuppan bu, 2012.
Ukai, Atsuko. "The History of Japonisme as a Global Study." In *Translation, History and Arts: New Horizons in Asian Interdisciplinary Humanities Research*, edited by Ji Meng and Atsuko Ukai, 70-84. Newcastle upon Tyne, UK: Cambridge Scholars Publishing, 2013.
Usui, Michiko. "Engeki Hakubutsukan korekushon ni miru, Nihon eizō shi no genryū" [The origin of the history of moving images in Japan seen in the Tsubouchi Memorial Theater Library collection]. *Yomiuri Online*. Accessed December 29, 2016. http://www.yomiuri.co.jp/adv/wol/culture/080711.html.
Vacche, Angela Dalle. "Cezanne and the Lumière Brothers." In *Film, Art, New Media: Museum Without Walls?*, edited by Angela Dalle Vacche, 39-56. London: Palgrave Macmillan, 2012.
Vacche, Angela Dalle. "The Difference of Cinema in the System of the Arts." In *Opening Bazin: Postwar Film Theory and Its Afterlife*, edited by Dudley Andrew with Hervé Joubert-Laurencin, 142-52. New York: Oxford University Press, 2011.
Vaughan, Dai. *For Documentary*. Berkeley: University of California Press, 1999.
Veyre, Gabriel. *Opérateur Lumière: autour du monde avec le Cinématographe correspondance (1896-1900)*. Lyon: Institut Lumière/Actes Sud, 1996.

Waller, Gregory. "Historicizing, a Test Case: Japan on American Screens, 1909–1915." Unpublished manuscript obtained from Sumiko Higashi.

Weisberg, Gabriel P. *Japonisme: Japanese Influence on French Art 1840–1910*. Cleveland: Cleveland Museum of Art, 1975.

"Western-Style 'Hokusai' Artworks Found." *Yomiuri Shimbun*, October 23, 2016. Accessed October 24, 2016. https://article.wn.com/view/2016/10/23/Westernstyle_Hokusai_artworks_found.

Wichmann, Siegfried. *Japonisme: The Japanese Influence on Western Art in the 19th and 20th Centuries*. New York: Harmony, 1981.

Williams, Alan. "The Lumière Organization and 'Documentary Realism.'" In *Film before Griffith*, edited by John L. Fell, 153–61. Berkeley: University of California Press, 1983.

Winter, O. "The Cinematograph." *New Review*, May 1896, 507–13. Accessed November 13, 2017. http://picturegoing.com/?p=4166.

Yokohama kaikō shiryōkan, ed. *Saishoku arubamu Meiji no Nippon: "Yokohama shashin" no sekai* [Colored album Japan in the Meiji era: The world of "Yokohama photographs"]. Yokohama: Yūrindō, 1990.

Yokoyama, Akio. "Mone to Nihonshumi sono ichi sokumen: Ra Japonēzu no ishō kara mieru mono" [A Thought on Monet and Japonisme: What We Can See in the Costume of *La Japonaise*]. *Bijutsushi Ronshū* 12 (2012): 127–39.

Yoshihara, Mari. *Embracing the East: White Women and American Orientalism*. New York: Oxford University Press, 2003.

Yoshihara, Mari. "The Flight of the Japanese Butterfly: Orientalism, Nationalism, and Performance of Japanese Womanhood." *American Quarterly* 56, no. 4 (December 2004): 975–1001.

Yoshimoto, Mitsuhiro. *Kurosawa: Film Studies and Japanese Cinema*. Durham, NC: Duke University Press, 2000.

INDEX

Page numbers followed by f indicate illustrations. Film titles in brackets are translations. Film titles in parentheses are English-language releases.

Abel, Richard, 31–32, 179n29
Acteurs japonais: bataille au sabre [Japanese actors: Battle with the sword] (film, 1897), 69f, 70, 166n70
Acteurs japonais: exercise de la perruque [Japanese actors: Exercise of the wig] (film, 1897), 69, 90, 112
actualité. *See* actuality film
actuality film, 1–3, 17–18, 33, 48, 60. *See also* realism
aesthetic, 5, 7–9, 22, 33–39, 48, 81, 84, 154n80, 178n13
The Aesthetics of Shadow: Lighting and Japanese Cinema (Miyao), 8–9
Ainos at Yeso, I. *See Les Aïnos à Yeso, I*
Ainos at Yeso, II. *See Les Aïnos à Yeso, II*
Ainu, 6, 72–77, 90, 165n47
Akita ranga, 25–26
Allan, Michael, 46
America, 14–15, 17, 104, 117, 129–44, 178n13–14. *See also* Hollywood
American Academy of Dramatic Arts, 177n8
The American Film Institute Catalog 1893–1910, 178n14
Andersen, Hermann, 84–85
Andrew, Dudley, 37–38
anthropology, 73–78, 81, 84. *See also* Ainu; salvage paradigm
Antoine Lumière and Sons, 17
Aoki, Toshio, 129
Aoki, Tsuruko, 14, 129–44
Après le lancement: sortie des invités et du public [After the launch: The guests and the audience leave] (film, 1899), 160n137
archetype, 63–68, 81, 117–19, 131–32, 141
architecture, 63–68, 111, 117, 173n33
Arrival of a Train. *See Arrivée d'un train*
Arrival of a Train at La Ciotat. *See L'Arrivée d'un train à La Ciotat*
Arrivée d'un train (*Arrival of a Train*) (film, 1897), 70
art: cinematographic, 48–49; impressionist, 28–30; Japanese, 3–15, 34, 78, 103–4, 123–24, 129; photography as, 2. *See also* impressionism; painting; postimpressionism; Renaissance
Artistic Japan (magazine), 4, 150n31
Asakusa kōen [Asakusa park] (film), 125
Asano, Shirō, 102, 108, 113–14, 170n9, 172n27, 172n30
assimilation, 73–77
à travers: kinzō-gata-kōzu/chūkei-datsuraku/en=kin-hō composition and, 24–28, 39–57; in painting, 28–30; physiology and, 30–39; realism and, 11–23. *See also kinzō-gata-kōzu/chūkei-datsuraku/en=kin-hō*; panorama
attention, 30–31, 158n131
Aumont, Jacques, 31
Aurientis, Father P., 72
authenticity, 66, 70, 76–88, 95–96, 130–43, 167n77, 173n33. *See also* staging
automatism, 36–39
Avant l'inauguration: Arrivée des souverains [Before the inauguration: Arrival of the Sovereigns] (film, 1896), 50, 50f, 51

Index

Bad Weather on the Sea. See *Gros temps en mer*
Baignade en mer (Swimming in the Sea) (film, 1895), 113
The bailiff's stunned face. See *Shittatsuri no akiregao*
Ballet: *"Le carnaval de Venise," II* [Ballet: "The carnival of Venice, II"] (film, 1897), 156n91
The Banks of the Seine. See *Le Printemps a travers les branches*
Bao, Weihong, 14
Barker, Reginald, 130
Barthes, Roland, 10–11
Batchelor, John, 164n41
Bauer, Yevgenii, 146n18
Baxter & Wray, 102
Bazin, André, 36–39, 162n14, 179n29
Beato, Felice, 80, 168n101
The Beckoning Flame (film, 1916), 132
Belloï, Livio, 95–96
Berger, Klaus, 4, 23, 154n71
Berlin: Hallesches Thor (film, 1896), 160n140
Berlioz, Alexandre, 72–73, 164n41
Bernardi, Joanne, 138
Bernhardt, Sarah, 128
Bertellini, Giorgio, 64
Bey, Hamdi Osman, 61
Bigot, Georges, 80, 88, 167n74
Bing, Samuel, 4
"Black Mt. Fuji." See "Kuro Fuji"
blocking, 40–43, 46, 50, 55, 156n106, 161n143
"Bōen renzu nite satsuei seshi yuki no Fuji" [Snow-clad Fuji sketched by a telephoto] (photograph) (Shibata), 118–19, 121f
Boulevard des Capucines (Monet, 1873), 23, 151n34
Bracquemond, Félix Henri, 4
Bromfield, David, 28
Brown, Pat, 178n13
Bryson, Norman, 29, 61, 147n32
bunmei kaika (civilization and enlightenment), 117

Burch, Noël, 18, 31, 33
Burty, Philippe, 3
Bushido: The Soul of Japan (book) (Nitobe, 1900), 172n33
Buyū gi Genji: Momijiga, Taira no Koremochi [Brave Genji: Celebrating maple, Taira no Koremochi] (Kuniyoshi) (painting), 104

Cahiers du cinéma (magazine), 39
camera obscura, 20, 153n70
Camille Monet in Japanese Costume. See *La Japonaise*
capitalism, 9, 13, 97, 156n103, 173n33
Card Game. See *Partie d'ecarte*
The Card Players (Cézanne), 9
Centennial Exhibition of 1876 in Philadelphia, 129
Cézanne, Paul, 9–11, 28–31, 34, 154n71, 154n73
Chahine, Yossef, 47
Champs-Elysées (Manet), 9
Chanteuse japonais [Japanese singer] (film, 1898–99), 92–97, 113
The Cheat (film, 1915), 132
cherry blossoms, 66–68, 164n35
Christianity, 131–32, 164n41. See also religion
chronopotography, 32–33
chūkei-datsuraku. See *kinzō-gata-kōzu/chūkei-datsuraku/en=kin-hō*
Chūō Kōron (magazine), 137
Chutes du Rhin vues de près [Rhine Falls seen from close up] (film, 1896), 51, 51f
Cinématographe Géant, 127
Cinématographe Lumière, 2, 17–22, 32, 48, 60, 89–90, 108, 145n1, 155n86, 160n140, 162n4, 162n6
cinematographer-beholder, 34, 39, 149n22
Cinéthique (magazine), 39
close-up, 24, 51, 138–42, 160n137, 179n29
colonization, 8, 63–64, 74–76, 116–17, 131
The Colorist (book) (Hatt, 1908), 155n91

Comolli, Jean-Louis, 39
composition: depth, 4, 18–21, 34, 113, 160n140; *kinzō-gata-kōzu/chūkei-datsuraku/en=kin-hō*, 26, 39–56, 66–67, 84, 112, 119, 128, 134–35, 148n3, 152n52, 158n126, 160n137, 160n141, 161n143; of Lumière street films, 70, 151n34; pictorial, 13, 78–80; ukiyo-e, 10–12, 24, 57–60, 68, 72, 81–83, 122. *See also* ukiyo-e
Concours de Boules [Balls competition] (film, 1896), 52, 53f, 54
"Constant Girel: Mes deux esclaves et mon interprête à Kyoto" [Constant Girel: My two servants and my interpreter in Kyoto] (photograph) (Girel), 87, 87f
contingency, 33, 93. *See also* reality
contrast, 11–12, 17–22, 34, 39–40, 56, 60, 72, 79, 111–13, 134, 145n6, 161nn143–44
Corot, Jean-Baptiste-Camille, 27–28, 153n58
corporeality, 22–32, 57, 149n8
Cortège arabe [Arab parade] (film, 1896), 47–48, 48f
Courbet, Gustave, 22, 149n22
Crary, Jonathan, 10, 20, 29–30, 153n70
The Cuckoo. See *Hototogisu*
Curiassiers: en fourrageurs. [Cuirassiers: As foragers (load)] (film, 1896), 160n140

Daguerre, Louis-Jaques-Mandé, 20
daguerreotype, 20–21
dance, 69–83, 93–100, 112, 128, 143. *See also* Kabuki
Danceuses: la danse des éventails [Dancers: The dance of fans] (film, 1897), 70
Danjurō, Ichikawa, IX, 6, 14, 99, 102, 123–25, 176n58
Danse japonaise: I. Kappore [Japanese dance: I. Kappore] (film, 1898–99), 81, 82f, 113
Danse japonaise: II. Harusame [Japanese dance: II. Spring rain] (film, 1898–99), 93, 93f, 95, 113

Danse japonaise: III. Geishas en jinrikisha [Japanese dance: III. Geishas on a rickshaw] (film, 1898–99), 81, 83f
Danse japonaise: IV. Jinku [Japanese dance: IV. Lively dance] (1898–99), 93–94, 94f, 95, 113
Danse japonaise: V. Gocho Garama [Japanese dance: V. Gocho Garama] (film, 1898–99), 81, 82f, 113
Danseuses japonaises (Japanese Dancers) (film, 1897), 69, 81, 166n70
"Dans la Tour" [In the tower] (lithograph) (Rivière), 3f
Déchargement dans un port [Unloading at a port] (film, 1897), 70
Degas, Edgar, 23
Delluc, Louis, 179n29
Delsarte, François, 177n8
DeMille, Cecil B., 132, 141
Départ d'un bateau sur la Tamise [Departure of a boat on the Thames] (film 1897), 158n126
depth, 4–5, 18–21, 39, 54–55, 152n47, 157n109, 159n133; of field, 39
Des glaneuses (The Gleaners) (painting) (Millet), 78–79
dessin, 23, 150n26, 150n29
Deutelbaum, Marshall, 1
"The Development of How to Apply the Technology of Photography" (report), 115–16
dialogue, 7–9, 11, 15, 57, 61, 81–97, 103, 112, 125, 167n74. *See also* negotiation; smile
Dîner japonais [Japanese dinner] (film, 1897), 88–93, 113
Dixon, Laurinda S., 152n50
Doane, Mary Ann, 21, 33
documentary, 48, 60, 63–64, 70, 83–85. *See also* actuality film; realism
Domestic Industrial Exposition, 123
double bind, 13, 30, 125
Doublier, Francis, 158n131
The Dragon Painter (film, 1919), 132–34, 134–35f, 143

Duel au pistol (longueur: 12 mètres) [Duel with pistol (Length: 12 meters)] (film, 1896), 54, 54f, 55
Duret, Théodore, 23

the East, 6–7, 15, 80, 85, 131. *See also* Orientalism
Eastman Kodak, 17
Edison Kinetoscope, 32, 169n110
editing, 33, 44, 158n131
Edo period, 80, 104, 113
"Église d'une Mission Étrangère" [Church of Foreign Missions] (photograph), 66, 66f
Eiffel Tower, 1, 4, 34, 36
1899 film exhibition flyer by Sossen Nihon katsadō shashin kai, 112f, 113
Elsaesser, Thomas, 5, 15
Enjoying the Evening Cool near Ryogoku Bridge. See *Ryōgoku bashi yūsuzumi uki-e* (Okumura), 25f
en=kin-hō. See *kinzō-gata-kōzu/chūkei-datsuraku/en=kin-hō*
enlightenment, 64–72, 78, 131, 174n34
the Enlightenment, 20
Epstein, Jean, 179n29
Escrime au sabre japonais [Fencing with a Japanese saber] (film, 1897), 70
Espagne: courses de taureaux, II [Spain: Bull races, II] (film, 1897), 158n131
essentialism, 15, 62
Estocade, I (film, 1899), 158n131
ethnography, 73–74, 84, 116. *See also* Ainu; Orientalism
Europe: film export to, 102–13, 123, 125, 150n29; Japonisme in, 3–5, 119, 129, 152n50; Orientalist gaze of, 6–7, 11–14, 60–63, 74–77, 95, 113–17, 128. *See also* Orientalism
"Evaluation of the Contest Photos" (report), 116
exoticism, 11–13, 60–62, 70, 77, 90–92, 97, 108–19, 136, 173n33, 177n8. *See also* Orientalism

Expérience du ballon dirigeable de M. Santos-Dumont: I. Sortie du ballon [Mr. Santos-Dumont's airship experience: Balloon exit, 1900] (film, 1900), 158n126
export, 102–3, 123–29, 138, 144, 171n18
Exposition Nationale in Geneva, 47
Exposition Universelle, 1–4, 23, 45, 99, 103, 112, 125–29, 136
exterior, 11, 20–21, 24, 113
eye, 8, 10, 22, 28–50, 56, 84, 154n70, 155n91. *See also* corporeality; physiology; vision

Family Meal. See *Repas en famille*
fantasy. See Orientalism
The Far East (magazine), 86, 167n76
Farrar, Geraldine, 130
Faust: apparition de Méphistophélès [Faust: Appearance of Mephistopheles] (film, 1897), 159n133
Faust: metamorphose de Faust [Faust: Metamorphosis of Faust] (film, 1897), 159n133
Felicetti, Francisco, 160n137
femininity, 129–44. *See also* women
Fenollosa, Ernest, 132
Fenollosa, Mary McNeil, 132
Ferris Wheel. See *Grande Roue*
Fifth Domestic Industrial Exposition, 123
film: actuality, 1–3, 11–12, 17–23, 60, 164n40, 167n77, 179n9; à travers effect in, 11, 30–59, 161n142–44; Hollywood, 127–39, 178n14; Japanese, 13–14, 99–103, 113, 125, 138, 144; Japonism in, 4–7; narrative, 33–38, 130–32, 176n59; physiology of, 24–32, 155n85, 155n91; staged, 63–64, 68–70, 79–88. *See also* actuality film; Hollywood; the Lumière Company; staging
First Sino-Japanese War, 115–17
Fontainebleau (painting) (Cézanne), 30
Foucault, Michel, 7
Freedom and People's Rights Movement, 139
Fried, Michael, 149n22

Fugaku Sanjūrokkei (*Thirty-Six Views of Mt. Fuji*) (prints) (Hokusai), 4, 41f, 119, 122, 123f
Fujikan Theater, 125
Fujiki, Hideaki, 139, 141, 143
Fujin Kōron (magazine), 136
"Fujisan chōbō" [View of Mt. Fuji] (photograph) (Shibata), 118, 118f
fukoku kyōhei (wealth and military strength of a country), 117
Fuller, Loie, 128
Fushigi no kagami [The mysterious mirror] (film), 124
Futari Shizuka [The quiet pair] (film, 1917), 139

Ganjiō I, 69, 91, 112, 176n58
Gama no yōjutsu [The toad's witchcraft] (film), 124
Gartland, Luke, 74–76, 84
Gaudreault, André, 5, 145n4
gaze: foreign, 7, 12–14, 61, 63, 91–97, 103, 113–17, 124–26, 136–37, 144; returning, 112, 168n101; spectatorial, 28–31, 36, 43–44, 168n99. *See also* dialogue; Orientalism; smile
geisha, 12, 14, 63–69, 77–83, 92–97, 113, 124–29, 167n74, 167n77, 169n110, 170n9, 172n30
The Geisha (Jones, 1896) (film), 80
The Geisha and the Knight. See *La Geisha et le Chevalier*
Geisha no odori [Geisha's dance] (film), 125
Geisha no teodori [Geisha's dance] (film, 1897), 113
gender, 129–44
Gerow, Aaron, 117, 138, 171n18
Gifu no hanagasa seizō [Flower-umbrella making in Gifu] (film), 125
Gilbert and Sullivan, 80
Girel, Constant, 11, 50–51, 59–78, 83–90, 108, 128, 160n139, 161n142, 162n4, 163n19, 163n29, 163n31, 164n35–36, 166n70. *See also* Yokohama photographs

The Gleaners. See *Des glaneuses*
The Glory of Life. See *Sei no kagayaki*
Godard, Jean-Luc, 9
Gonzalez, Myrtle, 139, 143
"Gotenba yori nozomu yuki no Fujisan" [Snow-clad Fuji from Gotenba] (photograph) (Shibata), 118–19, 119f
Gozen-Meal Time (photograph), 86
Grand Café, 32, 48, 127
Grande roue (*Ferris Wheel*) (film, 1896), 159n133
Grau, Oliver, 20
"The Great Wave off Kanagawa." See "Kanagawa oki nami ura"
Gros temps en mer (*Bad Weather on the Sea*) (Lumière), 40–41, 41f, 42
"Groupe de geishas prenant le thé" [Group of geishas having tea] (photograph), 65f, 163n31
Gubijinsō [The poppy] (film, 1921), 141, 142f
Guillemard, Francis Henry Hill, 163n32
Guimet, Émile, 80
Gunning, Tom, 32, 38, 135n6, 155n85

"Hachigatsu nijūsan nichi yoru no denkō" [The lightning in the stormy night of August 23] (Shibata), 122, 122f
Hakubunkan Publishing Company, 115–16, 175n42
Hall, Stuart, 8
Hammond, Anne, 156n91
Hanayagi, Harumi, 138
Handbook of Physiological Optics (Helmholtz), 155n91
Harootunian, Harry, 13, 173n33
Harvesting rice. See *Recolte du riz*
Hase, Masato, 21
Hasumi, Shigehiko, 164n40
"Hataraku nōmin" [A working farmer] (photograph), 167n74
Hatt, Arthur J., 155n91
Haworth Pictures Corporation, 134, 179n29
Hayakawa, Sessue, 9, 129–37, 179n29

Hayashi, Chōjirō, 9
Hayashi, Michio, 30
Haystacks (Monet), 24
The Heart of Youth (film, 1919), 141
heliography, 20
Helmholtz, Hermann von, 29, 153n70, 155n91
high-angle shot, 134, 151n34
Hiromeya, 102
Hiroshige, 5, 24, 26, 34, 35f, 122, 152n52
Hofer, Franz, 146n18
Hokkaido, 6, 60, 72–77. *See also* Ainu
Hokkaido Former Natives Protection Law, 73, 75
Hokkaido kyūdojin hogo hō, 73, 75
Hokusai, 4–5, 23–24, 26, 34, 119, 122
Hollywood, 14–15, 129–44, 179n29
Hototogisu [Cuckoo] (film, 1922), 142
Humbert, Aimé, 80, 86

Iampolski, Mikhail, 153n70
Ichikawa, Danjurō IX, 6, 14, 99, 102, 123–25, 176n58
Ichikawa, Sadanji I, 70
Ikeda, Gishin, 142
Ikita dōzō [A living statue] (film), 124
illustration, 80, 112–13
impartiality, 19–20, 23
imperialism, 8, 77, 174n35
Imperial Palace, 13, 60, 108, 111–12
Important Cultural Property, 14, 100, 103
impressionism, 4–5, 9–12, 21–26, 34–39, 57, 60, 111, 151n31, 156n91, 156n103, 180n29
"Impressionnisme et naissance du cinématographe" [Impressionism and Birth of the Cinémotagraphe] (exhibition), 10
Inabata, Katsutarō, 12, 59–60, 84–96, 111, 162n4, 162n6
Inaga, Shigemi, 25–26
Ince, Thomas H., 129–31
Ince films, 137
Indochina, 6, 59–60, 163n29
industrialization, 10, 33, 56, 103. *See also* modernization
Inoue, Takejirō, 102, 123
In Praise of Shadows (book) (Tanizaki), 172n33
instantaneity, 23–24, 29, 37, 56–57, 59, 155n85
Institut Lumière, 5–6, 9, 47, 146n15
interaction, 61, 92–97, 146n18. *See also* dialogue
Irie, Yoshirō, 100
"Iseyama kara Kitanakadōri 6-chōme o miru" [A view of Kitanakadōri 6-chōme from Mt. Ise] (photograph), 67–68
Ishitani, Haruhiro, 20–21
Īzuka, Tōkin, 143

Janssen, Pierre-Jules-César, 32
Japan: early film in, 99–108, 169n5; locked-door policy in, 13, 117; Lumière cinema in, 6, 11, 59–62; modernization of, 13–14, 74–78, 108–15, 125–26, 136–38, 144, 173n33, 174n35, 178n13; nativized orientalism in, 83–92, 114, 119–26; Orientalist fantasy about, 114–15, 129–44; Yokohama photos of, 63–73. *See also* Meiji government
Japanese Dancers. See *Danseuses japonaises*
Japanese Saber Fencing (film, 1897), 70
Japan Punch (magazine). See *The Far East* (magazine)
La Japonaise (*Camille Monet in Japanese Costume*) (painting) (Monet, 1876), 104, 105f
"Japonais posant devant leur maison" [Japanese posing in front of their house] (photograph), 67f
Japonisme, 3–15, 112–13. *See also* composition; dialogue; kinzō-gata-kōzu/chūkei-datsuraku/en=kin-hō; the Lumière Company; Orientalism; Shibata Tsunekichi; ukiyo-e; woodblock prints
Javal, Louis Emile, 29, 49

Jay, Martin, 168n99
Jeffries, B. Joy, 29
jiyū minken undō, 139
Jones, Sidney, 80
Joueurs de cartes arrosés [Card players watered] (film, 1896), 53f, 54
jun'eigageki undō, 138, 171n18
jūyō bunkazai, 14, 100, 103

Kabuki, 6, 13–14, 69–70, 99, 102, 112, 124–28, 138–39, 164n40, 166n70, 176n58. *See also* shinpa
Kabukiza Theater, 99, 102, 123, 176n58
Kachiku dorobō no chie [The knowledge of the cattle thief] (film), 124
Kadoza Theater, 162n6
Kaeriyama, Norimasa, 138
Kakan nai koi (film), 124
Kamata (magazine), 143
Kamiyama, Akira, 103
"Kanagawa oki nami ura" [The great wave off Kanagawa] (woodblock print) (Hokusai), 41f, 42
Kano, Ayako, 128, 137
Karadaru no gyōretsu [The march of empty barrels] (film), 124
Karatani, Kōjin, 117
Katō, Tsunetada, 177n7
Katsudō Gahō (magazine), 139, 143
Katsudō Kurabu (magazine), 137
Katsudō Shashin Zasshi (magazine), 139–40
Katsushika, Hokusai, 4–5, 23–24, 26, 34, 119, 122
Kawakami, Otojirō, 128–29, 139, 177n8
Kawakamiza Theater, 162n6
Kawaura, Kenichi, 103, 123
kendō, 69–70
"Kenshō shashin no shinsa" (report), 116, 175n43
Kettō daishōri [The great victory in the duel] (film), 124
Kiel: lancement du "Fürst-Bismarck" [Kiel: Launch of the "Furst-Bismarck"] (film, 1897), 158n126

Kiki kaikai jidō ryōri [Mysterious automatic cooking] (film), 124
Kikugorō, 6, 14, 99, 123, 125, 176n58
kimono, 104, 107, 112, 117
Kinema Junpō (magazine), 133
Kinema Record (magazine), 139
Kinkikan Theater, 124
Kinoshita, Naoyuki, 85–87, 94, 167n74
kinzō-gata-kōzu/chūkei-datsuraku/en=kin-hō, 24–26, 39–57, 66–70, 84, 112, 128, 134–35, 148n3, 152n52, 158n126, 160n137, 160n141, 161n143
Kobayashi, Yasuo, 153n62
Koga, Futoshi, 108
kokumin kokka shugi, 115. *See also* nationalism
Komatsu, Hiroshi, 2, 108
Komori, Yōichi, 75
Konica Minolta. *See* Konishi honten
Konishi honten, 102, 108, 170n9, 175n41
Kotani, "Henry," Sōichi, 141–42
Kume, Keiichirō, 111
Kuniyoshi, 105
Kurishima, Sumiko, 141, 143–44
"Kuro Fuji" [Black Mt. Fuji] (Hokusai), 122–23
Kyoto, 59–64, 69–72, 90–91, 112, 117

Labourage [Plowing] (film, 1896), 52, 52f
Lacambre, Geneviève, 7
La gare Saint-Lazare (*The Saint-Lazare Train Station*) (painting) (Monet), 9
La Geisha et le Chevalier (*The Geisha and the Knight*) (play), 128
La Japonaise (*Camille Monet in Japanese Costume*) (painting) (Monet, 1876), 104, 105f
LaMarre, Thomas, 26, 146n18, 173n33
La Martinière Institute in Lyon, 12, 48, 59
La musique aux Tuileries (*Music in the Tuileries*) (painting) (Manet), 9
Lancement d'un navire [Launch of a ship] (film, 1896), 43, 43f, 44

Lanciers de la reine, charge [Queen's lancer's charge] (film, 1896), 159n133
landscape, 11–12, 29, 63–68, 83, 109, 116–18, 173n33
La Revue Générale des Sciences (journal), 32
L'Arrivée d'un train à La Ciotat (Arrival of a Train at La Ciotat) (film, 1897), 9, 39, 44, 44f, 45
La sortie de l'arsenal [The exit of the arsenal] (film, 1899), 167n74
Laveuses sur la rivière (Women Washing on the Riverbanks) (film, 1897), 42, 42f
La vie et la passion de Jésus-Christ VI. La cène (Life and Passion of Jesus Christ: Last Supper) (film, 1898), 159n133
La vie et la passion de Jésus-Christ X. La mise en croix (film 1898), 159n133
layering, 26, 112, 134, 153n62, 158n131. See also depth
Le charpentier maladroit [The clumsy carpenter] (film, 1897), 160n140
Le Chat Noir, 88
Lee, Laila, 141
Le Japon artistique (magazine), 4, 150n31
Le Japon illustré (journal), 86
Le Moniteur de la photographie (journal), 32
Lenning, Arthur, 1
Le Printemps à travers les branches (The Banks of the Seine) (painting) (Monet), 26–27, 27f, 28
Le Progrès illustré (journal), 49
Les Aïnos à Yeso, I (Ainos at Yeso, I) (film, 1897), 73f, 76–77, 90
Les Aïnos à Yeso, II (Ainos at Yeso, II) (film, 1897), 74f, 76–77, 90
Les joueurs de cartes (painting) (Cezanne), 9
Les Meules à Giverney (painting) (Monet), 24
Les mines de charbon de Hon Gay [Hon Gay Coal Mines] (film, 1899), 158n131
Les Pyramides (Vue générale) (film, 1897), 46–47, 47f, 48
Les trente-six vues de la tour Eiffel [Thirty-six views of the Eiffel Tower] (Rivière), 3f, 4, 119

Letouzé, Maurice, 23
Levine, Steven Z., 9
Life and Passion of Jesus Christ: Last Supper. See *La vie et la passion de Jésus-Christ VI. La cène*
lighting, 19, 21, 24, 52, 138–43, 160n141
locked-door policy, 13, 117, 164n41
long shot, 47, 78, 81, 84, 100, 133, 139, 158n131, 160n137
Looser, Thomas, 19, 26
Los Angeles Examiner (newspaper), 129
Lumière, Antoine, 17
Lumière, Auguste, 1, 40, 155n85
Lumière, Louis, 1, 17–19, 22, 32, 36, 43–44, 148n3, 151n34
Lumière Autochrome, 32, 155n91. See also Girel, Constant
The Lumière Autochrome: History, Technology, and Preservation (Gandolfo and Lavédrine), 155n91
Lumière Cinématographe. See Cinématographe Lumière
Lumière Company: à travers cinema and, 39–57, 161n142; colonization and, 8; dialogue and, 83–92; impressionist influence on, 9–10, 156n91; in Japan, 59–77, 95, 128, 166n70; Japonism and, 1–5; Orientalist gaze of the, 8, 13, 89–90; physiological approach of, 24–32, 149n8; realist approach to film, 17–23, 36–39. See also actuality film; Cinématographe Lumière; Girel, Constant; narrative; Shibata Tsunekichi; Veyre, Gabriel
Lutteurs japonais [Japanese fighters] (film, 1897), 69
Lyon: débarquement d'une mouche [Lyon: Coming ashore from a boat] (film, 1896), 95–96

Mabuchi, Akiko, 26, 28
MacDonald, Margaret I., 133
Mace, Fred, 129, 131
Madama Butterfly (opera) (Puccini, 1904), 80, 130

Madame Butterfly, 129–44, 167n77
Maîtres de l'estampe japonaise [Masters of Japanese printmaking] (exhibition), 4
Malraux, André, 166n70
Manet, Édouard, 9, 156n106, 168n99
Manga (woodcuts) (Hokusai), 4, 23
Maple Viewing. See *Momijigari*
Marey, Etienne Jules, 32–33, 37
Maruhashi Chūya (play), 70
mass media, 14, 115–16, 125, 136
Masters of Japanese Printmaking (exhibition), 4
Matsumoto, Kōshirō VII, 102
Mauvaises herbes (*Weeds*) (film, 1896), 40, 40f
Max Factor cosmetics, 141
McDonald, Edward, 91
mechanicality, 10, 20–24, 30–37, 113, 149n8, 150n31, 167n77
Meiji government, 73–77, 88, 113, 117, 164n32, 174n35
Meijiza Theater, 170n9
Meisho Edo hyakkei (*One Hundred Famous Views of Edo*) (Hiroshige), 34, 35f
Memory of Mortefontaine. See *Souvenir de Mortefontaine*
Mesguich, Felix, 161n143
Mexico, 54, 60
mie (pose), 100
The Mikado (Gilbert and Sullivan), 80
Milan: les canotiers [Milan: The boaters] (film, 1896), 158n131
Millet, Jean-François, 52, 78
Mitchell, W. J. T., 63
Miura, Tamaki, 137
Miyazaki, Katsumi, 153n58
M. Loubet aux courses [Mr. Loubet at the races] (film, 1899), 158n131
modernization, 13–14, 62, 74–78, 108–15, 125–26, 136–38, 144, 148n4, 154n73, 165n65, 172n33, 178n13
Moisson, Charles, 160n140

Momijigari (*Maple Viewing*) (film, 1899), 6, 14, 99–100, 101f, 102–5, 108, 112, 123–26, 176n58
Momijigari, Kyoto dentō hatsudensho no kaji [The fire at Kyoto Electric Company] (film), 124
Monet, Claude, 9, 11, 23–29, 34–36, 104–5, 108, 112, 152n53, 153n62
motif, 7, 29, 34–36, 63, 77–83, 86, 104–8, 113, 131, 156n106, 158n126, 167n74, 167n77, 170n9, 172n30. *See also* archetype; architecture; dance; exoticism; geisha; landscape
Moulin à homme pour l'arrosage des rizières [Mill man for watering rice fields] (film, 1898–99), 78–79, 79f, 81
movement, 21–34, 112, 151n31, 157n109, 159n133, 177n8. *See also* à travers
Moving Picture World (journal), 129–30, 133
Mt. Fuji, 63–64, 75, 119–23, 176n54
Müller, Johannes Peter, 29, 153n70
Münsterberg, Hugo, 157n109
Muroran, 72–73
Museum of Modern Art, 1
Music in the Tuileries (painting) (Manet), 9
Mutual Film Corporation, 129
Muybridge, Eadweard, 32

Nagauta Ikioijishi [Long song: Vigorous lion] (film, 1898), 172n30
Naikoku Kangyō Hakurankai (exposition), 123
Nakamura, Ganjō I, 69, 91, 112, 176n58
Nakamura, Kasen, 138
Nakaza Theater, 176n58
Namo: panorama pris d'une chaise à porteurs [Namo: Panorama taken from a sedan chair] (film, 1900), 56f
Nanchi Enbujō Theater, 60
Naples: lancement du cuirasse [Naples: Launch of a cuirass] (film, 1897), 158n126
narrative, 1, 33–38, 130–32, 141–42, 146n18, 176n59

Naruse, Fukio, 24, 26
National Film Archive of Japan, 100, 169n5
nationalism, 14, 62, 74, 115–17, 125–26, 138, 172n33, 174n35. See also *kokumin kokka shugi*
naturalism, 7, 23, 74, 163n32, 179n29
negotiation, 8–9, 12–15, 81, 90, 97, 103, 112, 125. *See also* dialogue
New Art History, 7–8
New York Clipper (newspaper), 131
New York Motion Picture Company, 129
Nice: panorama sur la ligne de Beaulieu à Monaco, I [Nice: Panorama on the Line from Beaulieu to Monaco] (film, 1900), 161n143
Niépce, Joseph Nicéphore, 20
Nihonbashi uogashi [Fish market in Nihonbashi] (film), 125
Nihonjinron (theory of Japaneseness), 91. *See also* Japan
Nihon Taika Ronshū (anthology), 174n34
Nikkatsu Mukōjima, 139
Nisshin sensō jikki [Report of the First Sino-Japanese War] (book), 115
Nitobe, Inazō, 172n33
Nochlin, Linda, 64
Noh theatre, 99
"Notes sur la photographie" [Notes on photography] (Promio), 49

The Oath of O Tsuru San (film, 1913), 129
object, 6, 11–14, 20–21, 63, 91, 116–17. *See also* gaze; Orientalism
observer, 20–21, 95–96. *See also* gaze
Ōhashi, Sahei, 115
Ōhashi, Shintarō, 115
Ōhashi, Suiseki, 23
Okanesarashi (film, 1898), 172n30
Okayama Kōrakuen, Kyoto Chionin, Nara no Kasuga [Okayama Kōrakuen, Kyoto Chionin, and Kasuga of Nara] (film), 125
Okumura, Masanobu, 24–25

One Hundred Famous Views of Edo. See *Meisho Edo hyakkei*
onnagata, 69, 104, 124, 138–39, 143
Onna kamiyui no ie [The house of a female hairdresser] (film), 125
Onoe, Kikugorō V, 6, 14, 99, 123, 125, 176n58
"The Ontology of the Photographic Image" (Bazin), 36
Orientalism: enlightenment viewpoint and, 72–78; geisha fantasy and, 80–83, 92–94, 113–14, 167n77; in Hollywood, 136–44, 178n13, 179n29; internalized, 103, 113–44, 172n33; in Lumière cinema, 6–12, 60–62, 77; nativized, 13–14, 77, 83–92, 102, 108–15, 147n32, 172n33; in Yokohama photography, 62–64, 70. *See also* authenticity; exoticism; femininity; gaze; traditionality
Orientalism (Said), 6
Osaka Dōtonbori no nigiwai [The crowd of Osaka Dōtonbori] (film), 125
Otaru shimbun (newspaper), 60
Ozawa, Takeshi, 92

painting, 4–5, 12, 19–20, 23, 25–26, 28–30, 49, 78, 80, 151n37, 180n29. *See also* Cézanne, Paul; impressionism; Monet, Claude; postimpressionism; Renaissance; *specific paintings*
Panofsky, Erwin, 154n80
panorama, 36, 55–57, 161nn142–44
Panorama du funiculaire du Mont-Dore [Panorama of the Mont-Dore Funicular] (film, 1898), 55
Panorama pendant l'ascension de la tour Eiffel [Panoramic view during ascension of the Eiffel Tower] (film, 1897 or 1898), 1–5, 11, 18–19, 22, 30–31, 34–38, 46, 55
Panorama pris d'un ballon captif [Panorama taken from a captive balloon] (film, 1898), 161n141
Panorama pris d'un bateau [Panorama taken from a boat] (film, 1896), 161n143

Paris, 1–5, 23, 29, 48, 72, 112, 128–29.
  See also Exposition Universelle
Paris Foreign Mission Society, 72, 164n41
Partie d'écarté (*Card Game*) (film, 1896), 9
Passage d'un tunnel en chemin de fer [Passage of a railway tunnel] (film, 1898), 160n141
Pathé, 124, 177n61
perception, 29–37, 149n8, 152n50, 157n109
performance, 70, 76, 83, 90, 96, 177n8.
  See also dance; Kabuki; Orientalism
perspective, 5, 18–27, 39, 42–45, 48, 52, 55, 148n3, 149n8, 151n42, 160n140
photogénie, 179n29
photography, 1–5, 19–24, 32, 36, 49, 114–18, 155n85, 175n43. See also Yokohama photographs
photojournalism, 115–16, 122, 175n42
physicality, 33, 36, 150n31, 154n73. See also corporeality; movement
physiology, 5, 8, 22–39, 49, 149n8, 153n62, 155n91, 157n109. See also the eye
pictorialism, 3–4, 13, 63–64, 78–80, 83, 116–18, 122, 133, 145n6, 153n62
Picture-Play (magazine), 132
Pigeons sur la place Saint-Marc [Pigeons in St. Mark's Square] (film, 1896), 160n140
Pines and Rocks. See *Fontainebleau*
Pissaro, Camille, 29
Place Bellecour (film, 1896), 151n34
Plate-forme mobile et train électrique [Mobile platform and electric train] (film, 1900), 45, 45f
politics, 8, 12–13, 15, 60, 62, 116–17, 131, 136, 165n65, 174n35, 175n45. See also Meiji government; modernization
portraiture, 62–68, 140f
postimpressionism, 4, 10, 26, 29, 39, 57, 111, 151n37, 179n29
prints, 4, 11, 23, 29, 42, 57, 112, 119, 152n50, 156n103. See also ukiyo-e; woodblock prints

Procession shintoïste [Shinto procession] (film, 1897), 70
Promio, Alexandre, 45–50, 158n126, 159n133, 160n140
psychology, 20, 30, 130, 153n70
publicity, 113, 130–32, 139, 143
Puccini, Giacomo, 80, 130
Puppy Love (film, 1919), 141
pure film movement, 138, 171n18
The Pyramids (film, 1897), 46–47, 47f, 48

Rancière, Jacques, 37
Râyou, Father, 72
realism, 9–10, 19–26, 36–39, 128, 162n14, 164n40, 167n77; physiological, 36–39.
  See also actuality film
reality, 4, 22, 30, 37, 93–97, 109, 139, 142–43, 179n29. See also authenticity; corporeality; mechanicality; physiology; staging
Récolte du riz [Harvesting rice] (film, 1898–99), 78, 78f, 79
Reel Life (magazine), 129
religion, 64, 66, 72–73, 131–32, 164n40, 165n47, 174n34, 178n13
Renaissance, 4, 19–20, 24–27, 39, 149n8
Repas en famille (*Family Meal*) (film, 1897), 84–85, 85f, 86–91, 95, 111
representation, 10–11, 20–23, 39, 108–13, 122, 140, 145n6, 150n26. See also actuality film; authenticity
reproduction, 2, 8, 20, 138–39, 149n8, 167n77. See also mechanicality
Rivière, Henri, 3–5, 34, 119
"Rivière avec barque à voile devant le Mont Fuji" [River with sailing boat in front of Mt. Fuji] (photograph), 65f, 163n31
Robertson-Cole (distribution company), 179n29
Roi et reine d'Italie [King and queen of Italy] (film, 1896), 160n139
Romanticism, 20, 37
Ross, Sarah, 132

Rousseau, Jean-Jaques, 74
Russian encroachment, 73–74, 131
Russo-Japanese War, 131, 175n43
Rustling a Bride (film, 1919), 141
Ryōgoku bashi yūsuzumi uki-e (*Enjoying the Evening Cool near Ryogoku Bridge*) (Okumura), 25f
ryōsai kenbo (good wife, wise mother), 136. See also femininity

Sadayakko, 128–29, 136
Sadoul, George, 44
Saeki, Junko, 113–14
Said, Edward, 6. See also Orientalism
The Saint-Lazare Train Station. See *La gare Saint-Lazare*
Saitō, Takio, 165n65, 168n101
Salut dans les vergues [Salute in the yards] (film, 1898), 45–48
salvage paradigm, 73–77, 84. See also Ainu; Meiji government
"Sanka hakuu" [Rainstorm beneath the summit] (photograph) (Hokusai), 122–23, 123f
Satō, Morihiro, 63–64, 117
Saunders, Jackie, 140
Sauvage, Henri, 128
"A Scene of a Family" (Humbert), 86f
Scharf, Aaron, 23
science, 7–8, 28–34, 49–50, 154n70, 154n85. See also physiology
The Secret Garden (film, 1919), 141
Seguin, Jean-Claude, 46, 48
Sei no kagayaki (*The Glory of Life*) (film, 1918), 138
Seminary of Foreign Missions, 72
sensation, 29, 153n70. See also physiology
Seurat, George, 151n37
shakkei (borrowed scenery), 25–26
Shashin Geppō (magazine), 175n41
"Shashin jutsu ōyō no hattatsu" (report), 115–16
Shaviro, Steven, 180n29

Shibata, Tsunekichi, 13–14, 99, 102, 108–28, 170n9, 172n27, 172n30, 175n43, 176nn54–55
shidare, 34–36
Shiff, Richard, 23, 154n73
Shigeno, Yukiyoshi, 137
Shimabara tayū no dōchū [A geisha's walk] (film), 124
Shimooka, Renjō, 91–92
Shinan hikōki [The newly invented airplane] (film), 124
Shinmoriza Theater, 166n70
shinpa, 139–43. See also Kabuki
Shin Shakkyō (play), 69
Shittatsuri no akiregao [The bailiff's stunned face] (film), 124
Shiutome katagi [The mother-in-law character] (film), 124
Shōchiku Company, 141, 143
Signac, Paul, 151n37
Skladanowsky films, 32
smile, 92–96. See also dialogue
Smith, Henry D., II, 152n52
Société d'Encouragement à l'Industrie Nationale, 32
soft focus, 138, 140
Sortie d'un temple shintoïste [Exit from a Shinto shrine] (film, 1897), 71f, 72
Sortie d'usine, [I] (*Workers Leaving the Lumière Factory*) (film, 1895), 17–18, 18f, 19, 30–31, 36, 38, 147n3, 148n4, 158n126, 167n74
Sortie d'usine, [II] [Workers leaving the Lumière factory II] (film, 1896), 147n3, 148n4, 158n126
Sortie d'usine, [III] [Workers leaving the Lumiére factory III] (film, 1896), 147n3, 148n4, 158n126
Sortie d'usine, [IV] [Workers leaving the Lumière factory IV] (film, 1897), 147n3, 148n4, 158n126
Souriau, Paul, 22
Souvenir de Mortefontaine (*Memory of Mortefontaine*) (Corot), 27–28, 28f

space, 20, 25–28, 37. *See also* composition
Spain: Bull Races, II. See *Espagne: courses de taureaux, II*
Spate, Virginia, 28
spectator, 13, 30–33, 43–44, 57, 63, 123–26, 137, 154n80, 157n109, 168n99. *See also* gaze
Spivak, Gayatri Chakravorty, 62
staging, 63–64, 68–70, 79–88, 109, 113. *See also* authenticity; reality
Station du chemin de fer de Tokyo [Tokyo railway station] (film, 1898), 109, 110f
Stillfried, Baron Raimund von, 75, 84–85, 94, 165n65
Stucky, Charles F., 28
"Suishōsekai (Honnen ichigatsu yōka no asageshiki)" [The crystal world: The morning view on January 8 of this year] (photograph) (Shibata), 119, 121f
The Sun (magazine). See *Taiyō* (magazine)
"Suruga Gotenba no yuki no Fujisan" [Winter view of Mt. Fuji from Gotemba, Suruga] (photograph) (Shibata), 118, 120f, 122–23
Suspensions of Perception: Attention, Spectacle, and Modern Culture (Crary), 10, 29–30
Suzuki, Sadami, 115
Swimming in the Sea. See *Baignade en mer*

Tachibana, Teijirō, 139
Taira no Koremochi Togakushiyama kijo taiji no zu (*Taira Koremochi Conquering the Devil Woman on Mount Togakushi*) (woodblock print) (Tsukioka), 104, 106f, 107
Taiyō (magazine), 111, 115–18, 123, 174nn34–35, 175n43, 175n45, 176n55
Takashina, Shūji, 22, 36
Takayama, Chogyū, 174n35
Tanaka, Junichirō, 170n9
Tanaka, Stefan, 13
Tanizaki, Juni'chirō, 172n33
Tavernier, Bertrand, 47

Taylor, Fred W., 33
Taylorism, 33–34
technology, 1, 10, 13, 61, 103–4, 115–16. *See also* Cinématographe Lumière; mechanicality
temporality, 6, 33–34, 109, 112, 145n4, 159n133
Terada, Shirō, 136
the theater, 3, 6, 81, 128, 138, 177n8
theory of Chineseness, 91
theory of Japaneseness, 91
Thirty-Six Views of Mt. Fuji. See *Fugaku Sanjūrokkei*
Tokugawa, Yoshimune, 24
Tokugawa shogunate, 117
"Torii et cerisiers en fleurs" [Torii and cherry blossoms] (Girel), 66, 68f
Toulet, Emmanuelle, 127
tourism, 50, 88, 118, 167n76. *See also* Yokohama photographs
traditionality, 70, 76–93, 113, 117, 124, 137
transience, 11, 33, 38, 49, 154n73. *See also* the eye; vision
travelogues, 1, 80, 163n32, 167n77
Treatise on Physiological Optics (Helmholtz), 29
Tsivian, Yuri, 146n18
Tsubouchi, Shōyō, 174n35
Tsubouchi, Yūzō, 175n45
Tsuda, Kozo, 143
Tsukada, Yoshinobu, 162n4, 164n39, 177n63
Tsukioka, Yoshitoshi, 106f, 107

Ueda, Manabu, 102, 125
uki-e, 24–25
Ukita, Kazutami, 174n35
ukiyo-e, 4–5, 8–13, 22–28, 42, 57, 60, 72, 80–81, 104–13, 122, 148n3, 150n31, 156n103. *See also* composition; woodblock prints
Une avenue à Tokyo [An avenue in Tokyo] (film, 1898), 111, 111f

Une petit fête à la maison de thé [A little party at the tea house] (Bigot), 88
Une rue à Tokyo [A street in Tokyo] (film, 1897), 70, 71f, 81, 109, 110f
Une rue à Tokyo [I] [A street in Tokyo I] (film, 1898), 107f, 108, 111–12
Une rue à Tokyo [II] [A street in Tokyo II] (film, 1898), 109, 109f, 112–13
Une scène au théâtre Japonais [A scene at the Japanese Theater] (film, 1897), 69, 166n70
United States. *See* America
Un Pont à Kyoto [A bridge in Kyoto] (film, 1897), 70
Usui, Shūzaburo, 67
Utagawa, Hiroshige, 1, 5, 24, 26, 34, 35f, 122, 152n52
Utagawa, Kuniyoshi, 105

Vacche, Angela Dalle, 19
Vasari, Giorgio, 150n26
Vaughan, Dai, 22
Verhaeren, Emile, 24
Veyre, Gabriel, 11, 54, 56, 59–60, 83, 92–97, 108, 128, 166n70, 167n74
Vidal, Leon, 32
viewpoint, 26–28, 33, 44, 124–26, 161n141. *See also* the eye; movement; perception
vision, 8, 23, 27–29, 37, 50, 154n73; corporeal sense of, 5; disembodied, 20. *See also* the eye
visual cultural studies, 7–8
Vitascope, 102, 114f
"Vitascope niyoru 'Nihon shashin' kōgyō no tsuji bira" (flyer), 114f
Vue prise d'une baleinière en marche [View of a whaling boat on the move] (film, 1897), 161n144

Weeds. *See Mauvaises herbes*
the West, 6–7, 15, 80, 85, 131

Westernization, 66, 77, 84, 109–17, 125, 137, 139, 168n99, 173n33, 174n35. *See also* modernization
Wichmann, Siegfried, 156n106
Wilson, John, 92
Winter, O., 21
Wirgman, Charles, 80
women, 113–14, 129–44. *See also* geisha, onnagata
Women Washing on the Riverbanks. See *Laveuses sur la rivière*
woodblock prints, 4, 8, 22–26, 41f, 57, 105. *See also* ukiyo-e
woodcuts, 4, 23
Workers Leaving the Lumière Factory. See *Sortie d'usine, [I]* (film, 1895)
The Wrath of the Gods (film, 1914), 130–32, 138

"Yatsumi no hashi" [Yatsumi bridge] (photograph) (Hiroshige), 34, 35f
yellow peril, 131
Yokohama Archives of History, 67
Yokohama Kaikō Shiryōkan, 67
Yokohama photographs, 62–77, 83, 86–88, 91, 94, 113, 117–19, 125, 165n65, 167n74, 176n55. *See also* architecture; Girel, Constant; landscape; portraiture; Shibata Tsunekichi; staging; tourism
Yokohama shi gunjin kangei kai [Military reception in the city of Yokohama] (film), 125
Yokota shōkai, 176n59
Yokoyama, Akio, 105
Yokoyama, Taikan, 175n43
Yoshizawa shōten, 123, 177n59
Young, Thomas, 155n91
"Yuki no Fuji" [Snowy Fuji] (photograph) (Shibata), 118, 120f
Yoshitoshi, 106f, 107

Zhōngguórénlùn (theory of Chineseness), 91

www.ingramcontent.com/pod-product-compliance
Lightning Source LLC
Chambersburg PA
CBHW071818230426
43670CB00013B/2496